Case Studies in Abnormal Psychology

Kenneth N. Levy
Kristen M. Kelly
William J. Ray

Los Angeles | London | New Delhi
Singapore | Washington DC | Melbourne

FOR INFORMATION:

SAGE Publications, Inc.
2455 Teller Road
Thousand Oaks, California 91320
E-mail: order@sagepub.com

SAGE Publications Ltd.
1 Oliver's Yard
55 City Road
London EC1Y 1SP
United Kingdom

SAGE Publications India Pvt. Ltd.
B 1/I 1 Mohan Cooperative Industrial Area
Mathura Road, New Delhi 110 044
India

SAGE Publications Asia-Pacific Pte. Ltd.
3 Church Street
#10-04 Samsung Hub
Singapore 049483

Printed in the United States of America

ISBN 978-1-5063-5270-1

Acquisitions Editor: Abbie Rickard
Editorial Assistant: Jennifer Cline
Production Editor: Olivia Weber-Stenis
Copy Editor: Diane Wainwright
Typesetter: C&M Digitals (P) Ltd.
Proofreaders: Sally Scott and
                Lawrence Baker
Cover Designer: Rose Storey
Marketing Manager: Katherine Hepburn

This book is printed on acid-free paper.

17 18 19 20 21 10 9 8 7 6 5 4 3 2 1

Case Studies in Abnormal Psychology

Sara Miller McCune founded SAGE Publishing in 1965 to support the dissemination of usable knowledge and educate a global community. SAGE publishes more than 1000 journals and over 800 new books each year, spanning a wide range of subject areas. Our growing selection of library products includes archives, data, case studies and video. SAGE remains majority owned by our founder and after her lifetime will become owned by a charitable trust that secures the company's continued independence.

Los Angeles | London | New Delhi | Singapore | Washington DC | Melbourne

• Contents •

• Preface •

The purpose of this book, *Case Studies in Abnormal Psychology*, is to present the complexity of diagnosing and treating those with mental disorders. This is in contrast to the companion text, *Abnormal Psychology* by William Ray, in which case studies are presented to describe the essence of each disorder. As such, the core text focuses on the main features that illustrate the disorder.

This casebook expands that approach by adding culture, family, and work factors as context for how the individual related to the mental health professional during both diagnosis and treatment. These extended case studies include a follow-up that tracks the progress or difficulties experienced by the client during and after treatment. We have also included cases that demonstrate comorbidity and the complexity involved in real-world treatment of mental disorders.

Each case presentation is organized around a presenting problem and client description, a diagnosis and case formulation, the course of treatment, and the outcomes and prognosis. To help the student consider the case, discussion questions are presented at the end of the case study. When available, dialogues between the individual and the mental health professional are included to give a better picture of the person involved and their experiences.

Schizophrenia

Presenting Problem and Client Description

Demetri was 41 years old when he sought treatment at a university-based outpatient mental health clinic. He requested treatment in person, beseeching the receptionist in urgent tones, "I am in the homestretch of earning my PhD, but I'm quite sure if I don't get help soon I'm gonna blow it, and I simply can't let that happen."

Demetri was a Caucasian man of Russian and Italian descent, who stood over 6 feet tall and favored wearing cardigans and horn-rimmed glasses that made him appear somewhat older. Albeit still a little short of attaining his doctoral degree, Demetri already exuded a professorial persona, yet his build was more athletic than one would expect from a man who spent most of his time sitting at a desk and bent over books in the library. Living alone in a studio apartment next to the pizzeria where he ate most meals, Demetri reported having few friends and no family connections at the time he sought psychological treatment. His parents were long deceased, his father dying from lung cancer when Demetri was only 19. And sadly, his mother had been an alcoholic throughout his life and died of chronic liver disease just a few years later. Demetri had an unmarried younger brother, a successful computer engineer, but they lived on opposite coasts and rarely spoke. While there was also a large extended Russian Orthodox family with over a dozen first cousins, both brothers were atheists and neither had maintained contact with any of the aunts, uncles, or cousins for various reasons. Demetri indicated that he identified as heterosexual, had previously engaged in a few short-term relationships with women, but asserted that romance had been low on his priority list for the past several years.

Demetri's first appointment was scheduled for 8:30 in the morning, and he arrived on time, although unshowered and moderately disheveled. He seemed aware of his unkempt appearance and explained that he had been having difficulty getting up early lately and had felt anxious about accepting an early morning time slot. However, it was the first available appointment by more than a week, he'd been told; therefore, he was highly motivated to keep it. Almost immediately after sitting down, Demetri shared that he'd already completed multiple stints of psychotherapy over the past 20 years owing to the fact that he'd been diagnosed with schizophrenia nearly 2 decades ago.

It seemed that Demetri had been an exceptionally intelligent young man, graduating from high school and matriculating at an elite liberal arts college before age 17. Sadly, only a few months after he started college, his father was diagnosed with cancer, and early on the family was told the illness was almost certainly terminal. Demetri shared how he thought he had coped rather well during the first few months. "I think I always enjoyed studying more than most people, but I still had friends. That January, however, after returning to school after winter break, I began to feel a growing gulf between me and everyone else, like I was a two-dimensional entity lost in a three-dimensional world, and it was like my emotional architecture began to change." He said that he assumed the odd feelings he was having were related to the stress of his father's illness. Yet in response to his father's strong urgings he had stayed in school, in spite of feeling a strong pull to take a leave of absence.

After successfully completing the semester, he proceeded to return home to help his mother and younger brother care for his ailing father, who passed away shortly thereafter in August. Demetri had been close to his father and reported that he was pretty devastated by the latter's relatively brief illness and painful death, and was unable to return to school that fall. During the months following his father's death, Demetri began developing paranoid beliefs that his immediate family members also had cancer and that his entire extended family was cursed. He began hearing voices that accused him of terrible things, including feeding his father asbestos-laced foods that had caused his cancer. At one point, Demetri said he stopped consuming food and water for more than 3 days in the belief that it would cleanse him and his family of the sins that had sent their world into a downward spiral. It was at this point that he was hospitalized.

Demetri's hospitalization turned out to be the first in a long series of both short-term and long-term hospitalizations. He said, "I'm happy to provide more detail later, but in the spirit of efficiency, allow me to condense the next 2 decades in a rather direct, straightforward manner." Demetri proceeded to share a summary of his mental health history as follows: He suffered from active psychotic symptoms, such as auditory hallucinations and paranoid delusions, during most of his waking hours between ages 20 to 30. His schizophrenia was highly debilitating, making it difficult for him to live independently, never mind hold steady employment. Demetri was hospitalized multiple times during this decade, including an 18-month stint in a state-run mental institution. At age 31, he began taking a medication called clozapine, which dramatically reduced his symptoms and transformed his life. Within 9 months of starting the medication, his psychiatric symptoms almost entirely remitted, allowing him to live independently for the first time since becoming an adult. He spent a few years working for a parcel delivery service while quickly learning and consolidating virtually all of the skills required to function as a full-fledged adult (e.g., laundry, meal preparation, paying bills, taxes, etc.). Then, without any family support, he managed to complete his undergraduate degree in only a few short years, eventually gaining acceptance to a doctoral degree program at age 36. Demetri described how the first 4 years in his doctoral program were "smooth sailing," how he felt profoundly grateful that he had somehow successfully reconstituted some semblance of a normal life in spite of being diagnosed with a major mental illness—a life that revolved around gratifying academic pursuits and a small group of friends/classmates, the latter being a wholly new experience for him.

After providing this very organized, helpful summary, Demetri began describing changes he'd experienced during the past several weeks. As he did, his countenance noticeably shifted from one of reserved anguish to one of barely restrained agitation. He began bouncing his knee up and down as he spoke, creating an audible tapping sound that he didn't seem to notice. Demetri also began having more difficulty maintaining normal eye contact as he described how his academic progress began to stall a few months ago, shortly after beginning work on his dissertation. He shared how he began having difficulty falling asleep at night, often lying awake for several hours before finally drifting off. He observed that he had been socially withdrawing from others, avoiding meetings with his dissertation adviser, and skipping the reading groups he'd enjoyed attending so much since starting his doctoral studies. When his small number of friends asked him to go out to eat and/or just hang out, he had declined, protesting that he was too busy or too tired, not accepting a single invitation for 2 months. He also complained that he was suffering from low motivation and difficulty concentrating, which, combined with lack of sleep, made working on his dissertation increasingly miserable.

And then, in low, hushed tones, Demetri divulged the recent development that was the most anxiety provoking by far—the fact that he was experiencing auditory hallucinations again, a symptom he had not been forced to grapple with for several years. At first, they started out as vague whispers he heard only when alone, which he'd initially dismissed as signs of stress. A few weeks ago, however, he began hearing a few clearly distinguishable male voices that began making a running commentary about his thoughts and behaviors, "telling me I'm unworthy of eating that second helping of food, that I better watch out because my eyes are deceiving me as I start to cross the street, that I am a fool to trust this person or that person." He indicated the auditory hallucinations were typically quieter, sometimes even absent, during the first part of the day, but they had begun emerging in a pronounced way in the late afternoons or early evenings. When asked, he affirmed that this was the primary reason he had socially withdrawn from others and why he was having difficulty focusing and concentrating. He said he was feeling depressed, but he expressed confidence that his depressed mood stemmed from the stress and fear associated with experiencing hallucinations again. He added he felt sure that much of his exhaustion stemmed from not sleeping at night due to preoccupied feelings of horror that he could lose the life that he'd worked so hard to reconstruct for himself since recovering from his illness. Demetri denied experiencing other kinds of sensory distortions such as visual or tactile hallucinations, which are much less common in schizophrenia. He indicated he had been resisting the idea that he was suffering a setback for months, but after the auditory hallucinations emerged, the notion that he was suffering a relapse was no longer deniable, and thus he had scheduled today's appointment.

Sitting across from me, after sharing this much of his story, Demetri shed some tears despite visibly trying to contain them. In response to my calm inquiry, he offered that they were tears of relief, acknowledging that he hadn't realized how alone he had been feeling with fears he "was going crazy again" and "at risk of losing everything." Together, we developed a plan that included attending weekly psychotherapy sessions aimed at helping him understand the nature of his current stressors, as well as developing strategies to cope with them. Additionally, Demetri indicated that his general practitioner had been comfortable prescribing his antipsychotic medication so long as he was psychiatrically stable. But he suspected she would be reluctant to continue treating him now that it appeared clear he was in the midst of a relapse. To his credit, before I could even offer any input on the matter, he expressed a strong appreciation for the value of seeing a psychiatric specialist with expertise in treating psychotic disorders. Accordingly, we also arranged for him to meet with a psychiatric provider who would assess his current psychotropic medication regimen and likely recommend one or more adjustments or changes.

Diagnosis and Case Formulation

Schizophrenia is frequently a devastating, life-altering psychiatric disorder that typically develops during adolescence or early adulthood. Psychoses are the hallmark symptoms of schizophrenia, which are characterized by "positive symptoms" such as hallucinations and delusions. And these are frequently accompanied by "negative symptoms" such as impoverished emotions, speech, and interests. During our first meeting, Demetri reported that he experienced severe hallucinations as well as paranoid delusions during the worst phase of his illness, requiring round-the-clock supervision in a hospital setting for much of that time. He also endorsed having experienced some negative symptoms in his youth (e.g., affective flattening, decreased interest in the world around him), but he was clear on the point that he felt much of his social withdrawal, then and now, was largely an attempt to shield himself from the most distressing effects of the auditory hallucinations that plagued him.

In a manner that was helpful, and notably "nonparanoid," Demetri readily agreed to sign papers allowing his previous mental health providers to release copies of his medical records. And as expected, the information contained in these records was wholly consistent with the history Demetri had provided, confirming that he had been formally diagnosed with schizophrenia when he was 21. And as is often customary, the records showed Demetri was initially diagnosed with schizophreniform disorder, owing to the fact that an individual must suffer from psychotic symptoms for at least 6 months before a diagnosis of schizophrenia can be made.

Given that Demetri's psychosis developed shortly after his father passed away, his mental health providers at the time needed to consider whether he was suffering from other psychiatric diagnoses, such as either a severe major depressive disorder with psychotic features or a brief psychotic episode, which typically occur in response to a major life trauma or stressor. However, in Demetri's case, he did not recover in 6 months or less but rather remained severely ill and debilitated for several years.

Demetri's psychiatric records also contained some additional specifics that we had not yet had the opportunity to review. One of these specifics included the fact that while Demetri's mother had indeed died of liver failure secondary to chronic liver disease, records showed that her liver disease had been significantly aggravated by multiple suicide attempts when she had tried to kill herself using a combination of prescription medications and alcohol. According to the records, Demetri's mother also suffered from schizoaffective disorder, a variant of schizophrenia where a person suffers from both a major psychotic illness and a major mood disorder (usually depression) simultaneously.

This fact was diagnostically relevant for Demetri, as research has shown that both environmental and genetic factors play important roles in the etiology of schizophrenia; thus, Demetri's mother having a psychotic disorder increased the risk that her offspring could also develop a severe psychiatric disorder. Taken together, Demetri's current constellation of symptoms combined with the information obtained concerning his lengthy psychiatric history made confirming a diagnosis of schizophrenia a relatively straightforward matter. That said, the last essential piece of information gleaned from his previous medical records related to his course of recovery after starting a new medication called clozapine. Clozapine was the first of a new class of antipsychotic medications that did not become widely available in the United States until the early 1990s. It offered new hope to individuals like Demetri who were extremely ill and whose symptoms had not improved with the standard medications available at the time. Demetri took the medication, and for the first time in a decade his symptoms dramatically improved. Moreover, Demetri's records showed that his psychiatrist at the time described him as a "super-responder," meaning that he seemed to be one of the fortunate individuals who responded so well to the new therapy that he made a 100% recovery with no residual symptoms, which was uncommon and wonderful.

Course of Treatment

In his first psychotherapy session, Demetri lamented, "I feel so incredibly ambivalent about being in therapy again. . . . A part of me is eager to be here because I feel there is really nobody else in my life I can talk to. But another part of me feels such profound and overwhelming despair to be here because it signifies I'm losing everything and I'm starting all over again." The first part of his statement was easy to comprehend. Owing to the stigma he felt, none of his friends knew about his mental illness, and Demetri was intent on keeping it that way. Thus, at least in the short run, it seemed psychotherapy might be the single hour each week where he wouldn't have to hide the distress of his current reality. Underscoring this idea, Demetri bemoaned, "One of the most difficult things about this is that I feel like such a fraud—I sit in the library as if I'm just another normal doctoral student, which is a big fat lie!" He tried to soothe himself by highlighting his "lie" was an act of omission (i.e., withholding an important piece of information about himself from his adviser, friends, etc.) rather than commission, but it did little to help him feel less alone.

As his therapist, my first goal was to help Demetri contain some of his anxiety, especially as I suspected it played a major role in aggravating his psychotic symptoms. Thus, I asked whether we could shift our attention to the second part of his opening statement—his despair about "losing everything" and "starting all over." I suggested we step back and take a broader perspective about where he is in his life right now and compare it to where he'd been. And after empathizing with his distress, I commented, "I appreciate that this may be splitting hairs here, but doesn't the fact that you're so worried about losing all the gains you've made suggest that you haven't yet lost them?" We proceeded to clarify a large set of important facts—how *unlike* when he was severely ill (1) he was still meeting the requirements for independent living (paying bills, doing laundry, eating meals, etc.); (2) he was still a PhD student at a prestigious university; (3) he still held the respect he had earned from professors and classmates (he unsuccessfully tried to dispute this one, eventually conceding that he feared losing their respect but had not actually lost it); and (4) he was feeling guilty and glum about having recently withdrawn from his friends, which supported the fact that he had friends, unlike when he had been very ill.

We also observed the fact that while he was experiencing auditory hallucinations, an extremely disquieting symptom that needed attention and active intervention, their recurrence was not the functional equivalent of "losing everything or starting over." I highlighted the crucial fact that he understood the voices in his head were generated by his own mind rather than attributing the sensory perception to real people or entities taking over his brain or psyche (although he admitted fearing the latter). And while his auditory hallucinations often contained critical and paranoid themes, he confirmed that he was still free from the kinds of paranoid delusional beliefs that he suffered long ago, such as when he thought the hospital nursing staff was giving him "medicine" that would give him cancer, the same kind of cancer that killed his father.

Demetri was also able to validate and appreciate another major factor that distinguished his past illness from the present one—the fact that *he* had initiated seeking help. Instead of risking succumbing to a full psychotic relapse, he had acted to protect himself while he still retained the health, knowledge, and insight to protect his well-being, including his wealth of achievements. At last, I also pointed out that unlike what had been described in his old hospital records, Demetri was not exhibiting negative symptoms of schizophrenia: Despite difficulties with concentration, he was still passionate about his studies and he could still access his emotions. "Maybe even a little too much," he joked.

It appeared that an approach specifically clarifying and refining the scope of Demetri's current problems and differentiating them from those he had in the past reduced his anxiety a few degrees. But he was still experiencing psychotic symptoms; thus, keeping to our plan, he met with a psychiatrist who adjusted his medication, adding a low dose of a second antipsychotic and giving him an antianxiety medication to take in the early evenings. He complained that the new medications made him feel more tired and mentally sluggish, but he conceded that the trade-off would be more than fair if his psychotic symptoms improved. And over the next 8 weeks, Demetri reported that his auditory hallucinations indeed decreased in both frequency and intensity. He explained that instead of hearing voices 60% of the time, he was hearing only them 15% of the time. Moreover, he described how there were entire days "here and there" where he experienced no symptoms at all.

To his credit, Demetri indicated that he would rather not settle for anything less than the 100% symptom remission he had enjoyed for most of the past decade. Also to his credit, our early discussions revealed that as far as psychotherapy was concerned, Demetri was not at all "starting over." From the beginning of our work together, it was clear that he was benefitting from knowledge and insights that he had gained from his previous experiences in psychotherapy. One area of knowledge and insight was his understanding of the risk factors for relapse in schizophrenia: not taking medication as prescribed, medications losing efficacy, excessive stress, and excessive anxiety.

Demetri reported that he had always been diligent about taking his medication, and he was confident that this was not a contributing factor to his relapse. In addition, he felt that having grown to appreciate the strong connection between high levels of stress and his proneness to psychotic symptoms, he preferred to work on his stress and anxiety before making any additional medication changes, especially if it would mean taking higher doses of medication and risking even more side effects. Therefore, with the support of his psychiatrist, we placed our bets on utilizing psychotherapy to help meet his goal of 100% symptom remission, and we proceeded to delve more deeply into the areas of stress and anxiety that may have increased Demetri's risk for relapse.

One area of obvious stress and concern was Demetri's dissertation. In fact, it seemed the more persistent residual auditory hallucinations were often connected to it—voices saying, "it's a piece of junk, you should burn it," etc. He said that his work was no longer completely stalled as it had been a couple months ago; however, he self-consciously acknowledged that he was still avoiding his dissertation adviser and avoiding her requests for revisions. It didn't take all that much discussion to realize that most of his avoidance was an ineffective strategy to cope with fears of failure. "In order to be worthy of my degree, my dissertation needs to put forth one idea after another in a pithy yet elegant manner that supports my thesis and adds something thoroughly innovative to the academic knowledge base!" Moreover, he made statements implying that producing an acceptable dissertation was tantamount to proving "to everyone" that he was a normal and worthy individual, no different than his classmates.

After this statement, I asked him to pause for us to carefully consider the possible meanings of his words: Basically, he seemed to be saying that, like his peers, he had accepted the responsibility for producing an original piece of scholarship as part of earning his degree. However, he also seemed to be saying that, unlike his peers, his piece of scholarship carried the dual burden of proving he was a "normal" and "worthy" person. Moreover, given that he had kept his schizophrenia a carefully guarded secret, it seemed apparent that any burden to prove himself "normal" and "worthy" was aimed to reassure himself, not his faculty or friends. And upon unveiling these kinds of private assumptions, Demetri came to appreciate how these kinds of self-imposed pressures served to stymie his dissertation efforts. Yet another facet of working on his dissertation anxiety involved inquiring about what he knew about the status of his peers' dissertations. In short order, Demetri learned that when it came to dissertation anxiety, he had much more in common with fellow graduate students than he had previously assumed. Not only did this reduce some of his anxiety, it also served to reduce his self-consciousness in a manner that helped him resume social contact with his small but close-knit group of friends.

Gratifyingly, although not surprisingly, Demetri's residual hallucinations, the remaining "15%," disappeared as soon as he resumed steady progress on his dissertation, and he graduated with his doctoral degree symptom-free once more. Psychotherapy was able to continue beyond graduation thanks to Demetri's earning a postdoctoral grant that allowed him to stay at the university for another 18 months. The grant was a reward for his good work, work he had "exquisitely explicated" in his dissertation, according to his adviser, a compliment that gave both of us great pleasure. Thanks to Demetri's schizophrenia symptoms staying nicely in remission, we were able to direct our attention to issues such as his yet-unrealized desire to have a girlfriend and the communication skills that are helpful for creating and maintaining emotional closeness in relationships. Owing to the fact that Demetri was very ill throughout his late teens and 20s, the period when people usually consolidate these skills, it was not surprising that it was an area of personal growth that still needed some help and attention.

And finally, the last portion of psychotherapy was devoted to grieving. The need for grief work came about in a manner that neither Demetri nor I foresaw, yet in retrospect wasn't especially surprising. One day, Demetri arrived for his appointment uncharacteristically upset—initial words explaining his demeanor, "The voice is back. I woke up this morning and very first thing, it was back." I inquired about the nature of the voice, and Demetri paused. A searching expression was replaced by an incredulous one. "It was a woman's voice," he said. We both remarked about how that was quite unusual: In all this time, he had never specifically recalled hearing a woman's voice. "The voice was soft and kept saying, 'it's so sad, it's just so sad,' several times, almost like a quiet mantra." After a period where far-reaching exploration didn't seem to be going anywhere, we decided to shift to a different (though related) topic when Demetri suddenly appeared like he'd been struck by lightning, fleetingly sitting bolt upright and then literally falling out of his chair. That he might be having a panic attack or a seizure both seemed like reasonable possibilities at that moment, but then he gasped, "It's her birthday, today is my mother's birthday." He caught his breath, regained his balance almost immediately, and then began to shed quiet tears.

Outcome and Prognosis

We spent the next few sessions processing the events of that day and came to what seemed like both an obvious and logical conclusion. Namely, just as Demetri's illness had interfered with his developing social and emotional skills that people typically develop during their teens and 20s, his psychotic illness had almost completely foreclosed his ability to mourn his parents' deaths. Then he had spent his 30s and early 40s intently focused on claiming some of the normal developmental milestones his illness had stolen from him, leaving no reserves for grieving. Eventually, I shared another hypothesis concerning his delayed mourning that went beyond it rising to the top of his "psychological/emotional priority list." We knew from past experience that both stress and anxiety put him at risk of experiencing psychotic symptoms: We saw this again ever so briefly the day he heard the woman's voice, presumably a stand-in for his mother. Accordingly, one day when Demetri was criticizing himself harshly, interpreting his delayed feelings of grief as evidence that he had not sufficiently cared about his parents, I reframed it for him in very different terms. I said, "Actually, there is evidence to suggest that you loved your parents very, very much. In fact, it seems possible that your father's illness and death set your mental illness into motion. I'm not saying you wouldn't have developed schizophrenia if your parents had lived, but it seems clear that their deaths hurt you in terms of further complicating the course of your illness." I also explained that the fact that he had not yet devoted emotional reserves to mourning his parents' deaths could have very well served a protective function. Simply stated, he waited until he was ready, as approaching the grief any sooner might have risked more psychotic symptoms than the single auditory hallucination he experienced a few weeks ago.

Demetri accepted this rationale, and the ideas of "awareness," "readiness," and "listening to himself" became the concepts we often referred back to as we reviewed his progress as the end of the treatment drew near. While he slipped now and then, we also agreed on the considerable progress he had made in being more generous to himself, no longer automatically beating himself up for small transgressions of thought or behavior. Soon thereafter, Demetri found a job and moved to a different state. Yet on occasion he still sends me PDFs of papers he's authored and includes a short note assuring me he's still well.

Discussion Questions

1. Explain how Demetri's initial diagnosis of schizophrenia in his twenties was beneficial in his treatment at age 41.

2. What was the role of Demetri's family history in the development of his illness?

3. Describe the techniques Demetri's therapist used in Demetri's treatment.

2

Delusional Disorder

Presenting Problem and Client Description

Tyler is a 30-year-old mixed-race man who sought psychological treatment after experiencing considerable distress, including suicidal ideation in response to a series of unfortunate events that had unfolded over the past year. These events included (1) being informed by the school administration that he would not be allowed to continue in his PhD program in computer science, citing his failure to make adequate progress toward the degree; (2) being hit by a car and fracturing his leg; (3) losing his job as a result of being unable to work due to his injury; and (4) becoming homeless due to being unable to work and pay rent. On the eve of being evicted from his apartment, Tyler called the local community hotline very angry and distressed, claiming that he was considering suicide due to feeling hopeless about his future and feeling certain that he would not be able to survive homelessness. Emergency services mobilized in response to his crisis phone call, and emergency workers assessed him as being at significant risk of harming himself and transported him to the hospital for further evaluation and stabilization.

In the emergency department, Tyler said he continued to experience intense thoughts of wanting to die. He claimed that if he were released from the hospital, he "would go outside and jump in front of a city bus, and do it right this time." This statement was particularly worrisome to the medical staff given last year's traffic accident, as it called into question the possibility that his being hit by a car may have been intentional rather than an "accident." Upon being voluntarily admitted to the psychiatric unit, Tyler had the opportunity to provide staff with more detail concerning how his current situation came about. When queried about the source of his distress and suicidal thoughts, Tyler's responses revealed that his struggles extended well beyond his current housing crisis. He expressed feeling most angry and distraught about having been kicked out of his computer science doctoral program after only 2 years. Tyler cited that the decision to not allow him to continue was wholly unfair and claimed it was "motivated by academic and corporate greed at the highest levels." After he began telling his story, it quickly became apparent that Tyler directed the vast majority of the blame for his current circumstances at his academic adviser and fellow students in the computer science department.

Tyler provided the hospital social worker with a detailed explanation concerning how his academic adviser had recommended Tyler's dismissal "based on trumped-up accusations that I didn't complete course work or sufficiently participate in research." Tyler explained how "the reality of the situation was" that he had been conducting research in a wholly diligent manner, and during his first year he had made an innovative discovery that "would revolutionize and turn the entire computer chip industry inside out and upside down!" Clawing his fingers into his palms, rocking his body, and speaking in angry, agitated tones, Tyler described how at the end of his first year he made what would be "the absolutely most stupid and naive mistake of my entire life!" He went on to describe how during his first-year academic review, his adviser asked him to summarize his academic progress made over several months, and Tyler explained that he had devoted most of his time to his "innovation" rather than to work directly connected to his adviser's research program. "But before I could even share my discovery in my own time and on my own terms, Dr. X stole it from me and kicked me out of my PhD program!"

When asked to explain exactly how this had happened, Tyler provided an elaborate account of how his former university was actually a secret arm of the National Security Agency (NSA), how his academic adviser was a high-level NSA operative, and how his adviser had specifically recruited him when he was still an undergraduate "because he saw my full intellectual potential and knew that I was probably going to make a groundbreaking contribution to the field." In hushed, conspiratorial whispers, Tyler explained how after showing his adviser "merely the tip of the proverbial iceberg of my discovery," his adviser realized its huge importance and instructed the NSA to break into his computer workstation and steal his work. He shared how the worst part was not only did the NSA steal his work, but they planted a virus that wiped out not only his research but also all of the course work that he had completed over the past 9 months. Thus, when the time came for his academic review, he had "absolutely zero work" to show his academic committee, and the faculty quickly initiated "winding up all of the bureaucratic gears" needed to dismiss him from his program. "They stole my entire life's work, then they pretended the work never, ever existed, and then they kicked me to the curb like I was a stray animal!"

Since Tyler had been admitted to the same hospital after he had been hit by the car, the evaluator easily gained access to his medical records in order to ascertain what had happened several months ago. Medical records showed that Tyler had been intoxicated, and a friend/witness reported that he appeared to have walked into the path of a slow-moving vehicle when it hit him. At the time, too, Tyler explained in an adamant manner that the "accident" was in reality a "failed NSA assassination attempt," part of a concerted effort to keep Tyler quiet. During the evaluation process, he intermittently became angry and agitated in response to being asked questions and sharing his story. In one instance, his anger gradually gave way to tears and he lamented despairingly, "It looks like they [the NSA and his adviser] won. Look at me. I'm in the hospital. People are treating me like I'm some blubbering idiot espousing some kind of convoluted conspiracy theory. First they tried to murder me, then they nearly drove me to suicide, and now I'm sitting here in the hospital with everyone thinking I'm a crazy person. They have totally everything, and I have absolutely nothing."

During the next several days in the hospital's psychiatric inpatient unit, the intensity and frequency of Tyler's angry outbursts flanked by hopelessness gradually lessened. He socialized rather easily with the other patients on the unit, most of whom offered him a great deal of sympathy and support in relation to his plight. His depressed mood and suicidal thoughts rather quickly disappeared during the first 48 hours. Rather than seeming depressed, he appeared content and satisfied as he enjoyed the attention from the many people he encountered as long as they did not express any skepticism concerning his academic work or the manner he claimed it was sabotaged. In fact, he probably would have been discharged sooner except for the fact that he did not have a home to return to. Fortunately, his social worker addressed that problem during his 10-day hospitalization, helping him locate temporary housing to live in upon being discharged. Prior to leaving the hospital, Tyler agreed to continue his care with me at a community outpatient psychological clinic, including sending copies of his complete medical record, which is how I obtained the information described so far in this case study.

Diagnosis and Case Formulation

The hallmark symptom for diagnosing delusional disorder is the presence of one or more false beliefs. Such false beliefs are unshakable, rendering it impossible for others to use logic or irrefutable evidence to persuade the person to believe otherwise. Compared to schizophrenia, which typically develops in adolescence and early adulthood and affects approximately 1% to 2% of the population, delusional disorder typically occurs in middle to later adulthood and is much more rare. With schizophrenia, individuals might experience perceptual disturbances and disorganized thinking so severe that the illness interferes with being able to undertake basic tasks such as eating regular meals, maintaining lifestyle skills, and being able to maintain eye contact during a normal back-and-forth conversation. In contrast, individuals with delusional disorder often appear to socialize and function normally, not necessarily exhibiting any odd or bizarre behavior that would alert others that they are psychotic. Unless the subject of the person's delusion is actually broached, the problem may remain invisible to others during casual social encounters.

Additionally, in delusional disorder the false belief must be nonbizarre, meaning that it is a situation or condition that could conceivably occur in real life (e.g., having a very disfiguring scar on one's body, being stalked by a stranger, being convinced a specific celebrity intends to propose marriage, becoming the victim of an international conspiracy) as opposed to a bizarre belief that defies the laws of nature (e.g., that pigs *can* indeed fly). Delusional disorder should not be diagnosed if the delusional individual is suffering from dementia or some other organic brain disorder. And finally, it's worth noting that some delusions are benign and do not necessarily need any kind of psychiatric treatment, such as a person who is falsely convinced she is deathly allergic to nuts. Such a person could theoretically go about life carefully avoiding foods that contain nuts and live normally without further consequence. In Tyler's case, however, his paranoid system of delusions had completely derailed his education, caused him to fall into economic straits that led to homelessness, contributed to serious physical injury, and had left him estranged and isolated from family, colleagues, and friends. There was little doubt that follow-up treatment after his discharge from the hospital would be essential and possibly lifesaving.

Course of Treatment

One of the initial challenges of psychotherapy was working with Tyler to develop a shared understanding of why he needed ongoing psychological treatment. By the time he arrived for his first appointment, he had been discharged from the hospital for nearly a week, and the acute crisis that had led to his hospitalization had passed: Tyler was no longer suicidal. He indicated that he was not even especially depressed. He had a temporary place to live, and the county had provided him with an intensive case worker who would be meeting with him weekly for at least the next few months to help him find employment and permanent housing.

I knew from his hospital records that he was likely still very preoccupied with being forced to withdraw from his PhD program and by the thorny conspiracy surrounding his departure. But his inpatient psychotherapist had cautioned me that Tyler's paranoia existed on multiple levels. He expressed feelings of intense anger and betrayal toward his former academic adviser, and he was utterly convinced the NSA intended to resume electronic surveillance of all his communications and Internet usage after he was discharged from the hospital. In addition, Tyler was very distrustful of the hospital psychiatrist's strong recommendation that he take antipsychotic medication.

From Tyler's perspective, refusing to take medication just made logical sense because he had adamantly rejected the notion that his preoccupations and related anxieties were not tied to reality. Moreover, even a gently phrased suggestion to Tyler that he was suffering from psychosis had triggered Tyler's paranoia, causing him to accuse the psychiatrist of being a part of the espionage ring that was violating his rights and trying to harm him. His refusal to take medication was less of a setback than it would have been if Tyler had been suffering from schizophrenia, because while antipsychotic medication is the primary and often highly effective treatment for psychosis in people with schizophrenia, it is not nearly as effective for treating psychosis associated with delusional disorder. But while psychotherapy is the principal treatment, effective psychotherapy is predicated on being able to establish a therapeutic relationship built on a solid foundation of trust, which can be very difficult to achieve with a highly paranoid individual.

Not surprisingly, during the first half of our initial meeting, Tyler laid out the details of the conspiracy and the long list of people who were "determined to ruin my life." He concluded his tale with the deceptively straightforward statement/question, "Now that I have told you my story, you need to share your honest reaction. Do you believe me?" It was clear that Tyler was drawing a very clear line in the sand: If I indicated that I did not believe him, he might group me among those who he feels are conspiring against him, seriously jeopardizing any chance of continuing his treatment with me. Establishing trust between the client and psychotherapist is a basic tenet of good psychotherapy. Any explicit expression of disbelief about his story would understandably seriously undermine the chances of a successful psychotherapy.

At the same time, from my perspective as his psychotherapist, lying to him, telling him that I did, in fact, believe the intriguing saga he attached to his current plight, seemed like an equally poor option. While I internally winced at the idea of telling him I seriously doubted his story, I appreciated the importance of approaching the psychotherapy with as much honesty and personal integrity as possible in order to be worthy of any trust he might choose to place in me. The foundation of our therapeutic relationship needed to be built on something real and solid.

Beyond being dishonest, telling him that I believed him also risked a whole set of other unintended consequences. It might induce Tyler to want to pressure me to be his ally against his nemeses, not a healthy ally striving to help him navigate his way out of psychosis but rather looking to me for advice and input as he plotted and strategized against his perceived enemies, only to grow confused and/or suspicious when I redirected his efforts. Also, by permitting him to engage in accusations and tirades connected to his former adviser, the NSA, and whoever else he might set his sights on, I would be allowing him to draw our attention away from the things I could help him with, such as his alcohol use and his tendency to unintentionally intimidate others, resulting in few friends. Moreover, from a practical standpoint, I am a poor liar, and I had little confidence in my ability to maintain a charade for the many months, possibly years, that treatment would require to help Tyler. I was certain that the huge effort to perpetuate the lie would tax my morale and morals in a manner that would be exhausting as well as inevitably unsuccessful and detrimental.

Fortunately, ahead of our first appointment I had anticipated and prepared for this pivotal question. The following dialogue is a representative summary of a lengthier conversation we had during his first appointment:

Tyler: Now that I have told you my story, you need to tell me your honest reaction. Do you believe me?

Therapist: I think I appreciate the crucial nature of your question. But to be certain I do, perhaps you can share your thoughts on the matter? What would your reaction be if I told you that I fully believe you? And likewise, what would your reaction be if told you I didn't?

Tyler: Well that's pretty simple. If you believe me, I stay and we can meet some more, and if you don't believe me, this will have been a colossal waste of my time, and you won't see me again.

Therapist: I can see why it may seem simple, but from my perspective it seems like it could be more complicated than that. I agree that if I told you that I didn't believe you, you would have no good reason to trust me and you might very well choose to discontinue our working together. At the same time, I worry that if I tell you that I believe every word you said, our work will become thoroughly consumed by the extremely complicated situation you described to me, which then leads to another big problem—a problem that deserves equal consideration: Tyler, I am sorry to say that I have zero expertise nor a speck of experience in anything connected to the computer technology or the espionage you described, so I fear that I am not the right person to help you with those difficulties.

Tyler: Then maybe you should tell me why I'm even here.

Therapist: Because I do have expertise in helping people cope with the effects of extremely stressful situations like the one you are experiencing. I am well versed in helping people cope with stress, like the terrible anxiety and despair you were feeling shortly before you were admitted to the hospital. I feel hopeful that I could help you with those kinds of issues moving forward.

Tyler: I think I understand what you're saying (several second pause). But you are not saying that you don't believe me.

Therapist: I'm not saying that I don't believe you. I can see that the problems you described have deeply affected you.

Tyler: (Another long pause). I think I can live with that for now. But I guess that means you wouldn't be able to write a letter to the university provost, telling her that I'm not crazy and that if they don't reinstate me I will be forced to sue.

Therapist: Again, I have no expertise that would allow me to have a meaningful opinion concerning that, but I would very much like to work together to figure out how you might get through the weeks and months ahead with less pain than you have been suffering.

Tyler: Okay then. I guess I can give this a try.

Outcome and Prognosis

Tyler and I proceeded to meet weekly for the next few years. While we explicitly agreed that I would remain neutral/noncommittal concerning his conspiracy story, he was still consumed by feelings of having been betrayed by several individuals at his former university for the first several months of treatment. But over time, the conversation gradually shifted to discussing how there were many other people he felt cheated and betrayed by since his youth, revealing it was a theme that journeyed beyond more recent perceived injustices. He also began sharing his profound feelings of disappointment concerning how his technological brilliance was being wasted as a result of not being able to continue his studies. However, the grandiosity embedded in these kinds of lamentations gradually gave way to his being able to acknowledge that he occasionally struggled with self-doubt. He no longer obsessed about the technological innovation that had been stolen from him, but rather struggled with the angst connected to how he might have to cope if it turned out that he didn't have a second brilliant discovery to supplant the first.

Largely owing to the agreement that we would do our best to focus on the elements of daily living that I could help him with, I was gradually successful in helping him attend to certain issues that significantly affected the quality of his day-to-day life. For example, Tyler acknowledged that in the months prior to his hospitalization, he had been drinking eight or more beers most evenings in response to feeling angry and depressed about the state of his life. He shared how he had consumed a large amount of alcohol on the evening he had been hit by the car, showing some awareness of its potential harm and consequences if he continued to drink in this manner. Tyler also expressed anger and frustration about not having enough money, as well as feelings of depression and boredom related to spending too much time watching Netflix and not having any real purpose in his days. Thus, we began discussing the benefits of getting a job, at least a temporary one, in order to have an income and to add valuable structure so that he might also have an easier time resuming a healthy sleep/wake schedule.

Eventually, Tyler felt comfortable enough to share the heartache he suffered in response to his girlfriend breaking up with him shortly before his hospitalization. He alternated between angry accusations and tearful laments concerning how she had "abandoned" him during his "hour of greatest need." Thus, we were able to begin talking about the positive and negative aspects of that relationship and earlier romantic relationships, none of which had ever lasted more than 5 months. We identified and discussed his pattern of becoming absorbed in his own personal interests early on in relationships, not placing equal value on meeting his former girlfriends' needs, and then feeling angry and confused when the relationship deteriorated and ended. To his credit, Tyler was much less defensive and blaming than I thought he might be during these conversations, and he earnestly engaged in considering how he might approach future relationships in a healthier manner than he had in the past. We addressed these concerns one by one, and gradually over the next 24 months Tyler stopped drinking alcohol; he found a job selling advertising space in a community newspaper (which later led to a second job writing feature articles for the same paper); and he eventually met another girlfriend with whom he experienced more success in terms of having a longer, more intimate romantic relationship.

In place of being able to claim rightful ownership of his "innovative technology," he allowed himself to shift his energies to more ordinary tasks of daily living. One of my primary roles as his psychotherapist was helping him find meaning and value in things that he previously regarded as relatively unimportant. When his coworker gave him a birthday card, it provided an opportunity to reflect on how his attempts to be friendlier had paid off, helping him feel less of an outsider. When his sister invited him to share a major holiday with her husband and children, it was an opportunity to reflect on how his efforts to put aside past resentments and call her once a week over a period of months had allowed them to reconnect, helping him make room for the possibility that she had not actually abandoned him to the degree that he had supposed.

In terms of evaluating the success of the psychotherapy, it was not entirely successful in leading Tyler to wholly relinquish the belief that his former adviser and university had cheated him out of his technological innovation and his degree. His delusion did not evaporate, but it did steadily transform from being an obsession that dominated nearly every waking hour to a significantly thorny, painful issue that he was helpless to influence (owing to the unrelenting power and influence of the NSA). Without antipsychotic medication, Tyler's delusion successfully receded from the foreground to the background of his life, where it might permanently reside.

Discussion Questions

1. Compare the symptoms of delusional disorder to schizophrenia and explain why a delusional disorder diagnosis was ultimately made in this case.

2. Discuss why a trusting relationship is difficult to establish with a paranoid person, and how Tyler's psychotherapist establishes a trusting relationship with Tyler.

3. What specific changes was Tyler able to make during his treatment?

4. Why does Tyler's psychotherapist say Tyler's therapy was not completely successful? Do you agree? Explain.

3

Major Depressive Disorder With Comorbid Depressive Personality Disorder

Presenting Problem and Client Description

Ms. S. called my office late one night crying uncontrollably. Through her sobbing and in a soft voice she explained she was under a lot of pressure at work, she was having difficulty concentrating, unable to sleep, and frequently found herself in tears. As a result, she was having difficulty completing her work, which further contributed to her distress as she had a lot of responsibility as an executive vice president at a major corporation. She explained she was currently in treatment—a treatment I would learn later had been ongoing for 2 years—but that she was becoming increasingly dissatisfied with it. As I listened to the voice mail, I thought she sounded desperate, and I worried about her safety. She certainly sounded depressed and even in a brief phone message appeared to meet a number of criteria for major depressive disorder (MDD; e.g., reports of difficulty concentrating, difficulty sleeping, clearly sad with low mood). I returned her call the next morning. She sounded somewhat relieved but nonetheless depressed. Her voice was low and she spoke slowly. She assured me that although she had felt at her wits end, she was not suicidal. After a brief conversation, I agreed to see her for a consultation as a second opinion in order to give her recommendations about whether or not I thought her concerns merited a change in therapists.

During our initial meeting, I found out that Ms. S. was a 45-year-old woman of Arab descent with a master's in business administration from an Ivy League business school. She was the oldest of four children and had two brothers and a sister. Her father was a successful physician and her mother ran the household and was an amateur musician of local note. She described her family as religious Christians and strict, and that growing up she regularly went to church, although as an adult she identified as an atheist. She described being a very well-behaved and dutiful child. Her father and mother both had standing in their church, and her mother was particularly active within it. Ms. S. was substantially older than her sister, who was her youngest sibling. Ms. S. described her father as a kind and unassuming man but who allowed her mother to emotionally and physically abuse her. Although she described her father with much affection, she felt he had a blind spot when it came to her mother. The patient described a long history and many credible-sounding incidents of emotional and physical abuse as well as controlling behavior that intensified when the patient entered high school. The physical violence, which occurred throughout her childhood, began to happen more frequently, and her mother would scream at her, accusing her of having impure motives, questioning her commitments to the religion, the family in general, and to her. During these fights, her mother frequently called her names such as *slut* and accused her of desiring and engaging in sex. Additionally, the patient described her mother as attacking her during these incidents, which included slapping her, hitting her with open hands, punching her with a closed fist, throwing objects at her, throwing her into walls, knocking her down, and kicking her. The patient was tearful during these descriptions, sometimes angry, and other times appearing perplexed by her mother's behavior. Ms. S. reported that the mother showed little remorse during or after these incidents but instead described that the mother blamed her for having become so upset and for hitting her.

Ironically, the patient reported that she was not very interested in sex at that time but instead was interested in her schoolwork and friendships. She further noted that she had not engaged in any sexual behavior during her high school years and reported that her first sexual experience occurred rather late in her college career.

Now grown, all her siblings were highly successful. Although she described initially being close to her siblings, particularly her closest-in-age brother, she described having been estranged from her family after she went off to college. Rather than going to a small local religious college as her mother wanted, she chose to go to a large university with a strong reputation. This caused a lot of conflict with her mother and, according to the patient, led to her being "disowned," and turned the family against her. During her time as an undergraduate, she did not have many conversations with her father, siblings, or even extended family as she felt her mother spoke badly about her and limited others' contact with her by actively forbidding it. During this time, she felt very much alone and like a family pariah. When she did talk with her mother, it inevitably resulted in an argument. She described feeling hurt that her father abandoned her, but at other times spoke sympathetically about the dilemma he was in vis-à-vis her mother. As she described this time in her life, she became angry with herself, questioning the kind of person she was, and blaming herself for abandoning her family and her lack of loyalty. She was not able to show herself the same kind of sympathy she exhibited toward her father.

Upon graduating from college, she took a job at a major corporation and quickly worked her way up through her intelligence, hard work (e.g., long hours), and creativity in solving problems. A number of times, she developed very innovative solutions to problems facing the company. The company sent her to complete her MBA and promoted her. She continued to shine in her work and was responsible for important developments that resulted in the company making significant profits.

She dated a number of men off and on through college and her early work years. By her description, these men seemed kind and the relationships appeared healthy, but for various reasons, the relationships ended. She typically remained friends with these men. In her late 30s, she met a man who also worked at the same company but in a different division and responsible for very different concerns. He was very much a larger-than-life kind of person. He came from an extremely wealthy and connected family, had attended the best schools, and was highly successful within the company. Together, they were a power couple, a status she very much enjoyed. Both Ms. S. and her relationship partner were not only leaders in the company in their respective areas but within the corporate world. After a number of years dating, they were married. It was a big storybook type of wedding for her husband and his family's sake. She indicated she would have preferred to elope or not even get married but simply live together as they had been.

Despite the storybook description, by the time Ms. S. came to therapy there were significant problems in the relationship. Although he was brilliant, handsome, dashing, and highly successful, he had a prominent dark side. He was very needy with her and controlling of her. Although there was little reason to be jealous, he was very vigilant about her whereabouts and with whom she was interacting. He also needed her to dote over him, which she did, but in those moments where she was not attending to him or had to take care of her own concerns, he could become irate and angry with her. Although over the years he had never been physically abusive toward her, he had frequently lost his temper with her and, similar to her mother, called her all sorts of names, including derogatory sexual ones. A number of times, he threatened physical violence toward her or his suicide. One time during her treatment with me, he had even made a vague but serious threat of homicide against her.

Prior to beginning therapy with me, she had broken up and separated from her husband a number of times. These breakups/separations tended to be short, and neither of them would share with others that they were broken up or separated. One separation, however, was a bit longer than the others were, and during this breakup she began dating another man. She broke up with this other man when she got back together with her husband, but she kept this relationship from him for many years, fearing that it would hurt him deeply and make him infuriated. Over time, she was becoming comfortable with leaving her husband; however, he was easily able to guilt her into staying with him. This was easy to do in part because she had a very strong sense of loyalty and desire to "save" him. Additionally, she felt extremely guilty when she felt that she was not being loyal or committed, or perceived herself as abandoning him. However, he was also able to coerce her into staying with him because of her low self-esteem. Despite her obvious intelligence and successes, she felt undeserving of better. Finally, he was also able to manipulate her into staying in this relationship because the dynamics were familiar to her, as they were very similar to the dynamics of her relationship with her mother. Later in therapy, we would discuss how she was so committed to this relationship because in part it represented an opportunity to fix or correct the relationship with her mother.

Diagnosis and Case Formulation

Based on her description and presentation (beginning with the voice mail she left for me), the diagnosis of MDD was a clear consideration. Other considerations would include what at the time was called *dysthymic disorder* and is now called *persistent depressive disorder*. In order to meet criteria for MDD, a person must meet five or more of nine symptoms. At least one of those five must be either a depressed mood most days, most of the day for at least a 2-week period, or loss of interest or pleasure in all or nearly all activities, again for most of the day for at least a 2-week period. One then needs to meet either three or four additional criteria depending on whether or not a person meets both the depressed mood and loss of interests/pleasure criteria or not. Other criteria include what are referred to as *neurovegetative signs*, which include significant loss of appetite (with corresponding weight loss), insomnia, psychomotor slowing, and fatigue. Conversely, these neurovegetative signs can show themselves through increased appetite, hypersomnia, and psychomotor agitation (this display is often part of an atypical depressive presentation that also includes interpersonal hypersensitivity). The remaining criteria for MDD can be characterized as feelings of worthlessness, inappropriate guilt, and recurrent thoughts of death and suicide, and the cognitive symptom of difficulty concentrating or indecisiveness. As with depressed mood, these symptoms need to be nearly every day. Additionally, these symptoms must represent a change from previous functioning. In this way, MDD is conceptualized as an episodic disorder. The *Diagnostic and Statistical Manual of Mental Disorders* (5th ed.; *DSM–5*) also includes a number of specifiers for the severity of the episode. Also, the symptoms cannot be part of a psychotic-like disorder, substance abuse, or other medical condition.

Ms. S. met criteria for depressed mood by her report and my observation. Additionally, she reported that she had bouts of insomnia characterized by anxious worrying and rumination about unfinished tasks, tasks that awaited her, and rumination about decisions she made and her self-worth. However, she also described being able to work very hard on the tasks at hand, and although she would evaluate fruits of her labor quite negatively, much to her surprise her supervisors and coworkers saw her production as exemplary. Nonetheless, she complained of fatigue and loss of energy. She would spend days in bed feeling that she was a failure and a fraud who would soon be found out. The distress about failure would continue until she described it as unbearable, and then she would jump into action and work nonstop until she had completed what needed to be done. This was not a typical pattern for her as she typically had a large work capacity, but from time to time when she described being depressed, she would fall into this pattern. Her descriptions of "being depressed" tended to occur subsequent to her relationship difficulties, and although these feelings involved lowered self-worth, they were rarely precipitated by negative evaluations or failures but instead by relationship difficulties. Although not actively suicidal, during this time she occasionally thought her family and the world in general would be a better place without her. At other times, the thought of not being alive provided a respite from all the stress and tension she felt. There were no other neurovegetative signs, her appetite was good, she showed no psychomotor slowing and very little agitation, and she described her libido (sex drive) as normal—desiring and interested in sex with her partner a few times a week. She described both feelings of worthlessness and excessive and inappropriate guilt. Although these feelings were also characteristic of her typically, during this time they seemed worse than usual. Thus, the diagnosis of MDD was deemed appropriate. However, despite describing feelings of depression that had occurred throughout her life from the time she was young, she did not meet criteria for persistent depressive disorder because she reported never having had a period of feeling depressed that lasted 2 years without a period of being depression free that lasted more than 2 months at a time. Nonetheless, she reported a personality style that was consistent with the *DSM-4* description of depressive personality disorder, a disorder included in *DSM-4* for further study but not included in *DSM-5*. The concept of depressive personality or characterological depression has a long history in psychiatry; however, a number of authors have suggested that it could be subsumed under persistent personality disorder. Although the concept of a depressive personality disorder sounds similar to that of persistent depressive disorder, and the two disorders show some comorbidity (about 30%), the two disorders are conceptually different. Persistent depressive disorder focuses on somatic symptoms consistent with MDD but milder and more chronic. Depressive personality disorder focuses less on somatic symptoms and more on personality and cognitive/affective aspects. Ms. S. met five of the seven criteria, which was sufficient for the diagnosis. Criteria met included (1) having a self-concept that centered around beliefs of inadequacy, worthlessness, and low self-esteem; (2) being critical, blaming, and derogatory toward the self; (3) brooding and given to worry; (4) being critical and judgmental toward others; and (5) being prone to feeling guilty and remorseful. It was unclear whether or not her feelings of pessimism were sufficiently chronic to meet criteria, nor could it be said that her usual mood was dominated by gloominess, cheerlessness, joylessness, or unhappiness to the extent required to meet that criterion. She was certainly prone or susceptible to such feelings and was easily dejected, which is part of that criterion. Regardless, she met enough criteria to meet diagnosis for the disorder.

Another consideration was the diagnosis of borderline personality disorder (BPD). I considered this diagnosis for a number of reasons. First, it is important to evaluate a patient for a comorbid diagnosis of BPD whenever the criteria is met for major depressive disorder. This is because the two disorders are frequently comorbid, and such comorbidity is meaningful in that when that is the case, the presence of BPD negatively affects the course and outcome of MDD. Second, when the patient initially called and complained about her current therapist, I considered that her negative evaluation of the therapist might be consistent with the kind of devaluation that those with BPD are prone toward. However, during the evaluation it became apparent that the patient did not meet criteria for BPD.

The patient asked about medication and indicated a strong desire for something that would make her feel better quickly. Despite being highly educated, Ms. S., like many others, was unclear about who could and could not prescribe medication. She was surprised when I told her that as a psychologist, I was not able to prescribe medication. We discussed medication as an option for her. I shared with her my understanding of the empirical literature with regard to medication for depression and my belief that psychotherapy would be a good option for her given her pattern of symptoms. However, I also encouraged her to seek a consultation with a psychiatrist or other psychopharmacologist prescriber (e.g., nurse practitioner). I told her that I had colleagues I could recommend to her or that she was free to find a prescriber on her own. She decided to see someone whom I recommended but who was also on her independent list of providers. With the psychiatrist, as with me, she expressed a strong desire for a medication that might offer immediate relief from her distress. The pharmacologist explained that the medication might provide her some relief; however, it too would take time to reach therapeutic levels before beginning to work, and she additionally explained that the relief would most likely be partial in that many of her concerns would not be amenable to medications but instead would need to be worked out in the therapy. Nonetheless, it was explained that on the positive side, medication may help reduce her distress in a manner that would allow her to be more psychologically available for psychotherapy and, in addition, might provide her with more energy. On the negative side, it was noted that the medication had some minor side effects such as temporary dry mouth and blurred vision, and more long-lasting side effects such as decreased sexual desire, weight gain, and constipation. Additionally, a serious side effect of antidepressant medication can be manic-like symptoms and agitation associated with the increased energy. Ms. S. expressed concerns about these side effects in the context of preexisting concerns about her bowels, already feeling energized and agitated at times, and concerns about possible weight gain and diminished sexual functioning. The psychopharmacologist suggested that she continue without medication for now, that she and I closely monitor her for worsening symptoms, and that she be reevaluated for medication in 1 or 2 months. Additionally, Ms. S. expressed a concern about what it meant to her self-concept to be someone who needed medication.

Course of Treatment

Ms. S. began treatment in a very distressed state of mind, frequently asking for reassurance but continuing to talk in a way that precluded the therapist from having the opportunity to do so. Early on, I brought this up with her. In the discussion, I raised the possibility that maybe she was afraid to give me a chance to reassure her because she was concerned that my reassurances would not be enough or might run hollow. I offered that maybe there was a part of her that even wondered if I would offer reassurance. Maybe she feared I did not believe that things would get better for her, and talking the way she did prevented her from these difficult possibilities. She reflected on what I had just said and indicated that it resonated with her. My comment seemed to help in the moment, for she settled a bit and allowed me to engage productively in a conversation with her. As we discussed her feelings and concerns more directly, she described how she was afraid that I would tell her that she was hopeless and doomed to fail. She was also afraid that I would tell her that she had to leave her husband and that I would not understand her loyalty to him. Hearing about her husband's behavior during the assessment phase and during the course of the therapy did evoke feelings in me that she should leave him. Sigmund Freud referred to the feelings evoked in the therapist during the treatment as countertransferential feelings or as countertransference. As she described how the husband responded and treated her, I too, like her previous therapist, wanted to say something and encourage her to consider leaving him. It was difficult, and I restrained myself because although I wanted to be authentic and true to my feelings state, I also wanted to create an atmosphere that was open and that encouraged her to bring up her thoughts and feelings for us to explore rather than convey my values and make judgments about her perceptions and behaviors. I was afraid that if I responded by encouraging her to leave the husband, she would experience me as judging her and controlling her like the last therapist and her husband. Instead, what I did was lay in wait for those moments that she brought up her own concerns about him. I carefully crafted my comments as to acknowledge both sides of her conflict: the part of her that was committed to him, devoted, and loyal, and who admired him and loved him, as well as that part of her that felt judged, controlled, belittled, and emotionally abused by him. I tried to gently bring both sides of her experience into her awareness for us, as a team, to grapple with. It was difficult because she would vacillate back and forth between feeling committed to him and feeling fed up with him. It was like watching a tennis match with the ball going back and forth, back and forth. It was as if articulating one position for her forced her to rebound into the other position. Therefore, if she spoke negatively about her husband, she would eventually need to reaffirm her admiration and commitment to him. When she spoke negatively about him, she would often attack herself for doing so and question what kind of person was she who would say such things. In those moments, I felt she needed reassurance, but I was afraid that my reassurances would not be experienced as intended. When I tried to reassure her, instead of feeling reassured, she responded as if I were naïve or unable to see how truly bad she was. I not only failed to reassure her but I invalidated her experience and made myself look inept. Instead, I joined her in her commendation, but only in the mildest way and only briefly, before I questioned us both by asking her if she, or anyone, could be a good, well-meaning person and still have doubts or questions. She acknowledged that one could be a good person and well-intentioned and legitimately have doubts. Moreover, confronting one's doubts is inherently honest and genuine. When she acknowledged that, I asked her what got in the way of showing herself the same attitude she allowed others. As the therapy progressed, she would bring up her concerns about her husband more frequently and be able to stay with those concerns for longer periods before swinging back into a defense of him. Additionally, she was much more tolerant of her ambivalence toward him. This allowed us to discuss his attitude and behavior toward her more directly, and resulted in her becoming more aware of his limitations. Early on, she wanted me to tell her that he would change and get better. As the treatment went on, she became more aware and tolerant that he was not changing but that she was.

During the course of the therapy, Ms. S. separated with the husband a number of times. However, they tended to be in contact and he would exert great pressure on her to reconcile, which she did a number of times. However, during one separation she was particularly resolute about not getting back together. He responded by being more aggressive in his coercion, which generally followed a pattern of acknowledging that they were separated, admitting that he behaved badly but begging her until she broke down and agreed to have dinner with him or get together with him for pleasure or work. She often agreed to do these things. There were a number of reasons. Part of her held out hope that he would change; another part caved because she was worn down by his constant barrage of insistence, and another part of her also was trying to appease him. During these dinners and meetings, he would be especially charming, leaving her to doubt her decision. However, one dinner get-together during a separation evolved quite differently. As dinner came to a close, he pressed her to come back to his hotel with him. She refused and reminded him that they were separated. In public, he loudly accused her of having an affair and became visibly angry and threatening of suicide, all of which was common in these situations between them. However, her resistance was stronger than typical and he responded by angrily threatening to kill her. She was scared by his affect and words and called me. I was also concerned. While I was soothed by the fact that he had never previously been physically violent toward her, I was also very concerned given his affect and the seriousness of this threat, and therefore advised her not to return home but to get a hotel room, stay with a friend or relative (she had a sister within a few hours), or to go to the local women's resource center. This incident crystalized for Ms. S. the seriousness of the situation with her husband and led to greater resolve on her part to separate from him and to divorce him. Over a period of a few months, she was able to complete her separation and to resist his attempts to persuade her to allow him into her life. He found a permanent separate residence, and after initial threats of suicide and declarations of his need for her, he began to be more accepting of their separate lives. She began seeing the man whom she briefly dated during one of her previous separations from her husband. This relationship quickly became serious, although she did not share being in a relationship with her ex-husband. Both Ms. S. and her new boyfriend had reasons for wanting to keep their relationship private. Ms. S.'s new boyfriend was also a titan of the corporate world, in some ways even more so than her ex-husband. He worked in a similar but noncompeting capacity for another company, which provided her with some more freedom than did working at the same company with her ex-husband.

One aspect of the treatment that I found difficult was to keep the focus on her own issues rather than on her husband. Sometimes I felt it was the husband who was in therapy by proxy rather than Ms. S. (this despite the significant issues Ms. S. struggled with). She wanted reassurance about her husband and had a difficult time staying with her own experience or wanting to explore her own role in the dynamics with him. However, with the separation firmly in place and as she was able to proceed with the divorce, the focus on the treatment was more on her and similar dynamics that were playing out with a new romantic partner and with coworkers. The new boyfriend was emotionally intimate with her in satisfying ways when they were alone on trips but much less so other times. They both traveled for business and often to the same cities or were able to arrange rendezvous in nearby locations. While they were together, she experienced him as romantic, intimate, and close. He talked about getting married and even adopting children. This level of intimacy was belied by the fact that they kept their relationship private, and when out in public they acted as colleagues, not lovers. As time went on, Ms. S. wanted to be more open about the relationship. Her ex-husband now knew about the relationship and, although somewhat jealous, he was accepting of the relationship, he was doing well on his own, and he was even dating other women. Ms. S. wanted to proceed with his talk of getting married, albeit doing so relatively slowly. At this point, her boyfriend began to distance himself from her. He was less available when traveling and began expressing concerns about going public with their relationship and getting married. Ms. S. began to feel as if she were not really his girlfriend but instead his mistress. After discussing this in the therapy, the patient became more confident about confronting him regarding her concern. His response was very dismissive, and she was quite upset. Eventually, she broke up with him and began casually dating men who were both successful and appeared nice.

With coworkers, she often felt judged and persecuted, and this was a pattern that existed from her earliest years at the company. She was long considered one of the favorites of the CEO of the company due to her strong work ethic and outstanding performance. She had a knack for solving complicated problems in ways that could be described as win-win for the parties involved. When a win-win solution was not possible, she was able to fight hard for the company's interests. She was well liked by those with whom her company was negotiating, and her cultural background allowed her to work with foreign companies, particularly those in Saudi Arabia and other Middle Eastern countries. However, she and the person directly above her clashed on vision. This generally was not an issue because the company CEO held her in high regard, but it did cause tension at times in meetings. Ms. S. had a difficult time tolerating such tension. She often felt attacked and the victim of his and other people's mean-spirited aggression. She often perceived that others were bothered by her work ethic and success, and felt persecuted for it. What she described in session sounded well within normal limits for office politics, although at times understandably upsetting. Nonetheless, her response often felt exaggerated and more appropriate for a response to how she was treated by her mother and her ex-husband. From a nonjudgmental stance, we explored her response to her perception of others' provocations. In these discussions, her difficulty with her own aggression became central. Common in those prone to depression can be difficulties with one's own aggressive impulses. Depressed individuals often experience these feelings in magnified ways and experience intense guilt in relation to them. Ms. S. was no different. A turning point in our work about this occurred one session when Ms. S. arrived shaken. In tears, clearly upset with herself, she recounted how she had just "lost it" and had an inappropriate outburst at an important executive company meeting. She was afraid she would get fired and conveyed to me that if she were in charge she would have fired her on the spot. I asked her what happened. She began to describe the events in detail. I listened carefully for her outburst. The patient went on for about 15 minutes and still I had not heard the outburst, so I interrupted her and asked, "So when did your outburst occur?" She stared at me with a surprised expression and said that she had already described it. I stared back at her with a surprised expression, as I was unclear as to what part of what she had just described to me would constitute an "outburst," a sentiment I shared with her. She then recounted the "outburst" in which she described responding to something glib that a colleague said by suggesting that his comment was not helpful to the discourse, and then she went on to focus the discussion in a more productive manner. What she described sounded perfectly appropriate, contained, and even helpful to the dialogue. I thought about sharing my opinion but reckoned that it might not resonate with her and could be invalidating. Instead, I thought it might be more impactful to ask how other people responded to her comment. She shared with me that a number of other people came up to her after the meeting to thank her for her comment. The coworker was often experienced as bullying the group and making fruitless comments and contributions, and people felt that her comment appropriately contained him. I then asked her what she made of her reaction compared to what other people had shared with her. I then joked that it was a good thing she wasn't the boss because she would have fired herself rather than appreciate herself. She was able to laugh, and this led into a discussion about how she emotionally beats up on herself even when undeserved. We tied the pattern to how she experiences and responds not only to coworkers but also to relationship partners and family members. This discussion led into a discussion of a difficult dynamic regarding how she had taken on the role of her mother, who no longer was emotionally or physically abusing her, by emotionally beating up on herself. She described this as an "aha" moment of great insight that led her to treat herself differently.

Outcome and Prognosis

Ms. S. was able to weather the difficult breakup with her boyfriend and manage the relationship with her ex-husband and coworker openly and with healthy boundaries. She was able to begin dating again and showed an increased capacity to reflect and make decisions about how she felt about these men without feeling pressured by them or her own desire to have a relationship. She seemed more at peace with where things were and confident that she would find a suitable relationship. She became more tolerant of her mother, despite resentments toward her and difficulties with some of her mother's values. Her relationships with her siblings strengthened, particularly her younger sister, with whom she became more tolerant and friendly. At work, she continued to be successful but was now able to enjoy her success more fully. She was more tolerant of her coworkers and less entangled in their concerns. As she became more tolerant of herself, she also became more tolerant of others.

Discussion Questions

1. Describe the symptoms the patient displayed that met the criteria for Major Depressive Disorder (MDD).

2. Explain counter-transference, and how it played a role in the patient's treatment.

3. Describe an aspect of the treatment that proved difficult for both Ms. S. and her therapist.

Bipolar I Disorder

Presenting Problem and Client Description

Andrea is a 29-year-old Caucasian woman employed as the codirector of development (aka chief fundraiser) for a large nonprofit organization in the United States, a national charity that funded countless local efforts to support at-risk children and their families. Her job required her to travel to most of the major cities east of the Mississippi River, often several times per year, to meet with both established and potential donors as well as oversee the major fundraising events being coordinated by the local offices. Andrea was proud of her career success and very invested in and gratified by the humanitarian mission she served. Likewise, she also placed a high value on staying connected to her close-knit family; thus, she lived only 20 minutes away from her parents' home in the DC suburbs and usually saw them at least weekly in spite of her intense travel schedule. She typically enjoyed a sunny disposition and was outgoing and optimistic by nature, all of which had been major assets in her chosen profession.

Earlier in the year, Andrea had become engaged to marry a man named Shaun whom she had met at one of her fundraising events and had been dating for more than 2 years. He also had a demanding job working as a top aide for a U.S. government official, which likewise required long hours and significant amounts of travel. From the beginning of their relationship, he had been very open with Andrea that he had political aspirations of his own, a fact that Andrea embraced and admired. They had a lot in common, deeply enjoyed each other's company when they had time together, and found satisfaction in viewing themselves as a "power couple" of sorts. They both viewed themselves as approaching the prime decades of their lives closely bonded to their joint and individual aspirations, so it was rather surprising to both of them when Andrea reluctantly began to complain to Shaun that she feared she was "slowly but surely losing [her] mojo." She had noticed that she had begun sleeping poorly, often waking between 3 and 4 a.m. unable to return to sleep, causing her to feel tired and clamoring for a nap that her schedule never allowed. She began to have difficulty with focus and concentration to the degree that responding to 50-plus e-mails every day became an onerous chore in a way that felt different and demoralizing. Her previously effortless effervescence began to feel artificial and labored to the degree that she began turning down invitations from friends and avoiding social media. And most saliently, Andrea noticed that on most days she felt quite sad and morose in a manner that was "totally out of character" and for no apparent reason. She confided to a close friend, "I feel like I'm walking around like someone in my family suddenly died, when in fact nobody has."

After struggling with these difficulties for 2 months and realizing something was "really wrong" with her, Andrea made an appointment to see her primary care provider (PCP). To both her relief and disappointment, all of the tests came back normal, and her PCP suggested that she suspected she was experiencing a depressive episode. Andrea felt relieved that she wasn't suffering from something like leukemia or some other illness that could explain her symptoms of utter exhaustion, but she also felt disappointed that it wasn't something that a regimen of vitamins couldn't cure. Her PCP offered her a prescription for antidepressant medication, which she accepted but did not fill at the pharmacy due to feeling certain her depression was due to stress at work, which had considerably increased during the past year. Instead, she decided that she wanted to take a "natural approach" to treating her depression symptoms. Accordingly, she attacked the problem in the same direct manner she approached most things: renewing her efforts to exercise and eat healthily, seeking the support of friends, and most important, making adjustments at work by successfully lobbying to hire a second executive assistant to whom she delegated some of her travel-related responsibilities, allowing her to reduce her own traveling commitments considerably.

Although it required some patience on her part, Andrea slowly but surely began feeling better. Later on, she would report to her psychologist that her sleep pattern, energy level, and mood gradually all returned to normal during the following 4 to 5 months, so that when fall arrived, she was able to fully plunge herself into all of the countless smaller details needed to plan the kind of early-summer wedding she had hoped and expected to pull off for herself and Shaun the following year. Before she knew it, she had begun burning the midnight oil, giving her career her full attention and effort during the day, and then working on her wedding and honeymoon plans from 9 p.m. to 1 a.m. and later more nights than not. No detail was too small—from the various fonts she considered for her invitations, tracking down and evaluating the merits of 10 different varieties of roses that would be available in the early summer, to trying to accommodate the numerous food allergies and sensitivities plaguing some of her guests by constructing a menu that the caterer complained turned into an assortment of dishes that altogether seemed odd. Andrea would admit that she was allowing herself to be consumed by the planning, but simultaneously insisted to her fiancé and others, who were becoming a little concerned, that she was "having a ball" and "loving every second of it."

Unfortunately, 10 weeks or so prior to their wedding day, Andrea, along with the wedding plans and logistics, began to unravel. Shaun first noticed that Andrea seemed to be sleeping less and less. For the first week or two, he convinced himself that it was not a big deal, that she was merely excited about the wedding, which was to be expected. He discerned that it was not that Andrea could not sleep as much as she seemed to need very little sleep, which was quite different than when she had felt utterly exhausted but unable to sleep the year before. In response to his bidding, Andrea always agreed to lay down for 3 to 4 hours, but he suspected she had not slept more than 1 or 2. When Shaun expressed concern about this and the fact that he thought she was losing too much weight from not eating enough, Andrea insisted she felt "amazing," and this indeed seemed true—she was even more upbeat and energetic than usual, actually more buoyant than he'd ever seen.

At the same time, it had gradually become apparent to both Shaun and Andrea's boss that in spite of her high energy level, her daily efforts were steadily becoming much less focused. On one recent morning, the couple got into an argument when Andrea abruptly decided that she needed to expand their wedding invitation list by 50% owing to Andrea's burgeoning belief that they were at risk of offending countless people by not including them. However, the list included people like Andrea's favorite elementary school teacher, to whom she had not spoken in over 10 years, and Shaun's best man's estranged stepfather, whom she had never met. That same week, the wedding caterer fired Andrea in response to erratic, constantly shifting and bizarre requests, such as her insistence that each table be equipped with an electric blender so guests could make their own smoothies. Next, Andrea's boss overheard her preparing to cash out her entire savings and retirement accounts. When gently asked about her rationale, Andrea glowingly announced that in addition to working for her nonprofit organization, it was imperative that she become one of its major donors. Upon learning about this behavior, Shaun pleaded with her to explain herself (and accused her of jumping off the deep end). Andrea, in turn, launched a verbal attack, insisting in urgent, forceful tones that she and the First Lady of the United States shared "a unique mental connection" through which she had ordered Andrea to accept the position of "National Charity Adviser" to the president. The same day, soon after Andrea obsessively began making phone calls to the National Security Agency demanding to speak to the person in charge of providing passes required to gain entrance to the White House, Shaun also made a phone call—to Andrea's parents, expressing alarm and insisting they all needed to bring her to the hospital.

Unlike when she was depressed and able to recognize something was wrong with her, Andrea incredulously insisted she was "100% fine" and adamantly refused to go to the emergency room. Wanting to avoid involving the police or other emergency services, the family concocted a scheme, telling Andrea that her father was having mild chest pains and they all needed to go to the hospital to be certain there wasn't anything seriously wrong with him. She readily agreed to this, expressing great concern for her dad. Upon arriving at the hospital, Andrea's fiancé and father asked to meet privately with the emergency triage nurse and shared their concerns about the recent changes they had seen in Andrea: (1) how she had gradually all but stopped sleeping over the past few weeks; (2) her highly elevated mood and how it spurred grandiose, "crazy" ideas and plans that she wanted to implement for her wedding; (3) her impulsive and extreme decision to empty her bank account to pay for an "around-the-world" honeymoon cruise and other over-the-top wedding expenses;

and (4) erratic and sometimes irritable behavior that was alienating her in varying degrees from friends, family, and wedding vendors.

Not surprisingly, Andrea's concern for her father rapidly shifted to feelings of outrage and betrayal upon meeting with a psychiatric evaluator and gleaning her family's true motives. She was so angered and upset that she became physically combative in a manner that risked physical injury to both Andrea and the people trying to help her. Although it was emotionally difficult for all of them, Shaun and Andrea's parents agreed with the medical staff that Andrea was psychotic, unable to take care of herself, and needed to be involuntarily hospitalized.

Diagnosis and Case Formulation

Diagnosing mental illnesses where psychosis is a central feature can be challenging at times, as there are many distinctive psychiatric and medical illnesses where psychosis is prominent. Making an accurate diagnosis is essential for identifying and implementing the best possible treatment. Additionally, accurate diagnosis often has important implications in appraising the long-term prognosis of someone suffering from psychosis. An individual suffering from acute psychotic symptoms whose diagnostic picture is consistent with a brief psychotic disorder, for example, will probably suffer few, if any, long-term effects and will very likely experience a full recovery and proceed to lead a normal life. In contrast, an individual afflicted by identical psychotic phenomena whose pattern of symptoms warrants a diagnosis of schizophrenia will likely be coping with a lifelong psychiatric illness that may have a significant and enduring impact on his or her quality of life.

Arriving at the correct diagnosis is always first and foremost an information-gathering process that involves examining the patient, obtaining a clinical history, performing any diagnostic tests that appear to be warranted based on the person's presentation and history, followed by interpreting and synthesizing the available data and then generating diagnostic hypotheses. In situations where psychosis is a key element of the clinical picture, obtaining a history that elucidates the individual's symptoms and behaviors during the days, weeks, and even months leading up to the current psychiatric crisis provides crucial information for making a precise diagnosis. And this was certainly the case for Andrea and her family. In Andrea's case, the differential diagnosis, or the list of possible diagnoses that needed to be considered and either ruled in or ruled out based on the available data, are listed in Table 4.1.

When Andrea arrived at the emergency room, her delusional state was a conspicuous part of her presentation and immediately drew the staff's attention. Moreover, her delusions were fueled by an expansive and elevated mood punctuated by irritability. She explained her irritation to the hospital staff by claiming that their "interrogation" was a very rude disruption to her wedding planning efforts. She asserted that this visit to the hospital was putting her at grave risk of not mailing her invitations in time to meet the deadline for keeping the First Lady of the United States on the guest list. Consistent with the list of potential diagnoses listed in Table 4.1, the possibility that Andrea's behavior might be explained by a drug-induced psychosis was considered so

TABLE 4.1 ● Differential Diagnosis: Distinguishing Features of Disorders Characterized by Psychosis	
Brief Psychotic Disorder (or Reactive Psychosis)	A sudden onset of hallucinations, delusions, and/or disorganized speech/behavior lasting between 1 day and 1 month in duration
Bipolar I Disorder, Manic Phase With Psychosis	A distinct period of persistently elevated and/or expansive mood lasting at least 1 week accompanied by delusional thinking and marked increases in energy and goal-directed activity
Major Depressive Disorder With Psychotic Features	Severe depression symptoms accompanied by one or more delusions and/or perceptual disturbances that are nearly always depressive in nature (e.g., one's internal organs rotting or being consumed by insects, false belief of having caused another's death)
Psychotic Disorder Associated With Another Medical Condition	Hallucinations and delusions as a direct consequence of a medical disorder (e.g., brain tumor, Huntington's disease, thyroid abnormality, vitamin B12 deficiency, neurosyphilis)
Schizophrenia	A chronic condition of disordered thinking (e.g., delusions) and/or perception (e.g., hallucinations) accompanied by pervasive deterioration in social functioning; symptom onset is usually gradual and preceded by social withdrawal and isolation
Substance- or Medication-Induced Psychotic Disorder	Hallucinations and/or delusions caused by the physiological effects of a substance (alcohol, marijuana, opioids, etc.) or medication. Symptoms typically subside as blood levels of the substance decrease and disappear.

that it could be either confirmed or disconfirmed by a toxicology screen. In Andrea's case, the toxicology screen showed no evidence of any legal or illegal substances in her system. Additionally, the hospital staff questioned both Andrea and family members regarding any medications she might be taking, including specific queries about whether she was using corticosteroids or antidepressant medication. Corticosteroids, a very common class of medications used to treat a wide variety of disorders (e.g., asthma, rheumatoid arthritis, inflammatory bowel disease) are a well-known cause of mania and psychosis (Cerullo, 2006). Also not uncommonly, an individual taking antidepressant medications (e.g., sertraline, citalopram, duloxetine) may be at risk of developing psychotic mania; however, the staff learned that while Andrea's PCP had offered her a prescription of antidepressant medications several months ago when she was suffering from symptoms of depression, she had declined to take it. Moreover, even if Andrea had filled the prescription, medication-induced psychoses usually develop between a few days and a few weeks of initiating treatment.

During her first couple hours at the hospital, the staff determined that Andrea's symptoms did not stem from a reaction to medications or other substances. Her decreased need for sleep had steadily progressed over the past 3 weeks to the extent that it seemed Andrea barely felt the need to sleep at all during the past few days. Her fiancé, Shaun, reported that Andrea's wedding preparations had shifted from being focused and efficient to increasingly frenzied and sometimes bizarre, confirming that the First Lady of the United States was not among Andrea's friends or acquaintances. In addition, conversations with Andrea revealed that her speech was rapid and pressured, as if it could not keep pace with her mind as it seemingly raced from one thought to another. Andrea's excellent premorbid functioning, that is the manner and degree she coped with the demands of daily living prior to the onset of her current symptoms, was instrumental in ruling out schizophrenia and borderline personality as likely possibilities. And finally, the fact that Andrea's father was able to confirm both her paternal uncle and grandfather had been diagnosed with bipolar disorder during their 20s served to bolster the hospital staff's belief that she was experiencing the manic phase of a bipolar illness.

Course of Treatment

The episode of acute mania profoundly affected Andrea's capacity to regulate basic functions including sleep, eating, physical activity, mood, and attention; therefore, the initial emphasis of her treatment was to provide medication and a highly structured environment to address these areas of dysregulation. More so than for other psychological disorders, bipolar I disorder is virtually always treated with psychotropic medications, although psychotherapy is also a vital component of treatment for many individuals. Accordingly, Andrea was given a mood stabilizing medication called lithium, a naturally occurring salt. And while very effective, lithium often takes as long as 2 weeks to achieve complete mood restabilization; thus, she was also given a fast-acting antipsychotic medication called quetiapine. As expected, over the next 2 days Andrea's agitation and psychotic delusion began to subside, and she was finally able to sleep up to several hours at a time. By the fourth day, Andrea was well enough to begin participating in structured therapeutic activities, including a family therapy meeting with Shaun and her parents. During the meeting, it became clear that Andrea had recovered enough to feel embarrassed about the way she had behaved over the past couple weeks, issuing tearful apologies and needing reassurances from them that she "hadn't ruined everything." On the eighth day, Andrea was no longer psychotic and well enough to return home.

After being discharged from the hospital, Shaun, Andrea, and her parents all breathed a sigh of relief, feeling the worst was over and expecting that with their support, Andrea would "pick up the pieces" and resume normal life. And to some degree that is what she did; however, it was a long process, and often a painful one. As often happens, after Andrea's mania subsided, she gradually slipped back into a depressive phase of bipolar I illness. However, this time around, Andrea began to attend weekly psychotherapy. Her depression was complicated by several stressors: having to take an extended medical leave from her job, having to postpone (and possibly cancel) her wedding, and processing feeling around the fact that she had a long-term, albeit treatable, illness that would require taking mood-stabilizing medication(s) for the rest of her life. Early on, therapy helped Andrea contain her fears about passing on her mood disorder to any children she might have one day. But more distressing were the new doubts about marrying Shaun due to fears of burdening him with a partner that did not match up to the "power couple" image she had projected before her manic episode.

In addition to addressing emotional distress, Andrea's psychotherapist gradually but persistently introduced the facts about bipolar disorder, as this knowledge is one of the most important weapons for preventing future manic and depressive episodes. Due to its episodic nature, developing awareness around factors that may precipitate a relapse is a vital component of psychotherapy (i.e., work stress, relationship stress, skipping doses of medication, getting insufficient amounts of sleep). After returning to work, Andrea particularly struggled with the idea that she could no longer ignore her stress level and work 16-hour days at the expense of getting enough sleep. And for a few months this issue became an unexpected and repetitious source of tension between Andrea and Shaun—to the degree that they began to question if they could have a future together.

With some encouragement from Andrea's psychotherapist, they agreed to attend a series of appointments together in order to gain a better understanding of what was happening between them. Andrea was the first to speak in their first joint appointment by complaining that Shaun had been admonishing each time she worked a 12-hour day. Showing controlled frustration, Shaun countered saying, "She has to know that keeping up that kind of pace is playing with fire! She says she cares about our relationship, and she doesn't seem to see that when she ignores her health, she not only risks hurting herself, but it's like she doesn't care about our relationship." Andrea responded indignantly, arguing, "Ever since I was discharged from the hospital, Shaun has used my illness as a license to control every single freakin' detail of my life! He treats me like an 8-year-old, and I can't be with someone who treats me as someone less than an equal!"

With relative ease, the therapist discerned that Andrea's illness had upset the power balance in their relationship. Shaun felt Andrea did not appreciate that his efforts to encourage her to prioritize her health were motivated by feelings of love and concern, and he felt frustrated and misunderstood when she misinterpreted his efforts. Andrea, on the other hand, expressed feeling angry and scared that Shaun's behavior was a direct reflection of his no longer respecting and/or valuing her as much as he did prior to the events that led up to her hospitalization. In her mind, Andrea equated Shaun's attempts to show love by encouraging her to take care of herself to an accusation that she was weak.

With help from Andrea's psychotherapist, Andrea reluctantly acknowledged that her attention to taking care of herself had been slipping with greater frequency lately. Individuals diagnosed with bipolar disorder, like many chronic illnesses, differ in their ability to understand that they are suffering from the disorder. This may lead to an unwillingness to make necessary changes in their lifestyle to manage the disorder. The psychotherapist viewed one overarching goal for therapy as helping Andrea to value herself in a manner that was less narrowly defined. The therapist began to gently challenge Andrea's tendency to view herself through an overly narrow lens of "I must always be the absolute best in order to have any value at all." Eventually, Andrea was able to acknowledge that part of her "take no prisoners" attitude toward living was a need to prop up her own self-concept rather than a realistic reflection of the amount of effort she needed to exert in order to be successful in both her professional life and personal life.

Outcome and Prognosis

Not surprisingly, after allowing herself some time to adjust to the relatively new reality of having bipolar I disorder, Andrea was able to bring the same amount of diligence and optimism to maintaining her mental health that she had previously brought to the other areas of her life. Approximately 2 years after marrying Shaun, Andrea gave birth to a healthy son. Both of them would now say that the silver lining of Andrea's mood disorder was that it forced both of them to step back and reexamine certain assumptions about the kind of life they previously thought they wanted with each other. Today, they realize that much of what they thought they had wanted had been more tied to status than substance. Andrea takes pride in the fact that she has not suffered either a major depression or manic episode for years, and thanks to medication and therapy feels she is even healthier and more "whole" than she had been before her hospitalization.

Discussion Questions

1. Describe the symptoms Andrea was experiencing around the time she told her fiancé she was afraid she was "losing her mojo." Then compare them to the symptoms Shaun and Andrea's boss noticed in her about 10 weeks prior to the wedding.

2. Explain why it was significant that Andrea recognized her need to see a doctor when she was experiencing depressive symptoms, but did not recognize that something was wrong when she was experiencing manic symptoms.

3. What specific symptoms and factors were considered in Andrea's diagnosis?

4. Briefly describe what initial- and long-term treatment for Andrea entailed.

Reference

Cerullo, M. A. (2006, June). Corticosteroid-induced mania: Prepare for the unpredictable. *Current Psychiatry, 5*(6), 43–50.

5

Panic Disorder With Generalized Anxiety Disorder

Presenting Problem and Client Description

Mercedes was a 20-year-old African American college student, living at home with her mother in their apartment outside New York City at the time she sought help at the university's student counseling center. At our first meeting she was friendly and warm, shooting out a seemingly confident hand to shake mine. A tall, attractive woman, she was wearing a pair of fashionable black leather over-the-knee boots paired with a sweater and jeans. I would soon learn that her outgoing and self-assured manner disguised some ambivalence about seeking mental health treatment, for which she only called and set up the appointment because earlier attempts to address recent problems had been unsuccessful. From her perspective, her willingness to talk to a psychotherapist provided clear and troubling evidence concerning the degree she was feeling desperate for help. But to her credit, she countered her strong reluctance by jumping into our first session with both feet; like a sprinter charging toward the finish line, she provided a highly detailed history about the issues and concerns that caused her to seek psychotherapy.

In a matter-of-fact rather than a boastful manner, she described herself as a highly intelligent woman, one of only a dozen or so female biomedical engineering majors at her large urban university. She had accumulated a 3.8 grade point average over her first five semesters; however, this semester, Mercedes was struggling academically—straining to earn even Bs and Cs, a position that was both very unfamiliar and highly distressing to her. During the initial 2-hour assessment, Mercedes explained that she was seeking help because over the past 10 weeks she had suffered "three heart attacks, which were apparently not heart attacks but 'crazy attacks' according to the doctors." She shared this in a tone that seemed to convey embarrassment tinged with skepticism and went on to describe three separate and distinct episodes where she experienced a sudden, overwhelming fear that she was going to die, accompanied by a racing heartbeat and the physical sensation that her heart was going to explode. The first episode occurred on a Friday afternoon on her way home from school when she stopped at a grocery store to buy food for her and her mother to use to prepare meals for the following week, a joint activity they both enjoyed. Mercedes described how she was collecting food items based on a list her mother had given her when she suddenly suffered acute chest pains, shortness of breath, and dizziness. Her symptoms were so overpowering that she asked a store employee to find her a chair so she could sit, and she appeared so stricken that the manager promptly called 9-1-1 and an ambulance arrived to take her to the local emergency department. Mercedes had been diagnosed with a benign heart murmur when she was a child; thus, both she and her mother were very anxious that she was having a serious cardiac event. Taking her concerns very seriously, an emergency physician performed an electrocardiogram as well as a diagnostic cardiac ultrasound, and fortunately, both showed Mercedes's heart was as healthy as one would expect a 20-year-old's heart should be. The physician told her it appeared her symptoms "did not have a physical basis," but rather they appeared consistent with panic disorder. Accordingly, shortly after her first emergency room visit, her primary care provider had prescribed two antianxiety medications (sertraline and lorazepam). She reported that she had been taking them as directed, but due to significant and enduring anxiety and occasional severe attacks similar to those that brought her to the emergency room, she did not believe the medications had been adequately helpful.

After the first panic attack episode, both Mercedes and her mother, who insisted on accompanying Mercedes to her first appointment, did not agree with the emergency physician's panic disorder diagnosis. Both were adamant in their sentiment that Mercedes "had never been a nervous type" of person. Mercedes's mother regarded her middle daughter as the child who was most consistent and dependable with respect to fulfilling commitments and responsibilities. Mercedes's mother insisted, "No disrespect to you or the other doctors, but I always tell everyone that 'Mercedes is the rock of the family.' It really does not make any sense to me that her chest pains are really a mental problem. I just don't buy it." Indeed, Mercedes described herself as "a social person" with close emotional attachments to friends and family. She prided herself on having the kind of poise and "grace under pressure" that had helped her become a cocaptain and champion of her high school debate team. Her calm and level-headed nature led friends and family members to seek her counsel on matters that outpaced her own personal experience, such as last year when her cousin, only a few years older, came to her when the latter became pregnant. Throughout the first appointment, both Mercedes and her mother never yielded their resolve that she was quite simply not the kind of person who would be so stricken by panic or anxiety.

During the 30 minutes that Mercedes's mother had been present, she showed obvious pleasure in her daughter's accomplishments and obvious pride in her daughter's character and fortitude. Thus, it was noteworthy that while she largely radiated admiration, she somehow simultaneously maintained a controlling, sometimes dom-ineering stance in relation to her daughter. On more than a few occasions, Mercedes's mother disagreed with and corrected her daughter's descriptions. For example, when Mercedes described how she recently had difficulty concentrating while studying for an exam, her mother jumped in to say that Mercedes seemed to be studying fine, but rather she should not have been studying with music playing in the background, complaining that it was this error in judgment that explained Mercedes recently fail-ing an advanced physics exam. On another occasion, when Mercedes seemed to be describing feeling overwhelmed and at least mildly depressed, her mother broke in to say that "the truth is that Mercedes is tired—she had always taken on significant amounts of work, too much work, and it has finally caught up to her." And several times, Mercedes's mother substituted her own adjectives for Mercedes, asserting that her word choice was more accurate and helpful, implying that her daughter's was not. What seemed doubly noteworthy was Mercedes's reaction—which was seem-ingly none, at least not outwardly. Mercedes appeared to find comfort and security in her mother's presence. At the same time, Mercedes's attitude seemed to be one of acquiescence as her mother repeatedly refuted and revised her descriptions and nar-ratives. Also notable was observing that while Mercedes remained unvaryingly docile in response to her mother's interruptions, I found myself ever so slightly bristling on Mercedes's behalf.

During the longer portion of the assessment, after her mother departed and left Mercedes and me alone, her manner clearly shifted. She rather quickly relinquished her "stiff upper lip" veneer, which in turn permitted her to drop the invulnerable, almost indignant manner she had projected up until then. Almost immediately, she began to more openly share the extent of her distress—the fact that she was having much more anxiety on a day-to-day basis than she wanted others to know, especially her mother. She said that she felt anxious and apprehensive most of the day, nearly every day. While traveling back and forth between home and school, she worried that she was going to get hit by a bus or some other kind of moving vehicle—a fear that had caused her to skip several classes and social engagements. She described how the other day while studying alone in a quiet corner of the college library, she had been eating green grapes from a container she brought from home when she was suddenly gripped with an intense fear that she might choke on a grape. She realized that if she choked, she wouldn't be able to yell for help; thus, nobody would rescue her with the Heimlich maneuver, and she would surely die. Consequently, she had stopped eating alone in spite of the considerable inconvenience given that Mercedes's mother worked evenings as an administrator for the city's rapid transit system, typically not returning home until after 9:30 p.m. Mercedes clearly recognized that the actual risk of choking to death was quite low, which she said "makes me feel like I'm thoroughly weak and totally ridiculous."

Mercedes shared that she was also self-conscious about her lack of experience with men. She was aware that unlike virtually all of her friends, she had never been in a romantic relationship. She said that she was reasonably certain she was heterosexual, an assumption she based on never having had a strong sexual attraction to women.

But she said that while she would occasionally encounter a man and note how she found him "kind of cute," she felt out of step with her friends insofar as her level of interest in men was far less than theirs. She acknowledged that while she felt her virginity made her feel like an enigma among her peers, she said that she had very little interest in sex. In response to sensitively worded inquiry, Mercedes admitted she found the thought of emotional and sexual intimacy daunting. But she acknowledged there was also a willful quality associated with avoiding romantic relationships. She said that she had seen other women and men in her life lose their ability to focus on life goals upon entering into a romantic relationship, and she found this unacceptable. Moreover, between her close relationships with family members and close friends from high school and college, she had maintained many long-term friendships with young women and said that she felt she was currently meeting her needs for emotional closeness for the most part. Thus, at that time, she had very little interest in redirecting any energy toward cultivating a romantic relationship, especially now given the nature of her current concerns.

Mercedes also described how she had "lost almost all of my motivation for school." Unlike her anxiety/panic symptoms, which emerged rather quickly over a few weeks, her low motivation for academic activities had emerged gradually over the past several months. For many months, she had been pushing herself to get through school assignments, still getting good grades. However, at this point in the meeting, Mercedes began to weep for the first time, tearfully lamenting how this was becoming more and more difficult to do. She had always been a highly motivated, extremely disciplined student in a manner that was a source of great pride, a key part of her identity that she felt elevated her reputation among family members and friends. She sobbed that she "didn't know herself anymore," and she felt that her expectations, hopes, and dreams for her life were in serious jeopardy. Her dreams included applying to medical school and becoming an orthopedic surgeon, but she was having tremendous difficulty studying for the MCAT, the standardized test she was supposed to take in July, a prerequisite for applying to medical school. Finally, she further shared that so deep was her dejection and shame in response to her recent emotional and academic struggles, on two occasions she had experienced a sudden impulse to harm herself. In fact, just 2 days earlier she had been avoiding studying by doing laundry when she had the sudden impulse to drink the laundry bleach. She described lifting the bottle to her mouth, contemplating taking a gulp. However, when the pungent fumes hit her nose, she said it caused her to appreciate "the ridiculousness" of the idea. She quickly recapped the bottle and returned it to the closet. Follow-up questions clarified that Mercedes, after the fact, felt rather confident that she had not been at high risk of actually drinking the bleach—she eschewed any true wish to die or even harm herself. Instead, Mercedes clarified that her current anguish about the incident was connected to feeling ashamed that the thought of harming herself had even occurred to her. She explained how she placed a very high value on being a "rational person," not the type of individual who indulges in dramatic behaviors or impulses; thus, it reinforced the fear that she "was totally losing it," causing her a great deal of distress.

Diagnosis and Case Formulation

Whenever a client reports self-harming thoughts or impulses, a clinician must consider whether he or she may be suffering from either major depressive disorder (MDD) or borderline personality disorder (BPD), regardless of whether symptoms of self-harm are among the client's primary complaints. In the case of severe MDD, suicidal ideation is often characterized by a stable, day-to-day wish to no longer exist in response to feeling that life is too painful and burdensome. In BPD, wishes to die are usually impulses that erupt suddenly in response to an intense, stormy disagreement with a family member or friend.

Upon synthesizing all of the available data that emerged during her evaluation, it became apparent that Mercedes's reports of depressed mood and suicidal thoughts did not warrant either MDD or BPD diagnoses. Although Mercedes complained of feeling depressed and demoralized, these feelings were mostly related to her recent academic struggles. She did not manifest any neurovegetative symptoms of depression such as disturbed sleep or changes in appetite. She indicated that she was able to enjoy herself when she took breaks from schoolwork to share meals with her sisters and friends. And even though she had been going out less often out of fear of having a panic attack, approximately once a week she still enjoyed going to the movies or nights out dancing with friends. Moreover, her depressed moods nearly always occurred in the context of simultaneously feeling intensely anxious, with anxiety being the dominant form of distress. Likewise, while self-harm impulses are nearly always present in BPD, Mercedes did not suffer from persistent feelings of emptiness, intense fears of emotional abandonment, or chaotic relationship, all typical features of the disorder. Even though there was some evidence that Mercedes's relationship with her mother contained elements that might be contributing to her present problems, overall Mercedes's relationships appeared reasonably stable. Moreover, despite her claim that she "didn't know herself anymore," this statement seemed to be in response to Mercedes's feeling that her sense of herself had changed during the past year. But in fact, it seemed that prior to the past year, Mercedes's sense of her identity and values had been stable. She had long been able to set clear goals for herself and work assiduously toward them, and her interests in science and related academic pursuits were specific and longstanding. It became clear during the assessment that any relatively small areas of identity uncertainty were developmentally normal for a 20-year-old college student, and she did not meet criteria for BPD.

Proceeding down a list of diagnostic possibilities, Mercedes's most obvious symptom was her severe anxiety, which manifested in two distinctive ways. First, she described symptoms that indicated she was suffering from classic panic attacks. These included heart palpitations, feeling short of breath, trembling hands, nausea, and an intense fear that these sensations meant she was dying. Unlike severe anxiety, which typically develops more gradually and is often associated with an identifiable source or stressor, the feeling of utter panic associated with panic disorder grips a person suddenly, totally "out of the blue" with no readily identifiable trigger. This is why true panic attack sufferers so often misattribute its common symptoms (e.g., shortness of breath, chest pain, fears of imminent doom or death) to heart attacks or other serious medical emergencies that prompt them to seek help in hospital emergency departments. But in addition to panic attacks, Mercedes described other forms of anxiety such as difficulty concentrating on her school work, often prompted by anxious, racing thoughts, often related to fears of failure. She described having difficulty sitting still for more than 30 minutes at a time due to feeling a combination of fatigue, restlessness, as well as uncomfortable and distracting muscle tension in her legs, neck, and shoulders. And most significantly, for the past 8 months, Mercedes had been suffering from excessive amounts of anxiety and worry that were significantly interfering with her day-to-day functioning. Taken together, these symptoms showed that Mercedes met criteria for generalized anxiety disorder in addition to panic disorder. Finally, Mercedes also described fear of choking on food and, thus, preferred not eating alone. Nonetheless, in response to logistics and feelings of hunger, she reported that in fact she successfully pushed the fear away enough to eat by herself several times per week. So while she showed signs of a potential emerging phobic disorder, she did not meet criteria at the time she began therapy. This particular symptom could also be interpreted as part of the symptom picture for generalized anxiety disorder, as it could also fit within the criteria as an excessive worry that can be difficult to control.

Course of Treatment

Mercedes did not approach psychotherapy with enthusiasm. Her motivation was squarely rooted in desperation. She lived with chronic fear of having another panic attack, and her level of day-to-day anxiety was tremendous and difficult to tolerate. In her first psychotherapy appointment, I explained her diagnoses and then I proposed a therapeutic approach where she would come to weekly sessions and share her thoughts and feelings about issues causing distress, particularly focusing on areas of anxiety, although she was free to bring up other concerns as well. I explained how this would allow us to better understand multiple factors in her life: sources of stress in her life, how she understood and evaluated herself and others, and how these appraisals impact her emotions and psychological well-being. During the first two sessions, she expressed feelings of frustration as well as some mild indignation, complaining she "felt like a fish out of water . . . [she] simply didn't know what to say." In response to the not-so-subtle tension, I suggested that maybe she was also having mixed feelings about having to come to therapy in the first place. She looked at me sharply, a flash of anger crossing her face, and then just as suddenly it was gone, replaced by her best attempt at impassiveness. I waited a bit and then said, "You know, Mercedes, a little while ago I thought I saw a clear emotion, like annoyance or anger pass over you, although just for a short moment. Maybe that could be a place to start." In response, she quickly denied having any negative feelings, but with her next breath she proceeded to explicate the various reasons she was still unconvinced her chest pains and other symptoms were psychological in nature rather than medical. I inquired, "It seems you would prefer one of those causes over the other?" She replied "Of course!

If I have a medical problem, then whatever is going on with me is not my fault! But if my problem is psychological, then everything that has happened is all my fault, and everyone will see me as crazy or damaged in some way." Thus, it became clear that Mercedes's supposed resentments seemed to be an attempt to camouflage feelings of shame as well as fears of being rejected, both by others and herself. This revelation also spawned an animated discussion about her powerful drive to achieve the highest degree of excellence in every facet of her life—how her impressive level of motivation has helped her accomplish a great deal, including the high esteem of others. However, it was less clear whether she had permitted herself to accept a commensurate amount of self-esteem along the way. And perhaps her very vivid panic and anxiety symptoms were her mind's dogged, indomitable way of making her pay attention to that striking disparity—the difference between the way others regarded her relative to the way she regarded herself. With this observation, Mercedes wept softly.

At her next appointment, Mercedes's reticence seemed to have evaporated. She jumped right in, reporting that she had been experiencing a great deal of distress and anxiety that was interfering with her ability to study. When asked what she understood about the source of her anxiety, she answered with frustration, "I don't know. There isn't anything especially complex or challenging about the material." But then she went on to explain that it was crucial for her to master the content she was studying in order to be successful taking the MCAT exam required to apply to medical school. In response to additional queries, Mercedes blamed her difficulty on the temperature in her room being too hot, but then the temperature at the library was too cold. She joked, "I know I must sound like freakin' Goldilocks, but I'm serious, no matter when or where I study, it seems like I can't get comfortable enough to really sit down and focus like I need to. And time is growing short." So then, focusing on the theme of discomfort, I asked her about other discomforts she might have while studying, specifically any emotional discomforts. Initially, the only discomfort she could think of related to the mounting anxiety she was suffering due to the ongoing waste of precious study time. She said that upon arriving back home at the end of the day, she both longed for and dreaded her mother's returning home from work. She said that she looked forward to it to the extent that her mother would prepare a nice meal that they would share. But she said that she dreaded her mother's questions: "So how did it go today? . . . Were you able to study? . . . How do you feel?" Again she joked, "As much as I hate answering your questions in therapy, my mother's endless questioning makes me want to disappear into the floor. And then if I ask her to stop or get mad at her, she picks up her plate and walks away without saying another word. And I absolutely cannot stand that!! It makes everything even worse because then I typically go to my room and sit there in front of my books, staring at them, but then I'm too upset to study, which makes me even more freakin' anxious. I just sit there, frozen." I observed how in telling this story, Mercedes's knowledge of her different discomforts seemed to be growing. I suggested we might consider that in addition to anxieties about work and achieving, she might have strong feelings in relation to her mother—complicated feelings that might be expressed as anxiety due to being less comfortable with other feelings, such as anger. Mercedes responded that of course she felt angry with her mother for asking stupid, unhelpful questions, but she didn't have any reason to feel angry with her otherwise.

Mercedes's intricate relationship with anxiety and anger emerged as a consistent theme of her psychotherapy. Feelings of anxiety about turning in poor academic performances were balanced by feeling angry that various family members were demanding too much of her valuable time. Feelings of anxiety about disappointing friends who wanted to socialize with her were balanced by feelings of anger at them for lacking empathy for her and her recent problems, or even worse, for looking down at her because of them. Among countless examples of anxiety counterbalanced by anger, we observed how Mercedes was immediately aware of her feelings of anxiety but needed a therapeutic assist to see and acknowledge the anger side of the equation. In addition, on multiple occasions we both observed how often she attributed/misattributed emotions and sentiments to others that she might be experiencing toward herself. For example, on one occasion Mercedes came into her appointment on the brink of tears and immediately began explaining that she had just broken down in one of her instructor's offices. She said that she went to her organic chemistry teacher's office to get some extra help with a problem set that was due later in the week. Mercedes explained how the instructor referred to the fact that one of the problems was directly parallel to a problem they reviewed in class that same morning, but soon it became clear that Mercedes did not recall the example. Mercedes said, "She looked at me surprised that I didn't remember the chemical structure we had reviewed only a few hours ago, and it was clear that she thought I was a total idiot!" That said, upon processing the details of the exchange between Mercedes and the instructor further, it became more evident that it was Mercedes herself, rather than the instructor, who was accusing her of utter idiocy—a distinction that Mercedes, to her credit, was eventually able to grasp and acknowledge.

Over the first 6 months of psychotherapy, Mercedes's long-term professional and personal goals were also frequent topics of discussion. Gradually, Mercedes began to adopt the more nuanced and flexible ways of thinking about people and situations enough to begin considering that while some aspects of attending medical school were appealing, she was no longer confident that she wanted to be a physician. She knew that her career interests were firmly rooted in science, but she was beginning to recognize that she had more passion for medical research rather than applied medicine. Interestingly, Mercedes's increasingly more flexible and accepting attitude toward herself was mirrored by a corresponding decrease in her anxiety. She began to feel less overwhelmed and less fatigued; thus, she was able to resume accepting social invitations now and then. Her academics improved as her ability to concentrate normalized and her anxious preoccupations gradually subsided. Consequently, it was rather unexpected when in her ninth month of treatment, Mercedes called my emergency answering service, breathlessly announcing that she had just had a panic attack, and she urgently needed to make an appointment to meet as soon as possible.

We met early the following morning, Mercedes appearing still shaken by yesterday's incident but able to share what happened in a clear and cogent manner. She explained how she had decided to meet her cousin at a nail salon located around the corner from her apartment. They had decided to get their nails done ahead of the weekend because they had agreed to go on a "semiblind double date" on Saturday night with two guys who worked with this cousin. "Suddenly it was happening again. I noticed I was sweating even though I was not at all feeling warm. In fact, my hands and fingers became icy and suddenly I couldn't catch my breath. It was like all the air was suddenly sucked out of my lungs. I hoped it might have been due to fumes in the salon because the ventilation wasn't great in there, but when I stumbled outside, it wasn't any better. I still couldn't catch my breath. Please, please tell me what the heck happened! I thought I was done with this kind of thing." She said she was very fearful that the panic attack, the only one she'd suffered in more than 5 months, signaled that she had not made any progress after all.

I asked Mercedes to describe any situations or events that stood out during the past couple days. She responded to the question exasperatedly, "Nothing happened! It was a normal weekend, except maybe I had more schoolwork than usual because midterms are coming up." A few additional inquiries about other anxiety-laden stressors she'd discussed over the past few weeks (e.g., a man she only half liked asking her on a date; a major argument with her best friend) likewise did not offer any leads. Then I wondered out loud whether she recalled the interesting hypothesis we had developed—a pattern we recognized and wondered if it might have been related to her previous panic attacks. Specifically, our discussions revealed that all of her previous panic attacks seemed to occur within 24 hours of having a significant conflict with her mother.

It was true that over the past few weeks, Mercedes had lamented that she and her mother had been having more disagreements lately, "usually over really stupid stuff, like whether I was going to eat the close-to-expiring yogurt in the fridge or wait and buy something to eat at school." Mercedes had become more aware of how she usually lost these battles, saying, "Honestly it's just not worth it. If I don't give in, she just goes on and on about it. It's so much easier to just take the yogurt, besides, I like yogurt." However, in spite of minimizing its significance, we observed how after these kinds of incidents she would continue to simmer with anger for several hours, often bringing it up in therapy days later as a point of contention that she was eager to share. We began to explore the idea that her lingering feelings suggested that these disagreements were, in fact, quite significant insofar as they represented a major dynamic between mother and daughter: (1) Mercedes wishes to do something not in line with her mother's wishes, (2) Mercedes protests, (3) mother withdraws love in the form of walking away in a huff and continuing to ignore her, (4) Mercedes is aware of feeling anxious and guilty in response to the disagreement, and (5) Mercedes capitulates to mother's wishes, they both feel better, and things return to normal.

However, what came to light during the past few months of psychotherapy was the fact that Mercedes also felt quite angry (in addition to anxious and guilty) in response to virtually always giving in to her mother's demands. Mercedes had grown to appreciate that while she permitted herself to be angry with others (sometimes as a substitute for being angry with her mother), feeling anger, never mind expressing it, was nearly categorically unacceptable to both Mercedes and her mother. Upon gently reminding Mercedes about her therapeutic work that resulted in these insights, Mercedes's eyes grew big as saucers and began brimming with tears. She said, "A few hours before my panic attack, we had another argument where I basically told her that my feelings about becoming a doctor had changed and that I no longer planned to apply to medical school. Let's just say my mother totally flipped out, but I didn't say anything. I simply stood up and walked out of the house." Mercedes then explained how she'd immediately sought consolation from her favorite cousin. She described how she'd angrily fumed and seethed about her mother's reaction until her cousin, who had been very supportive, suggested that they should go see a movie together to help get her mind off of the fight, which they did.

During the next and final phase of the psychotherapy, Mercedes came to realize that while she always experienced her panic attacks as "coming out of the blue," closer examination always revealed one or more situations that likely precipitated it. We noted how during the argument preceding her most recent panic attack she had been the one to emotionally withdraw from her mother, instead of the other way around, by walking out of the house. She came to appreciate how the act of rejecting her mother, at least in the moment, helped her feel less dependent on and less controlled by her mother. However, Mercedes identified multiple occasions when her triumph was quickly replaced by intense apprehension, fear that her mother would retaliate by likewise rejecting her. That this fear was sometimes powerful enough to provoke a panic attack seemed like a reasonable hypothesis. In response to this insight, therapy shifted to focus on helping Mercedes understand the depths of this dynamic—how it seemed likely that her mother's longstanding attempts to control Mercedes and her choices were rooted in feelings of love and emotional dependence on Mercedes. She began to recognize that her mother's dependence on her was such that she was probably not at as much risk of losing her mother's love as Mercedes sometimes feared. This knowledge allowed her to continue to be more independent in making decisions while simultaneously expressing appreciation and affection toward her mother, thus allaying both their fears.

Outcome and Prognosis

Mercedes's panic and anxiety symptoms were entirely resolved by the end of the psychotherapy treatment. She reported experiencing the entirely normal anxieties associated with graduating from college and feeling apprehensive about how successful she would be in graduate school. She also experienced what was probably the overdue normal anxiety connected to moving out of her mother's home in order to pursue her doctoral degree in a different city. Five or 6 years after psychotherapy ended, Mercedes e-mailed me to share the good news that she had just graduated with a PhD in biomechanical engineering. She had accepted a job with a company that specialized in making cochlear implants, and her work team was trying to improve the fidelity of existing devices to translate complex tones so hearing-impaired individuals could hear things like music in a manner that much more closely resembled what hearing people can hear. She shared that she remained anxiety and panic attack free, but just as important, she wanted me to know that she was getting married in the next month and her relationship with her mother was quite intact.

Discussion Questions

1. Explain how the therapist arrived at a diagnosis of generalized anxiety disorder with panic disorder, and how major depressive disorder and borderline personality disorder were ruled out.

2. Summarize the two ways in which Mercedes's anxiety manifested, and describe the difference between severe anxiety and panic disorder.

3. How did Mercedes's mother contribute to her daughter's anxiety? How did therapy help to change their relationship?

6

Generalized Anxiety Disorder

Presenting Problem and Client Description

Mike is a 34-year-old male with one child. He entered therapy as part of a larger treatment study designed to evaluate the effectiveness of a cognitive therapy treatment for generalized anxiety disorder (GAD) developed by Tom Borkovec and his colleagues. This case shows a number of different approaches that can be used with GAD.

Diagnosis and Case Formulation

When he entered therapy, Mike reported no family history of anxiety, depression, or alcohol abuse. He was one of four children and felt pressured by his family to achieve. Mike described himself as being worried all his life and eager to please. He also saw himself as perfectionistic with high performance standards. In his life, Mike had a history of career success and a good social support network.

Mike's current worries focus on finances, work, and school performance as he is currently in graduate school. He is also concerned about his marriage and his child-rearing responsibilities. He has a number of bodily complaints including muscle tension in his neck and lower back, shortness of breath, accelerated heart rate, flushes, and sleep disturbances. He also describes himself as restless, easy to fatigue when stressed, irritable, and having difficulties in concentration. Mike reports feeling like he is inadequate and letting his family down. He worries that he will never get over his problems and that people will turn against him.

There are a number of stressful situations which contribute to his generalized anxiety. These include confronting authority figures, negotiating household and child-care responsibilities with his wife, public speaking, examinations, group projects, and meetings with his professors.

Course of Treatment

Mike's treatment included components from behavioral therapy techniques and cognitive therapy techniques. An additional component was a daily worry period. That is, Mike was encouraged to put off worrying to a particular time of day. During this 30-minute period, Mike could worry as he wished. However, he was also instructed on how to perform problem-solving behaviors and examine his catastrophic expectations during this period.

Mike received 12 individual therapy sessions on a twice-a-week basis with two follow-up sessions over the final month. The first five sessions were 90 minutes in length; all others were 60 minutes. The conceptual model underlying treatment stressed the importance of rapidly terminating chains of anxious responding, especially worrisome thoughts, to prevent further strengthening of anxiety networks in memory.

The behavioral techniques included relaxation. Initially, Mike was taught to tense and relax different sets of muscles. The goal at this point was to help him differentiate between a tense state and a relaxed state in 16 different muscle groups. Over the course of therapy, the focus was on fewer muscle groups and the ability to notice changes in tension level. Also, breathing techniques that emphasized slow stomach breathing were added. There was also an emphasis on helping Mike enjoy the pleasant feeling associated with a relaxed state. Pleasant imagery was also introduced at this point.

Outside of therapy, Mike was encouraged to check for states of tension in his daily life. For example, when he noticed tightness across his back and shoulders and shallow breathing when he was working on an assignment in the library, he immediately responded by taking four slow, rhythmic breaths and imagining his back muscles loosening up "like melted cheese." Mike discovered that early intervention was extremely effective in reducing his level of tension.

In the process of checking on his level of tension, Mike was surprised to discover the number of times that he thought about negative topics. These thoughts included the number of times he was critical of himself for minor incidents. Some of these cognitive beliefs centered around thoughts such as "I'm letting my family down," "I will never get over my problem," "I'm inadequate," and "People will turn against me." During the course of his therapy, Mike discovered it was easier for him to increase his state of relaxation than to initially reduce his cognitions.

Part of therapy was to help Mike challenge underlying beliefs as well as his catastrophic expectations. As noted, his underlying beliefs included such ideas as he was inadequate. His catastrophic expectations included such ideas as people will turn against him and his problems will exist forever. Through treatment, Mike came to see that he could remain in a stressful situation and reconsider what he was saying to himself. The following is an example he gave during therapy.

> I had done the whole routine, you know, the morning ritual, getting up, drinking coffee, and all that sort of stuff, and everything was just hunky-dory, and at 6:40 a.m. my wife said, "I have to go to town early today, so I'll drop you off on campus." Initially, I thought, "Well, that's fine," and then I thought, "Wait a minute, that

is not fine because I have, you know, we have to get everybody organized and out the door at the same time." In the morning, my son has his little routine and I have my little routine, and I talk to the same professor every Monday, Wednesday, and Friday morning on the bus and I sort of enjoy him, it's a lot of fun. I realized that, boy, my routine is going to get wrecked up this morning. Well, it really wasn't. I got in here to campus and was at my carrel at the same time and everything, and I had the same amount of time before class started and the whole business, but it seemed like for a while there that everyone, my whole world, had sort of been turned upside down and dumped on the floor, and I had to sort through it to get it back together. Afterward, I felt like it wouldn't have mattered 5 or 10 minutes one way or the other. I didn't have to be there at exactly the same time or earlier. I realized, before the bus was to arrive, I could have split, that I had a choice. I thought it was maybe better to deal with it than dash out the door and think about it. I thought it might be nice to see how well I could cope with it, and what I found interesting was that once I was out of the car and kissed everybody and said goodbye that it shut off and everything was OK.

Although he was embarrassed to talk about it, Mike believed that his worrying actually kept disaster from striking. In this way, his worry protected him. Somehow, if he focused on the worst possible outcome, it was less likely to occur, and he would be prepared for it if it did occur. Related to this was a fear of losing control; consequently, he was afraid to let go and relax.

To challenge these beliefs became an important task of therapy because successful treatment depended on Mike's willingness to let go of worry. As long as he believed it served an adaptive purpose, he would be conflicted about letting it go. Other beliefs that were central to Mike's generalized anxiety disorder related to the benefits of self-criticism and perfectionism. A belief that he didn't have enough time to do all he had to do was also present. Some of Mike's worries had to do with his social phobia, a condition he also met criteria for. Mike worried about the impression he made on others and feared their disapproval. This contributed to his anxiety about saying or doing the wrong thing. There were feelings of dread that "something bad will happen to my wife or son." Although he couldn't articulate any specific concerns, as is typical of many clients with GAD, he believed prior to the therapy that he would never get over his problem. Mike had worried all his life and said, "It's just the way I am."

Cognitive therapy techniques were used to modify such maladaptive cognitions. This included the self-monitoring of automatic thoughts that come about spontaneously. Also, logical analysis was applied to the catastrophic thoughts, a process referred to as *decatastrophizing*. One part of this is a search for alternative explanations. The original catastrophic idea could also be used in a relaxation procedure. The logical analysis of these ideas has also been referred to as the *Socratic method*.

Between sessions, the therapist had Mike gather evidence in support of alternative beliefs and practice substituting more adaptive cognitions in a range of situations in daily life. Within sessions, the therapist focused on possible alternative perspectives to the scenarios Mike presented. Because anticipating future disasters is inherent in generalized anxiety disorder, decatastrophizing is a particularly useful technique with this population. Mike was frequently asked what the worst possible outcome in a situation was, how likely it was to occur, how severe the damage would be if it did occur, and how he could cope in a worst-case scenario.

One example of a situation approached in therapy was a future comprehensive examination for his PhD that Mike had to take in his program at the university. Previously, he found himself freezing during an exam. He also knew that others in his class had failed. The therapist presented Mike's concerns in a logical manner as follows:

Therapist: What would happen if you failed?

Mike: Ah, well, I already checked that out. You have two options: one is you can take another one within 4 months or you can take an oral within 2 weeks.

Therapist: But you can't do both?

Mike: You can't do both, no. If you fail the second written [exam], you can take an oral 2 weeks after that.

Therapist: What is the likelihood you would actually fail this thing twice? Three times, basically—to take it and fail, and take it again within 4 months and fail it again, and take an oral and fail that?

Mike: Pretty slim chance from what I have been able to judge so far. I don't think they are out to cream anybody. I don't see any maliciousness in the department committees or anything like that. My concern would be that I'd go in there and choke.

Therapist: Your mind would go blank?

Mike: Yeah, which happened on an exam in the fall. A final and I sort of . . . it scared me.

Therapist: And what happened in that class?

Mike: I got a B.

Mike reported relief in going through the Socratic dialogue with the therapist. He also had an immediate reduction in anxiety. He was able to realize that he had blown the incident out of proportion by not including his past performance, which was acceptable. The therapist realized that Mike's desire to be perfect had pushed him only to consider optimal performance and create worry and anxiety by his thoughts of the possibility that this would not happen. In logically considering the evidence based on his past performance, Mike was able to see how he had created anxiety in himself by ignoring his own past performance. At that point, he was able to generate more adaptive self-statements that he could say to himself. In this way, he was able to prevent his past catastrophic thoughts from controlling him again.

Another part of therapy focused on Mike's worries. He was trained to recognize early signs of anxiety and worry, and to monitor his reactions. When he realized he was worrying, he was to use relaxation strategies as well as self-statements he had developed. If Mike was unable to remove the current worry or it returned, he would postpone thinking about it until his 30-minute worry period later in the day. It was suggested that Mike worry at the same time and place every day. Further, Mike was taught to divide his worry period into two types. The first type are those worries that can be helped through problem-solving techniques. As seen in the following exchange, Mike was able to postpone a worry and focus on the task at hand.

Mike: I saw that the professor was correct and there was a feeling afterward. Oh my God, if I can be that far off the mark on something that's relatively simple, I may be really in trouble in this course . . . But then that sort of passed and I kinda put it aside and hadn't really thought about it since.

Therapist: Do you have any idea of how or why it passed?

Mike: Well, because I consciously said that I would put it aside. I said, "You don't have time this week to worry about this stuff. Get the homework done, get it out of the way, hand it in on Thursday morning, and if you want to worry about it, worry about it some other time."

After about 3 weeks of using the worry program, Mike reported he had little to worry about.

Mike was also introduced to desensitization, which was used in sessions 4 through 12. With this approach, Mike was asked to imagine certain situations and notice both his bodily and cognitive reactions. These situational images were organized in terms of low, medium, and high levels of reactions. Seeing a snake produced a low-level reaction, whereas public speaking produced a high-level reaction. For Mike, doing financial transactions was of a medium level. High anxious situations left Mike feeling irritable and having his mind go blank. Medium ones induced a difficulty concentrating, feeling on edge, and increased heart rate. Low-level reactions would include being fatigued. In terms of cognitions, high anxious ones included Mike feeling that he gave a poor performance, or that he didn't express himself well, or that he was letting his family down. Medium-level ones included feeling different from others or thinking that he might fail. The low-level cognition was that he should have thought of that.

The desensitization from an early session is as follows:

Therapist: I want you [Mike] to imagine the following situation as vividly and realistically as possible, as if you were actually in the situation. Please signal by raising your finger at the first sign of anxiety and leave it raised until the anxiety has gone away. You are sitting in the examination room, looking at the exam. Your heart is beating rapidly and the muscles of your neck and shoulders are tense. As you read the questions, you realize you can't answer the first two. Your heart races as

you think, "I can't do this. I'm going to fail. My mind is going blank."
(Client signals.) Now, continuing to stay in the situation . . . relax
away the tension . . . slow, rhythmic breathing . . . slowing down
your heart rate . . . melting your thoughts . . . muscles loosening
up and unwinding as you focus on the pleasant feelings of muscle
relaxation . . . just continue visualizing being in the exam situation
as the muscles of your neck and shoulders continue to relax more and
more deeply, more and more completely . . . as you just let go.

The therapist continued to describe the scene until he could become relaxed. Mike
was then asked to continue the scene while relaxed. He was then asked to turn off the
scene but to continue being relaxed. After a time, another scene was presented and
the procedure continued.

Later, a cognitive component was added:

Therapist: You think to yourself, "I studied this. I feel confident I can do a
              reasonable job if I slow down, think it over, and take it one step at a time."
              You remain aroused, but relatively relaxed as you work on the exam.

Outcome and Prognosis

By the end of therapy, the situations which initially produced anxiety no longer did
so. Mike reported that he felt like a new person. Mike had worked hard in therapy and
was willing to complete his assignments outside of therapy. Mike was willing to work
with his therapist in a positive manner and was willing to complete follow-up proce-
dures, which continued to show gains begun in therapy.

Note: This case study was based on anxiety treatment research funded in part by Grant MH
13759 from the National Institute of Mental Health to Thomas D. Borkovec. A longer version
was published as a chapter in the *Comprehensive Casebook of Cognitive Therapy*, Plenum Press. We
appreciate Thomas Borkovec's willingness to let us use this case study.

Discussion Questions

1. Explain the behavioral therapy and
    cognitive therapy techniques used in
    Mike's treatment.

2. What was the benefit to Mike of
    challenging his underlying beliefs
    and his catastrophic expectations?

3. Describe the techniques used to
    help Mike deal with his excessive
    worrying.

7

Narcissistic Personality Disorder

Presenting Problem and Client Description

Mrs. N. was referred by a friend of hers in the field to a colleague who referred her to me for treatment. Her chief complaints were feelings of chronic depression and diffuse anxiety. The colleague who referred her had also indicated that she was prone to angry outbursts, which a number of times resulted in the police being called. These outbursts occurred in places of business, when traveling, with friends, family, lovers, and with neighbors.

Mrs. N. was a tall, attractive married woman in her mid-30s with three children, who looked slightly younger than her chronological age. She was the older of two children. Growing up, her father was an extremely successful businessman who had left her with a substantial inheritance. He was a self-made man who was "all business," hostile and very derogating of her, and generally too busy for his children. After her father's death, her mother remarried. Her mother was both physically absent and emotionally distant while Mrs. N. was growing up; although she provided for basic and nonemotional needs, Mrs. N.'s mother tended to use this support to coerce her children to do as she desired. This pattern of behavior continued into her children's adulthood. Mrs. N.'s mother often provided the patient with loans and helped her with her finances, as much of her inheritance was unavailable (i.e., in the form of stocks). Because of the unavailability of these funds, Mrs. N. had difficulty managing her money and often relied on her mother to organize her finances. In return, her mother often put pressure on Mrs. N. about where to live, where the children should go to school, and other major decisions in her life.

Despite her overt perception that she had superior intelligence and abilities, Mrs. N. reported constant difficulties doing well in school and in sticking with any one of her multiple hobbies (e.g., horseback riding, acting, and singing). She generally blamed her parents for not encouraging her or helping her develop her talents. She perceived herself as having difficulty concentrating or at least following through on tasks. She felt easily bored or frustrated with whatever she was doing. Despite her difficulties with money, she tended to hire assistants to carry out the more mundane aspects of her work and hobbies (e.g., she hired someone to take her horse riding for exercise because she found having to do so boring and an imposition). Her difficulties sticking with hobbies were sometimes made worse due to angry outbursts she would have with friends, colleagues, or others involved in these activities. She would frequently change her mind with regard to which hobbies were most important to her and where she wanted to invest her time and efforts. She once sold a horse she owned because she had not ridden it in years, and then a few days later bought a new horse after she saw one she admired. The result of these patterns was that as she entered her 30s, she had not yet developed expertise in any one area nor did she have a stable sense of what she wanted to do with her life.

To gain the approval of her parents, she married a man who, while supportive of her and tolerant of her rages, was unable to provide sufficiently for the family, in part because he was disproportionally responsible for the children and in part because he was probably identity diffuse himself. Her inheritance and support from her mother provided for the family and allowed both her and her husband to live comfortably but without steady career investments. She felt terribly put out by having children, found them to be quite a burden, yet needed them as an excuse for not having invested in a career path nor achieving tangible successes.

In addition to depressed mood and diffuse anxiety, the patient reported angry outbursts, significant alcohol and marijuana use, fleeting concerns about rapidly shifting interests, and unhappiness with the lack of success in her life. She felt considerably activated by routine situations and demands, and saw the alcohol and drug use as ways of dampening her internal experience. She shared that her husband was concerned that she was too disconnected from the children and overly frustrated with them—frequently losing her temper with them over developmentally normal stresses. By all appearances, she was quite brittle and needed much support. In addition to her mother's financial and logistical support, she had a housekeeper, gardener, au pair, and a number of babysitters to help her maintain the household and take care of the children. Additionally, her husband did not work regularly and was the primary caregiver who not only took care of the children's emotional needs but also brought them to all their lessons.

At times, Mrs. N. believed that her children and "unsupportive" husband were responsible for her "not making it" or becoming famous, and she had frequent fantasies of leaving her family and "making it big." She attended acting workshops and sang in a series of local bands, occasionally developing crushes on fellow actors or band members, particularly younger men. Sometimes these crushes resulted in affairs, sometimes in unrequited love relationships. She often fantasized about leaving her family and touring Europe with a younger man who would produce her music and help her achieve fame and fortune.

Diagnosis and Case Formulation

The case formulation for this patient was derived over a number of sessions using Kernberg's (1984) structural interview. This is a psychiatric interview designed to elicit information in order to make a differential diagnosis between those with personality disorders and those with neurotic-level functioning (as well as those organized at a psychotic level). The diagnosis and case formulation are based on a synthesis of reported and observed clinical symptoms, inferred intrapsychic structures based on the content and organization of narrative data, and the quality of the therapeutic relationship as experienced by the interviewer. During the structural interview, the clinician obtains the following information: mental status, a complete symptom picture, the patient's current function, and the patient's sense of self and others. The structural interview is not only important in establishing a diagnosis and case formulation with personality disordered patients, but it is useful in gathering information that can be shared with the patient when providing feedback and in developing collaborative goals for the psychotherapy.

From the data that emerged, it became clear that despite her complaints, Mrs. N. did not meet criteria for any axis I disorder. Although there were some somatic symptoms, she did not have any of the neurovegetative symptoms of depression, nor did she report feelings of worthlessness or excessive or inappropriate guilt, or recurrent thoughts about death. She did report depressed mood and occasional loss of interest in activities, but these states were variable, fleeting, and typically in response to a perceived interpersonal slight. In fact, rather than being anhedonic, she was particularly self-indulgent and pleasure seeking. Likewise, she did not meet criteria for dysthymia or depressive personality disorder, bipolar disorder, or an anxiety disorder.

Although at times she displayed elevated, expansive, and irritable moods, they never lasted at least a week (or even 4 days for a hypomanic mood); instead, these symptoms tended to be quite labile, quickly vacillating with depressed mood states as is more characteristic of personality disorders (Henry et al., 2001; Koeingsberg et al., 2002). This pattern was chronic as opposed to being present in discrete episodes as is the case with bipolar disorders. With regard to generalized anxiety disorder (GAD), her anxiety was diffuse, free floating, and variable. Her anxiety was also imbued with irritability and impulsivity, and the GAD diagnosis was contradicted by a variable presence of anxiety and long periods of lack of any anxiety, even in the face of anxiety-provoking situations. Although she had described an occasional panic attack, she did not meet criteria for the disorder.

As she discussed her functioning, she described situation after situation in which she flew into rages and made outrageous verbal attacks on those she was close to as well as strangers she encountered. She would fly into rages against her parents, her husband, her children, the au pair, her auto mechanic, her singing and acting coaches, lovers, and countless others. No one was safe from her wrath. When asked to describe herself and others, consistent with Kernberg's theory, Mrs. N. was able to provide a relatively intact and coherent, if grandiose, description of herself, whereas her descriptions of others were quite impoverished. In terms of narcissistic personality disorder (NPD), she clearly displayed a pervasive pattern of grandiosity in her fantasy and behavior and a need for admiration, and she described instances of clear lack of empathy for others. With regard to specific criteria, she (1) displayed a sense of self-importance that was exaggerated in terms of her achievements and talents, and she certainly expected to be recognized as superior without commensurate achievements; (2) described being preoccupied with fantasies of unlimited success, power, beauty, and ideal love; (3) indicated that she considered herself to be special and should associate with other special or high-status people; (4) described a clear need for excessive admiration; (5) displayed a sense of entitlement; (6) periodically was interpersonally exploitive; (7) had difficulty recognizing feelings and needs of others; (8) was often envious of others and believed that others were envious of her; and (9) at times behaved or displayed an arrogant, haughty attitude.

Based on her symptom picture, her functioning in work and love, and inferred psychological organization based on the quality of the narrative descriptions of self and others as well as the quality of her relatedness to others, it was felt that the panoply of symptoms she presented with could best be understood as occurring in the context of an NPD diagnosis. This is a woman who aggressively defended against feeling small and inconsequential to her parents—one of whom was hostile and derogating and the other cold and disengaged. Understandably, she deeply wanted to be with her parents, to be valued by them, and to be nurtured by them. She was angry with them and others, sensitive to any indication that she was being devalued, and prone to distort benign situations so as to feel belittled. In these situations, she quickly responded with extreme rage that often resulted in her being removed from a situation and/or the dissolution of previously established relationships.

I began working with Mrs. N. using a version of transference-focused psychotherapy (TFP; Clarkin et al., 2006) that was specifically modified for work with NPD. TFP is an empirically supported treatment for borderline personality disorder (BPD), a "near neighbor" disorder. This choice seems warranted due to the high level of comorbidity between BPD and NPD as well as the theoretical connection between NPD and BPD (Kernberg, 1975/1984). Additionally, there is some preliminary evidence that TFP is uniquely efficacious when compared with dialectical behavior therapy and a supportive psychotherapy for narcissistic patients (Diamond, Yeomans, et al., in press). Nevertheless, in recent years, a number of technical modifications of TFP have been made to accommodate differences in the pathology between these disorders (e.g., Diamond & Yeomans, 2008; Diamond, Yeomans, & Levy, 2011; Diamond, Yeomans, et al., in press; Stern, Yeomans, & Diamond, in press). These technical modifications are described below.

Course of Treatment

I could tell from the onset that I was about to begin a challenging treatment. Mrs. N.'s opening volley to me showed both her aggression and her neediness. The very first thing she said to me, referring to my office, was "Gee, this is the nicest broom closet I have ever seen," which was quickly followed by reprimands for a series of perceived failures on my part: I had no watercooler in my faculty office, my office was too far from where she had to park, the weather did not suit her. Each of these comments was embedded in an angry "put-out" affect and resulted in my feeling both criticized and sad. She was hostile, but I hypothesized that part of her wanted me to care for her. She wanted me to provide nourishment, intimacy, and atmospheric comfort. And even before I said anything more than "come in," she was angry at me because she wanted these things from me. Her comments invited interpretations, but to do so would have been too early, too exposing, and too penetrating. She would feel as part of me was feeling—that is, attacked without any good options. Immediately, I had a sense of the link between her neediness and her feelings of abandonment with her aggressiveness and superiority. I felt she wanted these things from me and she was sad that I could not provide them, but she was also angry at me that I had not provided them and that I evoked such desire in her. I also sensed that she took great pleasure in knowing that I was incapable of making a watercooler appear or moving the parking garage. And even if I could get her some water and find her a closer parking spot, I could not change the weather. Thus, it was me who was incapable, not her.

This dynamic continued, for as I explained my practice to her, she dismissed everything I said as if I were telling her things she already knew (despite the fact that this was her first therapy). When I told her my fee, she told me that I "would never get rich charging so little." She followed this comment with stories of all the people who wanted a piece of her financially, as if she were made of money and others were corrupt users who wanted nothing more than to have what was rightfully hers. Infused in these comments was my presumed greed (i.e., that I was using her for my financial gain) but also its opposite—that I was not charging as much as I could, and therefore, maybe I was not a greedy money-hungry user. Additionally, she was scoffing at my fee as if it were inconsequential to someone with her money but at the same time expressing her concern that I didn't really care about her besides the money. Early on, it was clear that her communications were complicated and represented a condensation of overt and covert narcissistic concerns.

Despite my experience of the patient as critical of me, she also spoke very glowingly about me, and it became apparent that her experience of me was very different than the way she talked to me. Mrs. N. described multiple situations in which she was hostile, disparaging, and rude toward others, and I experienced her as that way toward me, despite the intermittent idealizations. However, she saw herself as someone others attacked, derogated, coerced, imposed upon, and controlled. She could not acknowledge it, but it seemed to me from her affect and the content of what she was saying that she found me and my questions a terrible imposition. Someone was being imposed upon and controlled, and someone was imposing and controlling, but it was unclear to her who had what roles. She and I in the consultation room, and others outside it, vacillated back and forth in her scenarios.

As we continued the structural interview and I gathered information about her relationships and experience of others, she frequently talked about people in her life whom she thought were narcissists or had a personality disorder. She often spoke to me as if we were colleagues discussing her family members who were "our" patients.

I began to experience dread about sharing my diagnostic impressions with her. I fretted regarding how she was going to take it and imagined that she might lash out at me and end the treatment (part fear, part wish upon reflection). This was an unusual feeling for me. Although it can be difficult to share a personality disorder diagnosis with patients, it is important that clinicians convey diagnostic impressions in order to collaboratively set the treatment frame. I am not only an advocate of sharing diagnoses with patients but usually feel quite at ease and skilled when doing so. Despite my apprehension, I knew what I needed to do and dutifully did so. I did my best to be tactful and precise in my language and to utilize the material she shared in ways that I thought would resonate with her. To my surprise, she took the news very well. My descriptions of her experience and the psychological rationales I described resonated with her, but most important, despite her disparagement of those she perceived as narcissistic in her circle of family and friends, she disclosed that she had long suspected that she herself was diagnosable for NPD (in fact, she reported that she wondered about this for almost 10 years!). This was an important moment of both reflection and connection between us. We had a shared experience that I could now refer back to as needed. It was not just me who thought she was narcissistic; she too believed this.

The discussion of the treatment frame was easier now that we were both on the same page about the problems, and we discussed each of our roles and responsibilities in the treatment as well as the rationale behind them. She was less defensive, but I knew that this state was only temporary. When working with personality-disordered patients, it is important to have a clear discussion of the treatment frame or what is called the *treatment contract* in a TFP model. The contract-setting phase has multiple purposes. First, it educates the patient to psychotherapy. This is important for both the therapy-naïve and therapy-experienced patient because even those patients who have been in multiple treatments may have only minimal understanding of this particular type of therapy, in part because they may have been in therapies that utilized very different stances (e.g., supportive treatment, medication management, or cognitive behavioral therapy).

A second goal of the contract-setting phase is to establish a clear treatment frame that allows the patient and therapist to address and reflect on the material that arises in treatment, including feelings both in and out of session. The treatment contract creates a safe environment for patients that allows their dynamics to unfold with the therapist. By providing structure and clear expectations, it also provides a safe environment for the therapist to work within. Having an explicit agreement of the tasks and responsibilities of each party also provides an avenue for discussing and understanding deviations from the frame or contract. As Diamond et al. (2011) outline more fully, the contract-setting phase is more difficult with narcissistic patients because the expectations and responsibilities confront and limit patients' grandiosity and omnipotent control, and often results in their perceiving the therapist as controlling and imposing. The frame or contract is often initially rejected or tested in ways that may threaten the treatment. It is important when setting the treatment frame with personality disordered patients that the therapist utilize patients' past treatment experiences and relationship patterns to predict the kind of difficulties they might experience in the treatment. It is also important for the therapist to examine a patient's responses to the treatment frame to ensure that he or she is not simply acquiescing to the goals proposed by the therapist but is making a true commitment. With Mrs. N., I stated that although she felt what I was suggesting was reasonable right now, we might predict that at some later time she might feel differently and that it would be important to discuss those feelings as they arise.

It is not uncommon for NPD patients to begin therapy with either a haughty, devaluing attitude toward the therapist or conversely with an idealization of the therapist as one who can magically provide solutions to all problems. Both of these stances result from the need to sustain the grandiose sense of self and from the envy the patient experiences in relation to others. In both cases, the patient envies the therapist's functioning and psychological health. This conflict often leads the patient to devalue the therapist or aspects of the therapy and to either subtly or explicitly reject the therapist's interventions. In Mrs. N.'s case, she prefaced every acceptance of what I offered with "Of course." At other times, she made small tweaks to my wording, and still at other times she would reject what I said, only to come in the next week or some time later and share with me her newfound understanding that was exactly what I had offered earlier but which she had rejected.

One important technique when working with narcissistic patients is to work outside the transference—that is, to discuss the transferences that patients show with people outside the therapy setting. These interpretations can have great immediacy and impact for the patient, and although they have been looked down upon within traditional psychoanalysis, they are consistent with the widening scope model (Bender, 2012). Another useful intervention with this population is to use "analyst-centered" rather than patient-centered interpretations (Steiner, 1994; Stern et al., in press). This type of interpretation focuses on the patient's experience of the therapist, typically in that moment, and is considered analyst- or therapist-focused because it stops short of interpreting the patient's motives to see the therapist in a particular way. Instead, the therapist allows the patient to hold this view of him or her without immediately challenging it, facilitating the examination of the patient's experience of the therapist more deeply and thoroughly. These extratransferential and therapist-centered interpretations with a focus on the patient's affective experience are ideally experienced by patients as validating but should not be delivered in a way that reinforces patient distortions. This is accomplished by maintaining technical neutrality and attending carefully to one's word choices and paralinguistic communication. From this nonjudgmental stance, therapists comment on patients' representation of experience rather than actual reality; over time, therapists introduce an alternate perspective that facilitates a more integrative sense of self and other. For example, a therapist might say: "When I asked about X, you experienced me as attacking you, rather than seeing me as concerned." The value of providing such validation while simultaneously providing an alternative perspective in a gentle and matter-of-fact manner is that it invites reflection in a nonthreatening manner and provides a base from which to build deeper understandings of the patient's experience. In this way, a therapist-centered interpretation, like extratransferential work, is preparation for a later transference analysis and transference interpretations.

These techniques were central to my work with Mrs. N. One theme that presented itself repeatedly was her sense that her various doctors and assorted helpers were not providing relief but instead making her worse. Over the course of weeks, she described how the various ministrations of her trainer, masseuse, chiropractor, and dentist left her feeling in pain. This led to discussions about whether she might be feeling the same about our work—that although she recognized she was "getting better," including experiencing more satisfying family relationships, she might also feel that there was a terribly painful downside to therapy. Over time, we were able to focus more on the transference, and she found it more tolerable to discuss our relationship and possible distortions of it. This discussion led to deeper discussion about whether the work we were doing and the improvements she was experiencing were worth the effort, especially given her continued feeling that I was imposing my expectations on her.

Another turning point in the therapy came after I charged her for a missed session. The first few sessions after she received the bill were unremarkable, but a few weeks later she brought up how angry she was that I would charge her for a missed session. She reminded me that she had been up late the night before performing at a local venue and had overslept. We explored how she had held this feeling for a few sessions and the reasons why she might not have told me right away. It became clear that she wanted to protect me from her wrath and that only weeks later could she even broach the subject without flying into a rage. We discussed her need to protect me and her fear that I might cower, be destroyed, or abandon her. The fact that I could tolerate her anger, discuss it openly, not act defensively, and not retaliate was important to helping her integrate her own feelings into a productive discussion. I modeled maintaining a thinking stance in the context of an affect storm. We discussed how part of her worried about my motivations and if I was only interested in her money. I wondered aloud if one could be interested in being compensated for one's time but also concerned about and wanting to be helpful to another.

The main vehicle for change in the treatment was being vigilant for indications of mental shifts that provided momentary windows into Mrs. N.'s more reflective, nondefensive spaces. The occurrence of these shifts between grandiose self-states and depressed, defeated, and vulnerable states are difficult to predict. Nonetheless, these are highly valuable opportunities, and the therapist must be vigilant for them and seize these moments. With Mrs. N., these moments came frequently, and we developed a shared responsibility for noticing their occurrence and reflecting and exploring them. As we explored them in the context of her discussions of others, she also gained more awareness of when she was having this experience in relation to me and more tolerance for our examining her experience of me not as truths but as representations of me that might include distortions similar to the ones she had about others in her life.

One aspect that the therapist needs to be prepared for as the NPD patient improves is the true feelings of depression that arise with a more integrated experience and a greater capacity to take responsibility for one's behavior and mistakes. As Mrs. N. improved, she began to feel closer to her husband and children. She increasingly described more satisfying interactions with her children and delighted in their genuine appreciation of her. She began to be more attracted to her husband, ended affairs, and lost interest in potential other relationships. She also became more forgiving toward her parents, recognizing that they did the best they could and that they had experienced difficult childhoods themselves. She also recognized that, despite their shortcomings, they wanted the best for her and her sibling. However, she also began to feel very depressed and even guilty about missed opportunities with her family and her past behavior toward them. This represented a new stage in the treatment.

Outcome and Prognosis

Over the course of the treatment, Mrs. N. made a number of concrete, tangible, and clinically significant improvements. These included marked decreases in frequency and intensity of angry outbursts, alcohol and marijuana use, and feelings of detachment from her family. In addition to these changes, she showed a marked increase in her tolerance for distressing thoughts and feelings, motivation to work and capacity for ordinary functioning, and time spent with her children and husband.

In sum, Mrs. N. is now more productive at work, getting along better with coworkers, happier and more engaged with her children and husband, and happier in general. She drinks socially but does not smoke marijuana. Although she still feels tension quite often, she nonetheless is in much better behavioral control and only rarely loses her temper. Her internal experience of herself and others still is inconsistent at times, and she is not completely free from symptoms of NPD. However, she is on the path toward more stable, realistic, and positive experiences of herself and others, and her prognosis is much better than when she entered treatment.

●

Discussion Questions

1. Describe the specific symptoms displayed by Mrs. N. that led to a diagnosis of NPD. Explain why this diagnosis was made rather than bipolar disorder, depressive disorder, or anxiety disorder.

2. Discuss the primary treatment technique used in working with Mrs. N. and how it can be effective in working with patients with NPD. Briefly summarize the other treatment techniques used in working with Mrs. N.

3. What are the ways in which Mrs. N.'s therapist began to see changes during the course of treatment?

References

Bender, D. S. (2012). Mirror, mirror on the wall: Reflecting on narcissism. *Journal of Clinical Psychology: In Session, 68*(8), 877–885.

Clarkin, J. F., Yeomans, F. E., & Kernberg, O. F. (2006). *Psychotherapy for borderline patients: An object relations approach.* Washington, DC: American Psychiatric Press.

Diamond, D., & Yeomans F.E. (2008). Psychopathologies narcissiques et psychotherapie focalisee sur le transfert. (Narcissism, its disorders and the role of transference-focused psychotherapy). *Santé Mentale au Québec, XXXIII,* 115–139.

Diamond, D., Yeomans, F., & Levy, K. N. (2011). Psychodynamic psychotherapy for narcissistic personality. In W. K. Campbell & J. D. Miller (Eds.), The handbook of narcissism and narcissistic personality disorder: Theoretical approaches, empirical findings, and treatments (pp. 423–433). Hoboken, NJ: Wiley

Henry, C., Mitropoulou, V., New, A. S., Koenigsberg, H. W., Silverman, J., & Siever, L. J. (2001). Affective instability and impulsivity in borderline personality and bipolar II disorders: Similarities and differences. *Journal of Psychiatric Research, 35,* 307–312.

Kernberg, O. F. (1984). *Severe personality disorders: Psychotherapeutic strategies.* New Haven: Yale University Press.

Kernberg, O. F. (1975/1985). *Borderline conditions and pathological narcissism.* Northvale, NJ: Jason Aronson, Inc.

Koenigsburg, H. W., Harvey, P. D., Mitropoulou, V., New, A. S., Goodman, M., Silverman, J., et al. (2001). Are the interpersonal and identity disturbances in the borderline personality disorder criteria linked to the traits of affective instability and impulsivity? *Journal of Personality Disorders, 15,* 358–370.

Levy, K. N. (2012). Subtypes, dimensions, levels, and mental states in narcissism and narcissistic personality disorder. *Journal of Clinical Psychology, 68,* 886–897.

Steiner. J. (1994). Patient-centered and analyst-centered interpretations: some implications of containment and countertransference. Psychoanalytic Inquiry: A Topical Journal for Mental Health Professionals, 14, 406–422.

Stern, B.L., Yeomans, F., Diamond, D., & Kernberg, O.F. (2011). In J. Ogrodniczuk, (Ed.). Transference-Focused Psychotherapy (TFP) for Narcissistic Personality Disorder. American Psychiatric Press: Washington, DC.

8

Schizotypal and Narcissistic Personality Disorders

Presenting Problem and Client Description

Nathan James was a 30-year-old, never-married Caucasian man who had lived his entire life with his mother and various siblings. When he was a small child, his father left; shortly afterward, the patient was repeatedly sexually abused by an older man who lived across the hall from the his apartment. The sexual abuse typically included being forced to perform oral sex and occasionally involved anal penetration. The patient's first hospitalization occurred when he was 8 and made a suicide attempt and had reported visual and auditory hallucinations. Since that time, he has been psychiatrically hospitalized three additional times but not since he was 18. Following his initial hospitalization, he had numerous outpatient treatments. At the time I began working with him, he was being seen in treatment at an outpatient clinic at a university medical center. He was in his eighth year of treatment at the medical center, being treated in a specialty clinic within the outpatient department for adults suffering from schizophrenia and related psychotic disorders. Nathan had been diagnosed with a range of disorders, including schizophrenia, schizoaffective disorder, bipolar I and II, and obsessive-compulsive disorder; however, most recently, he carried a diagnosis of schizophrenia, residual type, because he had denied having hallucinations and delusions for many years now, and there was little evidence of such. Nonetheless, Nathan was peculiar in his physical presentation and mannerisms, and although not frankly delusional, the content of his speech was also peculiar and often paranoid—replete with stories of how he was mistreated and resulting revenge fantasies, fantasies that he occasionally enacted to his disadvantage. When I was assigned him as a patient, Nathan had just been transferred from the schizophrenia specialty clinic to a day hospital for people with personality disorders. During his time in the schizophrenia clinic, he had a reputation for being very difficult to deal with, often threatening to sue the psychiatric resident assigned to treat him or, worse, threatening to ruin the resident's career. During my initial interview with him, Nathan regaled me with tales of how his previous treater was inept, misdiagnosing and mistreating him, and how he "ran him out of town." Nathan declared that he would not stop pursing his former treater until he was no longer able to practice medicine and instead had a humiliating job selling women's shoes. During my initial interview with Nathan, consistent with previous reports, he denied having hallucinations and delusions. He indicated that it was something he said when he was a child in order to avoid going to school because he was rejected by a girl he liked and teased by other kids. He also thought that having hallucinations would make him special and interesting to his peers. Upon questioning, it was clear that he was ostracized by peers because he behaved in peculiar ways with them, including claiming to experience hallucinations. In a brief moment of vulnerability, Nathan admitted that it was a mistake to have feigned hallucinations, as it sent him on a path he regretted. He shared that he did not believe he had schizophrenia and that his previous treaters were naïve or foolish for believing he had schizophrenia. When I questioned him about why, then, did he spend so many years in the schizophrenia clinic, he glibly declared, "I was training residents." At some level, he was not kidding. Nathan had a reputation for being difficult to treat, and he put the residents through the ringer.

At the time treatment began, Nathan was living at home with his mother and was unemployed. In fact, despite evidence of high intelligence based on IQ testing, Nathan had never lived outside his mother's home nor had he ever had sustained paid employment. He had also never held a job for more than a few days before being fired. This included volunteer work for which he was fired after a few days since he came across as odd, peculiar, and hostile. He would often say competitive and derogatory things toward others. He volunteered for a political campaign where he had many ideas that were different than those of the campaign. He told others that his low-level volunteer position was one of great responsibility. He has a hard time reading the emotions of others and thought at times others were jealous of him. He had little insight into how his behavior influenced others. At the time therapy began, he was receiving disability for his emotional problems. He had volunteered at a number of places, all resulting in his being let go because of difficulties with peers. Similar to when he was in school, he acted in peculiar ways with coworkers, often antagonizing them, acting competitive with them, and behaving and speaking in inappropriately sexualized ways with women coworkers on whom he often had unrequited crushes. Nathan's history was also remarkable because although he desired intimate relationships with women and despite being 30 years of age, he had never had an emotionally or sexually intimate relationship with a woman. He was very much humiliated and bothered by the fact that he was a virgin and that he missed out on opportunities others have had, such as losing one's virginity at the prom with the girl of one's dreams. Nathan reported having friends, including women friends, but bemoaned that either he was not interested in these women because they were unattractive to him or they did not return his interests. Upon further questioning, however, it was clear that none of these individuals were long-term friends or people who he confided in or who confided in him.

Rather, Rather, he was in contact with people through the services he received, and he mistook politeness and friendliness as friendship.

Nathan reported that as a child he felt "odd" compared to his peers in elementary school. Although somewhat bothered by this feeling, he also took great pride in being eccentric. He saw himself as highly intelligent compared to his peers and envied by them because of this; however, he did not like to take exams or be in situations that would test him. When he was 8 years old, he reported to teachers that he saw skeletons dancing in the front of the classroom. Nathan indicated to me that he did so only to avoid taking an exam and thought he would be sent to the nurse's office, only to return later when he reported feeling better and the exam was over. However, this incident began a long series of psychiatric hospitalizations and neuroleptic medication trials. As a child, he was hospitalized twice, and as a teen, he was hospitalized twice more. He reported feeling suicidal as a teen. Despite his hospitalizations, Nathan was able to graduate from high school on time. Upon graduating, he attended a local commercial business school where he was trained in word processing; unfortunately, not one of the word processing programs were in demand at the time. He also took gun cleaning and handling classes by mail; however, he did not complete the training due to a dispute over the grading of one of his exams. Psychological testing performed at age 28 revealed a full-scale IQ of 128 with a score of 19 on vocabulary.

Growing up, Nathan had no significant friendships. In childhood, his friendships were characterized by one of three main scenarios: (1) friendship with other awkward and strange boys. He would occasionally make friends with someone awkward and weird like himself but then the friendship would wane due to his intolerance of the other person's "weirdness"; (2) he was sometimes befriended by more popular and occasionally older girls who typically saw him as sweet but not as a romantic interest. These girls would confide in Nathan about their relationship troubles with romantic partners, and Nathan would invest hours to help them with little, if any, emotional reciprocity. Nathan would frequently develop a strong unrequited love interest in these girls, and often these relationships ended when Nathan's feelings became known; and (3) friendships in which Nathan tended to be a "mascot" for a group of other kids and in which he would frequently be the object of jokes and pranks. These friendships were formed mainly through proximity, and his friends would change with location. He would rarely be able to maintain a friendship over time or through change of circumstances, despite the fact that he sometimes tried to do so through calling or writing letters (this was before smartphones, texting, etc.) On a number of occasions, he was told by these friends to stop harassing them. During young adulthood, most of Nathan's friendships developed through psychiatric treatment programs. His friendships were invariably with women for whom he often had a rather transparent "secret crush." He would often take the role of protector and take up battles on their behalf against what he perceived as "terrible injustices" perpetrated against these women. For instance, on one occasion he smuggled caffeine pills into an inpatient unit for a peer who he felt was being denied her basic right to coffee. This peer was hospitalized for a very serious eating disorder from which she almost died and was at the time being restricted from coffee and tea use because of their diuretic properties. His peer was caught with the pills and lost status on the unit, which affected her upcoming pass. She was terribly angry with Nathan and did not want to see him. He perceived himself as a knight in shining armor and the hospital as oppressive.

Although Nathan presented himself as an industrious and exemplary worker, his work history was very poor. He reported that as a preteen he had a large paper route, which by this report he was able to complete quickly and efficiently. With much pride, Nathan claimed to have never called in sick. Of note, however, he complained bitterly about not being appreciated by his customers or treated fairly in terms of payment and tips. In high school, Nathan worked in a local store, and he reported that this job was satisfying and that they were happy with him. The store closed at about the same time he graduated from high school. From ages 18 to 22, Nathan attempted to work, mostly in low-level clerk type positions and temp jobs. Nathan reported with great disdain and amazement that he had a difficult time getting hired, although he also reported dressing and behaving in provocative ways during the interviews. Nathan reported being fired from each of the positions he was able to obtain. For instance, Nathan had a job at a bookstore for a short period of time. He was fired after ostracizing his peers by trying to show them up. He reported having been driven to show his employers what a good employee he was compared to others; however, this plan backfired as he ostracized himself from his peers and they began teasing him. The conflict escalated until the point that Nathan's mere presence at work was highly disruptive to the functioning of the store and he was fired. In another clerk job, he was fired after showing female workers a picture of a naked male action-movie actor and making fun of the actor's genitalia. He was also fired from jobs at a local library, a telemarking firm, and even volunteer jobs, including one at the local chapter of the American Heart Association. At the time, Nathan was generally indignant and felt he had been mistreated in each of these incidents. At this point, he set his sights on bigger and better jobs, using his word processing skills to develop what he called a sure-fire winning resume that he sent out for various high-level jobs advertised in the *New York Times*. He was particularly interested in high-profile political jobs as well as executive jobs at major corporations such as director of programing at a major TV station. He was surprised when he was unable to garner any job interviews. This increased his paranoia. He perceived that he was being unfairly rejected and could not see why he was unqualified for the jobs he was applying for. Frustrated and desperate for work, he began looking for stores with help-wanted signs in their windows. However, he had a number of experiences where he entered establishments with help-wanted signs displayed prominently and was refused an interview after being given what he, probably correctly, believed to be excuses. Nathan was probably being rejected because of his odd and eccentric mannerisms, which were readily apparent to those he interacted with, even in only a short interaction. Examples of his oddities include wearing prominent cowboy boots, a cowboy hat, and a thin-string cowboy tie to job interviews where such attire was clearly not the norm. Additionally, his voice tends to be excessively loud and he would often tell off-color jokes or take up controversial viewpoints during conversation (e.g., he often made sure to mention his support of the National Rifle Association and would call prominent political figures wimps, etc.). After about 4 years of being fired from jobs and another 2 years of not being able to find a job, Nathan stopped job searching. During this period, Nathan claimed to have applied to "literally a thousand jobs." He believed that his lack of success was because others were jealous of his obvious superior intelligence and were closed-minded in their inability to appreciate his unique characteristics and eccentric behaviors. He was unable to evaluate the limited extent of his accomplishments and the lack of appropriate education and training for the jobs to which he was applying. Instead, he overvalued his raw intelligence and his unique way of thinking as making him qualified for positions he had no background in.

With no job prospects and a history of emotional difficulties, he began receiving disability and continued to live at home. At home, he was frequently in conflict with his mother. He was able to volunteer for a local political organization, and although he had a lot of conflict with other members of the organization, he was able to work in a nonpaid, unelected position that was of little interest to others. However, he saw the position as central to the local party and that it would prepare him to eventually fulfill his aspiration to become a congressman or senator. Consistent with other inter-actions, he held a number of loudly expressed positions that were completely contrary to the party platform (and more consistent with the opposing party). He would engage in very heated arguments with others, and eventually, he was asked to step down from this position.

Diagnosis and Case Formulation

Based on the information Nathan was presenting, the diagnosis of schizophrenia was ruled out. He denied hallucinations and delusions, and there were no observations or reports of his experiencing them. He provided a credible narrative that he had feigned hallucinations for secondary gain (e.g., impress others, avoid school when he was upset). Although he had a number of strange beliefs across multiple domains, these did not rise to the level of being delusional. Instead, his presentation was con-sistent with a diagnosis of schizotypal personality disorder. Nathan reported or dis-played six of the nine criteria for schizotypal personality disorder, including (1) odd beliefs or magical thinking; (2) odd thinking and speech; (3) suspiciousness/paranoid ideation; (4) inappropriate and constricted affect; (5) behavior and appearance that is odd, eccentric, and peculiar; and (6) a lack of friends or confidants. Nathan also met criteria for narcissistic personality disorder (NPD), including: (1) a grandiose sense of self-importance (e.g., exaggerates achievements and talents, expects to be recog-nized as superior without commensurate achievements); (2) a belief that he is special and unique, and can only be understood by special people; (3) preoccupation with fantasies of unlimited success, power, brilliance, and ideal love; (4) lack of empathy toward others; (5) envy of others or the belief that others are envious of him; and (6) arrogant, haughty behaviors and attitudes.

After completing the evaluation, the therapist provided Nathan with feedback about his understanding of the difficulties Nathan was experiencing as well as a diag-nostic conceptualization. This information is shared in order to establish a collaborative and shared understanding of the nature of the patient's difficulties and treatment plan. From a cognitive-behavioral therapy perspective, Beck (1976) has been explicit about the collaborative nature of treatment; however, such a stance is also consistent with humanistic and psychodynamic perspectives. The treatment goals, the therapist and patient's roles and responsibilities, and the techniques used in treatment all follow directly from one's understanding of the underlying mechanisms or functions of the patient's difficulties. Nathan began by telling me that he didn't have schizophrenia and that previous treaters were too stupid to realize that. However, he was perplexed about how to understand his problems. He shared that he questioned whether or not he had a problem at all or if it was society that had the problem; society was just not ready for someone of his intellect and vision. I asked him to elaborate on that and then pointed out that although part of him questioned if he had a problem, another part of him clearly recognized that something was amiss because he had brought himself to treatment even though he had not been forced to do so. He wondered if he had depression but then doubted it. I asked him to say more about his thinking, and he noted that although he often did feel demoralized about his situation, he recognized that he was not depressed in ways similar to the depressed patients he had seen around the outpatient department or the descriptions of depression in the *Diagnostic and Statistical Manual of Mental Disorders* (4th ed.; *DSM-IV*). Together, we noted the differences between his experience and that which is more typical of depressive disorders. He noted that although he was not typically anxious in a chronic sense, at times he was very anxious. As we explored those instances, it became apparent that rather than anxiety about negative evaluations of himself, his concerns were more readily characterized as paranoid fears about others' intentions and/or narcissistic concerns about others not recognizing his value.

I shared with Nathan that I agreed with him that he was not suffering from schizophrenia for similar reasons that he articulated—namely, that he did not have hallucinations. Nonetheless, I told him I thought his problems were serious, long-standing, and unlikely to improve without a very direct focus on issues that might be difficult for him to tolerate at times. I continued that similar to the concerns he articulated, I did not think that his problems could be understood in terms of a depressive or anxiety disorder. Instead, I suggested that his problems could be understood in terms of personality-related issues. I pointed out, as he might be aware, that the *DSM-IV* includes, among the various difficulties it notes, a set of problems related to personality that they called *personality disorders*. I then explained the main characteristics of personality disorders to him. *DSM-IV* describes personality disorders as "an enduring pattern of inner experience and behavior that deviates markedly from the expectations of the individual's culture." This pattern is manifested in two (or more) of the following areas: (1) cognition (i.e., ways of perceiving and interpreting self, other people, and events); (2) affectivity (i.e., the range, intensity, lability, and appropriateness of emotional response); (3) interpersonal functioning; and (4) impulse control. Initially, he agreed that his problems have been long-standing and that there was a pattern to his problems. He also agreed that his behavior deviated from what was expected by society. Although part of him was indignant about society's expectations, he saw himself as an iconoclast, a perception in which he took great pleasure. I was able to point out that while part of him felt this away, a consequence of this way of being is that he often felt like an outcast and was not accepted. I went on to describe how in *DSM-IV* the enduring pattern is inflexible and pervasive across a broad range of personal and social situations, and that this enduring pattern leads to clinically significant distress or impairment in social, occupational, or other important areas of functioning; that this pattern was stable and of long duration, and its onset could be traced back at least to adolescence, and in his case even childhood; and finally, that this enduring pattern is not better accounted for as a manifestation or consequence of another emotional disorder such as schizophrenia. Nathan readily agreed with all these points. Once we agreed on the general premise that he was suffering from a personality disorder rather than depression, anxiety, or schizophrenia, I shared with him that in the *DSM*, different types of personality disorders are described and that it would be important for us to determine which, if any, best characterize his difficulties. With agreement on the goals of the treatment as well as the frame, we began the therapy.

Course of Treatment

Over the course of the psychotherapy, Nathan made remarkable strides. Nathan went from living at home to having his own apartment, from never having a romantic relationship to having a committed romantic relationship, and most important, Nathan went from having been unemployed his entire life to having a professional position. However, these changes were not easily accomplished and were met with apprehension and resistance.

Nathan began treatment in a day hospital specializing in the treatment of personality disorders and individual therapy with the author. The individual psychotherapy approach employed with Nathan consisted of a combination of expressive and supportive psychotherapies. Although it was believed that Nathan's NPD would best be treated using an expressive approach like transference-focused psychotherapy, his difficulties associated with schizotypal personality disorder required a more supportive approach. The support was directed at two main issues. The first was working to help Nathan move into a more independent living situation and support himself through sustained employment. The second was to provide advice, direction, and support to refrain from behaviors that typically led him to be fired or might put him at risk for maintaining more independent living.

Nathan's attitude toward the therapist was generally one of idealization. Idealization occurs when the positive view of the therapist represents a defensive distortion or exaggeration rather than an authentic, reality based, positive regard. Typically, idealizations are considered defensive evaluations because such an attitude is used to protect the patient's positive feelings from being overtaken by any negative ones—even relatively minor negative feelings—that the patient may be experiencing toward the therapist. Although Nathan tended to idealize the therapist, he tended to denigrate other staff associated with the day hospital. While he would refer to me as Dr. Levy, despite the fact that at the time I had yet to complete my doctorate, other staff with doctorates were often referred to by their last names only, often with a tone of disdain (similar to the way Jerry Seinfeld used to utter the name "Newman" on the *Seinfeld* show). Theorists disagree with how best to handle patients' idealizations of the therapist. Some, like Heinz Kohut (1971, 1977), believe that it is important to allow the patient these idealizations in the beginning of treatment. In contrast, others, like Otto Kernberg, believe it is best to confront the idealizations as distortions. For much of the therapy, my attempts to confront the idealizations were largely unsuccessful. Nathan would routinely idealize me and derogate my colleagues. In a group session and individual session, I would be praised for almost any comment I made, whereas Nathan would criticize my co-leader's comments, phrasing, and even word choice. Referring to the co-leader by her last name only, he would continue with "well actually what you meant to say was . . ." or "what you are saying makes no sense, either conceptually or grammatically." My own non sequiturs, word-choice mistakes, and grammatical errors were not only left uncorrected but often highlighted instead for their importance. But as the therapy progressed and he improved, the need to maintain the idealization began to weaken. For instance, one time he began his individual session railing about how stupid everyone in the world is, and he went on about this one's stupidity and that other person's stupidity. I noted to him that when he says *everyone* in the world is stupid, I would be included in that statement, and I wondered if maybe I had done something that he thought was stupid, too. He responded with "Oh no. Not you Dr. Levy (I recall I did not have my doctorate at the time). Not you, I mean everyone else." I gently reminded him of how he is typically very precise with his wording, often criticizing others for their lack of precision, and thus I wondered if his word choice was meaningful. I said this as a very gentle confrontation. He assured me that I was not included in his statement and that I was the only person he could count on to not act stupidly. I decided not to push against this idealization, at least for the time being. Over the next 10 minutes or so, as he continued to speak, he elaborated about why everyone was stupid, which among other things included not following through on commitments. He gave the example of a number of people who canceled on him or changed appointments on him. In that moment, I suddenly recalled that the previous week I had a clinical emergency arise that I needed to attend to during what would be my normally scheduled time with Nathan. I had time to call him to reschedule before attending to the emergency. The evidence was clear, regardless of the legitimacy of my request, that I had behaved in a manner consistent with what had him riled and believing others were stupid—that is, changed an appointment on him, a commitment, and I had behaved stupidly by his definition. Mindful of this need to protect his image of me, I gently reminded him that a week earlier I had called him to reschedule and wondered what that was like for him, noting that I typically have not rescheduled with him. He reminded me that I had never rescheduled with him before. I pointed out that it sounded like he was aware of that, and he agreed. I said, "Given that, maybe you had some feelings about my needing to reschedule." He said he understood, I had an emergency arise. I continued, "Well, maybe part of you understands that I had an emergency arise and was aware that I had never rescheduled with you before, and certainly intellectually you might understand that, but maybe another part of you, maybe even just a small part, was upset with me for having to change the appointment, even if another part of you realized it was not done on purpose or out of malice or even stupidity. But nonetheless, you might have been a little upset, if not at me, then the situation." Once again, he denied being upset with me. However, he was able to acknowledge that he was very much looking forward to our session that day. Rather than say he was disappointed or upset, he focused on the positive of looking forward to the session. I added, "It must have been disappointing then." He sighed and acknowledged that it was. I asked if he recalled what he wanted to talk about that day. He did. Interestingly, it was something that he had not yet shared with me. I told him I was curious why he did not share this with me when we did finally meet later that week. This led to a discussion that maybe he withheld as a way of punishing us both.

Another theme in the therapy concerned his revenge plots against those with whom he had grievances. Early in the treatment, Nathan recounted to the therapist the many grievances he had with people who had done him wrong. The list of past offenders was long and, among others, included neighbors and classmates who mistreated him as far back as elementary school to women who rejected him in high school, to coworkers who sabotaged and reported him to superiors, to incompetent treaters. In every story of his failure there was a villain to blame, and with anger he elaborated on his plans for revenge. His revenge plans were often very colorful and Rube-Goldbergesque in design with many moving parts. Nathan spent hours planning and elaborating these schemes, although he rarely attempted them. However, at times he did. One time when he was actively searching for jobs but having little luck, he missed a scheduled interview due to poor bus service. He was livid, having believed that he would have received the job had he made the interview. He blamed a local politician whom he felt was responsible for the bus service's poor performance and developed an elaborate and bizarre plot to target the politician, writing the person a letter detailing what he had in mind for him. This resulted in a visit from the police, who after meeting with Nathan deemed him harmless.

Although he was 30 years old, there was a very young, childlike quality to Nathan. This quality was quite prominent, in part because much of what he discussed focused on his high school years and stories of boys half-heartedly befriending him only to tease and humiliate him, and of unrequited love interests. He was quite bothered by the fact that he was still a virgin and never had a physical encounter with a woman. Session after session he bemoaned the fact that he did not go to his prom. He often spoke about wanting to meet someone and take her to a prom. At times, in an almost dreamlike quality, he spoke as if he could turn the clock back some 15-plus years and correct the great wrong that had been carried out against him. Other times, he would discuss a fantasy, as if it could be real and without the awareness of how it would seem to others, about meeting a high school girl whom he could take to a prom. He gave little thought to how it would seem to school officials or the girl's parents for an 18-year-old girl to show up to her prom with a man 12 years her senior. In both cases, these powerful fantasies were relived over and over as a way of mitigating the great injustice that was imposed on him. Meanwhile, he was wasting the present day stuck in a fantasy about correcting the past.

Distraught about his virginity, he talked about taking an ad out in the local paper to advertise his willingness to provide cunnilingus. He would share his ideas with glee and excitement, as if it was a good idea that would work to solve his virginity problem. Nathan seemed impervious to my attempts to confront these ideas. To him they made sense. As the therapy progressed, he began to recognize that both his focus on the prom and the idea of placing an ad offering oral sex were unrealistic, and the fantasy of both became less satisfying and less gripping. He was becoming more interested in meeting a real woman with whom he could be in a relationship. He was now living in a group home where he shared an apartment with a roommate. As such, there were other residents in other apartments, including women, and at a residents meeting he met a woman whom he would eventually begin dating. As he dated this woman, a different side of Nathan emerged.

Meanwhile, in the reality of the day hospital, Nathan was not well liked. The women seemed not to notice him and certainly did not interact much with him, except when verbally attacking something provocative he said during a group session. The men, particularly the antisocial ones, interacted with him but treated him like a mascot and tended to toy with him, a dynamic to which he seemed oblivious. In groups, he was often attacked because he was proactive, and a number of women, who themselves had been traumatized in the past and some relatively recently, treated Nathan as if he were a perpetrator. The irony was that Nathan himself had suffered sexual abuse as a child.

A combination of support and encouragement, along with tactful confrontations, was used early in treatment to help Nathan move out of his home, moving into an independent living situation, and to help him not only obtain a job but to maintain it by giving him specific advice at times. In psychotherapy, the technique of a confrontation is not what we typically think of when we hear that word. In psychotherapy, a *confrontation* is the clear and tactful pointing out of some discrepancy in the patient's experience or behavior. It is meant to bring disparate aspects of experience in confrontation with one another in order to allow the patient to grapple with and integrate them. In this way, it is meant to promote insight or productive reflection, and it is delivered with an attitude of concern and warmth, not aggression as the word might otherwise imply. Initially, Nathan moved into a group home with other chronic but functioning, capable outpatients. This move turned out to be critically important to Nathan's improvement because it was at this group home that Nathan met a woman whom he began dating and with whom he would eventually have both an emotionally and physically intimate relationship. Later, he moved into housing with a roommate and eventually out of supervised housing and into his own apartment.

The new living situation, with other housemates and the politics of governance as well as his job and relationship with a girlfriend, provided ample opportunity for important issues to arise, be discussed, and understood. There were conflicts, jealousies, and competiveness with housemates, roommates, and coworkers that Nathan had to manage. At work, Nathan performed better than he had done previously. Although he was competitive with coworkers, he was able to keep his behavior in check. This allowed him to thrive at work, and although he was not close with his coworkers, he was not universally ostracized either. His supervisors also seemed to appreciate Nathan's competence, commitment, and work ethic, despite his quirkiness. Still, there were land mines to navigate. One session, Nathan arrived furious with some of his coworkers. They had been teasing him, playing small jokes on him, and generally trying to undermine his performance. He was angry and frustrated with their disrespect. In session, he angrily cursed them and shared with me an elaborate revenge fantasy designed to expose them and humiliate them. It had been a long time since I had heard one of these revenge plots from Nathan, and I worried that he might try to enact this one and that the result could be his losing his job and all the opportunities it provided. I shared with him that "I could understand why he would be upset with these particular coworkers," and furthermore, "I could understand the impulse to seek revenge and the value of fantasizing about doing so." But I also wanted to express my concern about what might happen if he was to act on his impulse and how it could put the important gains he made over the last year at risk. I further articulated the gains and how if he were to act on his revenge impulse, he might end up losing his job, and that losing his job would put his housing at risk, which might interfere with his relationship, and so on. He agreed. Acknowledging the legitimacy of his feelings and his impulse appeared to satiate his desire for revenge. In the beginning of the treatment it would not have sufficed, and my mention of the potential negative consequences would have been experienced as invalidating and an imposition. Having navigated this land mine, Nathan continued to impress his supervisors. Over a relatively short time, supervisors came to rely on Nathan, and while other workers came and went, Nathan moved up the ladder, the pinnacle of which was when he was selected for a management trainee program.

Another important event in the therapy concerned Nathan's relationship with his girlfriend. Nathan was thrilled to have a girlfriend. They met at the group home Nathan had moved into and spent a lot of time together. Although he had been desperate to have sex, he spoke of her in an idealized manner and was quite chivalrous toward her. However, as their relationship unfolded, both wanted it to become physically intimate. This created a number of conflicts for him. He wanted her to desire him but questioned her desire. Was it truly for him or could he be anyone? In addition, her sexual desires in and of themselves bothered him. He desired her and wanted to have sex with her, but her willingness to do so and her own sexual desires made him feel she was too lascivious. Such conflicts are not unusual for those suffering from narcissism. Moreover, he was having his own conflicts about his sexuality secondary to his sexual abuse, which caused him great pain. He was frantic to have sex, and yet as the opportunity presented itself, he found himself uncomfortable with being sexual, and he particularly had difficulty in the moments where he would be expected to penetrate her. It is not unusual for those who are victims of sexual abuse to have difficulties in sexual relations. It is not uncommon to see one of three types of responses to sexual abuse: (1) extreme promiscuity, often with disregard for one's safety, such as having sex with strangers, unprotected, and/or while blackout drunk; (2) avoidance of sex and/or frigidity; and (3) the capacity to physically engage in sexual behavior but without an emotional connection or physical enjoyment of it. Nathan's conflictual feelings about both his sexuality (believed to stem from his sexual abuse) and her sexuality (stemming from his narcissism) and the subsequent discussions provided an important area for exploration and resolution. Together, we determined that it was difficult for him to perform intercourse because he associated being the penetrator as being a perpetrator. It took time to work through the associated feelings that in penetrating her during intercourse he was now the aggressive one abusing another. But over time, with exploration of both his conscious and unconscious concerns, he was able to engage in intercourse in a conflict-free manner.

Another avenue to explore was Nathan's narcissistic defenses that occurred in the exploration of our relationship. Initially, and for a long period of time, Nathan tended to idealize me, which showed in a number of ways, some of which were described earlier. Another way that the idealization showed itself was in Nathan's insistence on calling me Dr. Levy despite not yet having my doctoral degree confirmed. As interns at the site where I trained, we were instructed to inform our patients to refer to us as Mr. or Ms. rather than our first names. Because, as interns, our doctoral degrees were yet to be confirmed, we could not be called *doctor*. Throughout my internship year, Nathan loudly referred to me as Dr. Levy. I would correct him to no avail. Every time he saw me, it was Dr. Levy, Dr. Levy. However, that abruptly changed after my doctorate was actually conferred. I defended my dissertation about halfway through the 2-year period that I treated Nathan. Nathan was aware of the impending change, as we discussed it per my supervisor's direction. He seemed uninterested in exploring what it might mean to him. With my dissertation defense, the sign on my office door was changed to reflect my new degree and move from an intern to a postdoctoral fellow. From that moment on, Nathan would refer to me as "Mr. Levy," which was also said loudly and with the following emphasis: "Miiister Levee." At first, he denied that there was any meaning to his change in salutation. But this change was a harbinger of a move from an idealization to a devaluation. I never wanted to be the good or idealized therapist, but I also did not want to be the derogated one either. Not because I could not tolerate it but because being the integrated therapist in Nathan's mind would represent the needed improvement. With this move from the idealization, we were able to work toward a more integrated view of me, his girlfriend, and himself.

Outcome and Prognosis

Nathan made remarkable progress over the 2 years I saw him in psychotherapy. In contrast to his previous functioning, he was now living in his own apartment, he was in a long-term, committed relationship, he was engaged in a satisfying emotional and sexual relationship, and he had stable employment that was satisfying to him and in which his performance was recognized. As a result, he was promoted and no longer on disability, a state of affairs that was almost unimaginable before beginning treatment. Along the way, there were a number of relationship and work challenges. Both he and his girlfriend had to work through intimacy issues related to past sexual abuse, and at work, Nathan had to weather both difficulties with coworkers and the impact of outside market forces. In the past, these types of challenges often derailed Nathan.

In the context of newly developed capacities and with the support of the therapist, Nathan was able to navigate what previously would have been treacherous terrain but now was experienced as mere bumps in the road.

Discussion Questions

1. Explain why Nathan's therapist ruled out schizophrenia despite a diagnosis of schizophrenia in the past.

2. Describe the advantages of a collaborative approach in cognitive-behavioral therapy and the ways in which Nathan's therapist used such an approach in Nathan's treatment.

3. What were the two primary issues Nathan's therapist sought to help him address? Describe at least three specific techniques that were used during treatment.

References

Beck, A. T. (1976). *Cognitive therapy and the emotional disorders*. New York, NY: Meridian.

Kohut, H. (1971). The analysis of the self. New York, NY: University of Chicago Press.

Kohut, H. (1977). The restoration of the self. New York, NY: University of Chicago Press.

9

Histrionic Personality Disorder

Presenting Problem and Client Description

Amy Porter is a 50-year-old divorced woman with two young children. She was referred to one of the authors when her current therapist was leaving the outpatient clinic in which Ms. Porter was seen at the time. Ms. Porter had been in treatment off and on over the past 20 years. She would typically enter treatment after becoming distressed by stressful life circumstances, particularly interpersonal ones. Often, she would end treatment precipitously after the start of a new romantic relationship. At that point, she would feel excited about the new person she was dating and idealize the person, and, feeling good about her future, she would feel little need to continue in treatment. It was as if with the promise of the new relationship all her ills vanished into thin air. At the time of the transfer to the author, Ms. Porter had been in therapy for about 1 year with her previous therapist. Ms. Porter reported feeling ambivalent about the previous therapist. At times, she felt she liked her, but she also felt in conflict with her. Ms. Porter reported that she admired the therapist, who she saw as successful, but she sometimes felt jealous of and competitive with the therapist, whom she viewed as a highly competent woman who probably had a perfect life and was thus unable to understand her situation. Sometimes she felt judged by the therapist, assuming that a highly competent person like the therapist would look down on someone like herself. On the other hand, Ms. Porter also reported that at times she was concerned about the therapist's competence, believing that the therapist was unsure of how best to treat her. She reported that she believed the therapist was often overwhelmed by her distress and/or felt exasperated by her inability to help the patient. Other times, she felt that the therapist was not taking her distress and difficulties seriously enough.

Diagnosis and Case Formulation

The mental status examination (MSE) is an important part of the diagnostic assessment and provides a standardized way of observing and describing the patient's current state of mind. It is important to have a baseline assessment of the patient and to monitor the patient's mental status for any changes that might suggest important issues to attend to. Monitoring the mental status of a patient is useful for identifying the occurrences of psychotic, manic, or depressive episodes, or suicidal or homicidal risk. The domains of the MSE include appearance, attitude, behavior, mood, affect, speech, thought processes, thought content, perception, cognition, insight, and judgment. In terms of mental status, Ms. Porter arrived for her initial sessions on time, dressed professionally and consistent with her level and type of employment. She appeared kempt although a bit frazzled after what she reported was a long day. She was slightly taller than average for a woman and appeared of normal weight. She appeared slightly younger than her chronological age. Although her attitude was generally cooperative, she was distressed and easily irritated. Initially, she was extremely pleasant and outgoing. Her mood appeared upbeat. However, her mood would quickly shift with the content of what she was discussing. At times she was tearful and other times smiling, making subtle jokes, or even laughing. Although her affect was generally consistent with the content, either happy or sad, at times her affect was incongruent with what she was talking about; most notably, she would often giggle or have a slight laugh when discussing some distressing events. Her speech was normal in terms of rate, rhythm, and volume, although she sometimes became pressured in her speech. Her thought content was logical, but at times she went on slight tangents. She was oriented to person, place, and time.

During the initial evaluation, Ms. Porter complained of being very unhappy and appeared in a lot of distress. She was very activated, talking quickly, somewhat perturbed and even agitated at times about perceived failures on other people's part to attend to or understand her. She was upset with her parents, siblings, ex-husband, children, and previous therapist. The author hypothesized that Ms. Porter's pattern of being dissatisfied with others, including her previous therapists, would also likely happen with him. Sure enough, even in the very first session, he perceived that Ms. Porter was annoyed with him at times for not allaying her distress and/or for not being sympathetic enough. The author felt that the patient wanted him to wave a magic wand and cure all her ills in one quick swoosh, and anything short of that was disappointing. The patient also seemed to be "fishing" to get the therapist to agree to her many grievances about having been mistreated by others. The therapist attempted to be sympathetic and concerned for Ms. Porter; however, anything short of a strong acknowledgement by the therapist of the injustice suffered by Ms. Porter appeared to annoy her. The patient reported worrying about a host of concerns, including her work situation, child care, and meeting an appropriate romantic partner. She also reported episodes where she became increasingly anxious and felt panicked. However, her most pressing concerns and complaints centered on her relationships and her sense of herself, as described in more detail below.

Given her complaints, a number of diagnostic decisions had to be considered. Was Ms. Porter's unhappiness sufficient for a diagnosis of major depressive disorder (MDD), or chronic and sufficient for a diagnosis of persistent depressive disorder? Was her lability, agitation, and pressured speech an indication of a bipolar disorder? Was her worry sufficient for a diagnosis of generalized anxiety disorder (GAD)? What about her reports of panic attacks? Given the consideration of these disorders, as well as her concerns about relationship functioning and her sense of self, personality disorders such as borderline personality disorder (BPD) and histrionic personality disorder (HPD) would also need to be considered.

Although Ms. Porter was quite unhappy, she did not meet any other criteria for major or persistent depressive disorders. Although she reported currently feeling depressed, her mood reactivity was such that she did not meet the criteria for depressed mood (i.e., most of the day, most days, for a 2-week period). Additionally, inconsistent with the depressed mood seen in MDD, Ms. Porter both described and displayed ample mood reactivity, including sustained positive emotions, joy, excitement, and laughter. Instead, she reported a pattern that suggested her mood was closely tied to events in the moment. As such, it rapidly shifted between feeling depressed, happy, irritable, and even angry. The author observed such reactivity within and between the initial sessions. Ms. Porter also showed no evidence of anhedonia such as loss of pleasure in activities she usually enjoyed. In fact, one reason she was unhappy was that she did not have enough time for those activities and could not attend as many social events as she desired. Ms. Porter showed no neurovegetative signs such as appetite or weight loss, insomnia/hypersomnia, psychomotor slowing, or loss of libido. In fact, she described an active and healthy sex drive, albeit currently unsatisfied. Although she complained of lack of energy at times, it appeared that she felt this way when confronted with undesirable activities but had plenty of energy for activities that she enjoyed. She showed little guilt or blame more typical of MDD but instead was critical and blaming of others. Although she complained of being frequently indecisive, she did not have difficulty concentrating, and her indecisiveness tended to be long-standing, chronic, and not restricted to an episode. Instead, her indecisiveness was more consistent with the kind of difficulties seen in individuals who suffer from dependent personality disorder in that she had difficulty making everyday decisions without an excessive amount of advice and/or reassurance from others, or the kind of indecisiveness seen in HPD in which people feel unsure of themselves and need the reassurance of others. She became quite upset with those in her life when they would not provide her with the level of advice and reassurance she desired. Finally, she was not suicidal. For these reasons, MDD was ruled out. Similarly, she did not meet criteria for persistent depressive disorder, and in addition, she had long periods of not feeling depressed. Bipolar disorders, particularly bipolar II, were also ruled out as none of her symptoms met the threshold for that disorder. Although she reported previous depressed episodes, she never reported a hypomanic episode. She did report irritability, which would be consistent with a hypomanic episode, but the irritability tended to be chronic and part of her normal functioning. Certainly the irritability occurred outside of any discrete episode. She also reported rapidly shifting emotions; however, again the report and observation made by the author indicated that it was inconsistent with that typically experienced in bipolar disorder. For example, the patient's emotions shifted very quickly, moment to moment and minute to minute, as opposed to what is typically seen in bipolar disorder where the shifts occur over many days, even weeks or months. Additionally, the shifts were tied to events in Ms. Porter's life and, consistent with histrionic personality, tended to be of more shallowly experienced emotions.

With regard to GAD, by her report, Ms. Porter appeared to meet each of the criteria for the disorder according to the *Diagnostic and Statistical Manual of Mental Disorders* (4th ed.; *DSM–IV*) criteria, which was in use at the time. (The only changes between *DSM–IV* and *DSM–V* have to do with the number of associated physical symptoms having been reduced from six to two.) Ms. Porter reported excessive worry that was occurring more days than not and with regard to a number of activities such as work, her children, and dealing with family. She found it difficult to control the worry. And the anxiety and worry were associated with a number of identified symptoms of GAD such as feeling keyed up or on edge, being easily fatigued, her mind going blank, and irritability. The focus of the anxiety was not confined to the features of another axis I disorder nor was it due to the direct physiological effects of a substance or other medical condition. Finally, by report, the anxiety and worry did cause clinically significant distress, which was consistent with clinical observation. It was difficult to disentangle if the anxiety and worry were causing impairment versus other contributors, however. Given her report and clinical observation, GAD was strongly considered as a possible diagnosis.

With regard to panic disorder, there were a number of inconsistencies between her experience and the criteria articulated by *DSM–IV*. First, rather than peaking quickly, her anxiety during her "panic attacks" tended to be prolonged. Additionally, she did not feel that the panic came out of the blue but rather was tied to very specific events. Finally, her descriptions of her panic attacks were not consistent with the typical symptoms but instead appeared to be more about poor distress tolerance and about feeling overwhelmed in the moment about something that was going wrong (e.g., fight with parents, kids not listening) rather than a fear or concern about something that might happen in the future. Finally, her feelings of being overwhelmed would dissipate very quickly if she was reassured or if people accommodated her.

Other diagnostic considerations included BPD and HPD. Although BPD was considered, it was determined that Ms. Porter did not meet the threshold for it. Although Ms. Porter was highly preoccupied with romantic relationships as well as with her relationships with her parents and siblings, and these relationships could be quite entangled, she did not consistently engage in frantic efforts to avoid real or imagined abandonment. And with the exception of a few incidents (e.g., stalking ex-boyfriends) that happened when she was in her 20s, neither did any of her behaviors approach the threshold for this criterion. Although her relationships could be characterized as with intense and alternating between idealizations and devaluations, the vacillations between idealization and devaluation were less frequent, and the vacillations occurred over longer periods of time than what is typical for BPD. Additionally, the nature of these relationships was more characteristic of what is seen in HPD, in which relationships are perceived as more intimate than they actually are and tied to rapid shifts in more shallow expressions of emotion. Most important for the differential diagnosis with BPD was that her sense of identity, particularly in terms of her sense of self, goals, and values, as well as her ability to work toward these goals and behave in ways consistent with her values, were more developed and stable than what is typically seen in BPD. Although at times she could seem identity disturbed in that she reported not being sure of who she was and feeling empty at times, given her stability in goals, values, and her sense of self, these reports about being unsure of who she was were understood as being related to a histrionic style of speech that tends to be excessively impressionistic and lacking detail. Such a speech pattern in those with HPD is believed to be related to a histrionic style of not thinking precisely or deeply about things, including oneself. Importantly, Ms. Porter was not prone to the kind of aggression and impulsivity seen in BPD nor was she suicidal, threatening suicide, or ever made a suicide attempt.

Thus far, Ms. Porter did not meet criteria for MDD, persistent depressive disorder, bipolar I or II, panic disorder, or BPD. However, she did meet criteria for HPD. Consistent with the criteria, Ms. Porter enjoyed being the center of attention and was uncomfortable when not. Her need to be at the center of attention caused problems with friends and with family members. She relayed stories of fights with family members who thought she was too loud and attention seeking at other people's events such as weddings and graduations, and even the funeral of her grandmother where she cried uncontrollably and fainted despite not being particularly close to that grandparent. Both her mother and sister, who felt they had closer relationships with that grandparent, were upset with Ms. Porter for making herself the center of attention. Related, she often dressed and used her physical appearance to draw attention to herself. During the workday, she generally dressed appropriately, but she dressed very stylishly and somewhat flamboyantly so as to stand out. Additionally, she had a long history of dressing to garner attention, including dressing provocatively. When she went out at night with friends to parties or bars, she dressed to be the center of attention. In fact, she shared with joy scenes that sound right out of Carly Simon's 1972 song *You're So Vain* about walking into parties where all the men's heads turned to check her out and her belief that they all wanted to be with her. With glee and pride she declared that she used to look like a Barbie doll, which quickly turned to distress as she noted that as she aged, she was less able to elicit the kinds of reactions she wanted out of men. She prided herself on her ability to flirt and her skills in the art of seduction. As discussed earlier, she displayed rapidly shifting and shallow expressions of emotion, although she viewed herself as very empathic and sensitive. It is not unusual for those with HPD to feel that they experience emotions more deeply than others but for others to experience the patient as appearing or sounding shallow.

At the time Ms. Porter entered psychotherapy, she was working in a position far below her intellectual level, college education, and her aspirations. As an undergraduate, she had wanted to major in psychology with the goal of attending graduate school to become a clinical psychologist. However, she was unsure if she would be competitive for doctoral programs in psychology, so instead she majored in sociology with the goal of becoming a social worker. After a few years of working in a bachelor's-level social work position, she decided to go to graduate school to obtain her master's in social work (MSW). She gained entrance into a strong program and completed her degree in a timely manner. Although initially after graduating she worked a number of years doing administrative tasks related to social work, she wanted to be a psychotherapist. Over the next few years, the same work pattern emerged. She would begin a job with excitement and hope. She brought a lot of energy to the position and was generally well liked and social with her peers. But eventually, Ms. Porter would have minor run-ins with coworkers and/or supervisors, which would leave her feeling underappreciated and disillusioned. As a result, her work performance would suffer, sometimes she would become mildly but noticeably oppositional, and then she would either begin looking for another job on her own initiative or be advised to do so. This process would typically take 2 to 5 years to fully play out. Thus, she had some good work years in which she enjoyed her work, was valued by others, and was working toward promotion. However, each time this trajectory was altered, and after working in the field for 25 years, she had not achieved the kind of standing typical of people her age who have worked in a field for the amount of time she had. In fact, when the author began seeing her in therapy, she was underemployed, working a job that required only a bachelor's degree and not the master's degree she held. She was underpaid as a result, which caused her great strain. Additionally, she felt stifled, unsatisfied, and in a rut. Nonetheless, she was easily stressed in her job and frequently overwhelmed by the tasks and the politics. Meanwhile, her siblings, who were about the same age, were consistently moving ahead in their careers, achievements, and in family life.

Prior to her marriage, Ms. Porter reported a pattern of serial dating in which she would date one man after another, with each relationship lasting a short time. She described herself as having been very attractive when she was a young woman and often dressed in a provocative manner so as to gain attention from others. She even described herself as looking like a Barbie doll when she was younger and reported that she very much enjoyed all the men looking at her when she entered a room. Her view of relationships could be described like those from a romance novel. Similarly, she reported that she identified with the characters "Carrie" and "Ally McBeal" from the TV shows *Sex in the City* and *Ally McBeal*, respectively. Ms. Porter frequently described her ideal scenario for meeting a life partner in which she would walk into a party and all eyes would focus on her as the center of attention, and as she panned the room she caught eyes with the handsomest man in attendance. She described that the experience would be like fireworks exploding, which would only intensify as he approached her. They would have a witty banter and then leave together for a night of romance and sex. In her mind, this romantic evening would be the prelude to a life of living happily ever after, filled with fun and success. And she and her partner would be the envy of all. When she was younger, she did indeed have experiences akin to her fantasy except that the relationships would only last a few months to a few years. Over time, she had many relationships like this. However, as time went on, she found herself getting older without the life she imagined and became increasingly pressured, distressed, and irritable about her life situation. Additionally, as she got older she very much wanted to have children and was aware that there was a time press for doing so. Although her interest in having children was earnest, it was also fueled by her friends and siblings who were doing so and her envy of their lives. Ms. Porter described becoming desperate to find a life partner with whom she could have children. But as she aged, she became more and more unsatisfied with the men who were attracted to her. She complained that these men were too old, too short, too balding, too heavy, not handsome enough, or inadequate sexually. Eventually, however, she met a man whom she felt good about. He was not as tall, thin, or handsome as the man she imagined that she would marry, but she described that she was very attracted to him nonetheless. After a relatively short time dating, they married. For a short time, Ms. Porter reported that she was very happy. She got pregnant quickly and then again shortly after the birth of her first child. She reported that she enjoyed being in a stable relationship with a man she admired, to whom she was attracted, and with whom she had a satisfying sexual life. She also reported that she enjoyed being a mother and parenting as part of a couple. However, she also described some significant dissatisfactions: She described frequent fighting between herself and her husband, often over inconsequential issues but also over disagreements about how to parent the children. Additionally, although she described her sexual life as satisfying, she also complained that at times she felt objectified by him, particularly when he was interested in sex. Other times, she complained that she felt ignored by him and that he was uninterested in her. Still other times, she said he made derogatory comments about her body that made her feel self-conscious sexually. Independent of his comments, as she aged, she also noticed changes in her body that made her unhappy and self-conscious. Despite these difficulties in the relationship, she was shocked and unprepared when he asked for a divorce. Initially, she felt devastated and overwhelmed. She had financial concerns as well as feeling overwhelmed with the prospect of being a single parent. Although her ex-husband continued to be involved in caring for the children, the disagreements about how to parent the children intensified, and he often interacted with her in ways that understandably annoyed her (e.g., arriving early or late to pick up the children, returning the children early or late, changing plans at the last minute, and frequently not communicating these changes to her).

Single again, Ms. Porter began dating in a pattern that was similar to the one before her marriage. Although she was still attractive, she noticed that she no longer drew the attention of others the way she did when she was younger. Although she was now 50 years old, she found herself attracted to men in their late 20s to mid-30s. She complained that men her age tended not to be as fit, virile, or attractive as she desired, going as far to describe men her age derogatorily as "trolls" (as in the mythical cave-dwelling dwarf, ugly in appearance, not the Internet type). She was clearly bothered by the signs of aging in these men. And while a 50-year-old woman has every right to date and establish a relationship with a man younger than herself, the younger men that Ms. Porter was exposed to tended not to be interested in her. Although these men were often attracted to her for short-term sexual relations, rarely did one of these relationships last more than a few dates. This pattern bothered Ms. Porter very much as she still clung to a romantic ideal of walking into a party and catching eyes with the love of her life. In this fantasy, the men had model-like looks, were smart, successful, and interested in her both sexually and emotionally. Although part of her recognized that these men may have only been interested in a short-term sexual relationship, another part of her was indignant and upset that she couldn't seem to find someone who shared her romantic vision. She bemoaned getting older, declared she did not feel 50 years old but rather 20 years younger, but at other times would cry while describing her humiliation about her aging body. Although she stated quite clearly she wanted emotional intimacy, it was unclear that she had a sense of what that would entail. Conversely, she judged others and herself not with regard to their values, beliefs, aspirations, and psychological traits but by concrete, external physical appearance.

Course of Treatment

To treat the patient, the therapist used an expressive/insight-oriented psychotherapy approach based on a specific treatment called transference-focused psychotherapy (TFP). Expressive/insight-oriented approaches are also called *insight* or *insight-oriented psychotherapy* or sometimes referred to as *depth psychology* (particularly in Europe, and especially Germany). Expressive/insight-oriented psychotherapies are geared toward helping the patient gain awareness of the multiple, sometimes conflicting, views or perspectives on their experience of themselves, others, and events. The thoughts, feelings, and behaviors associated with these views can be very much in one's awareness, sometimes even flooding the person, or can be outside of one's awareness to varying degrees at various times. In Ms. Porter's case, it was observed that she vacillated between both feeling flooded and overwhelmed, and at other times feeling unsure of what she was thinking and feeling. Because these views can be contradictory and outside of one's awareness, the patient may think, feel, and behave inconsistently and not fully consider important aspects of a situation when making decisions. This was certainly the case for Ms. Porter. From a psychodynamic perspective, the contradictory experiences that are outside one's awareness are called *unconscious thoughts and feelings* or sometimes *subconscious* to highlight that the thoughts and feelings are just outside one's awareness (as opposed to being buried deep down in one's mind). Additionally, from a psychodynamic perspective (PDT), this process is typically seen as a defensive one. That is, the patient, at some level, is motivated to be unaware of these thoughts or feelings because they are bothersome and/or difficult to tolerate. From the behavioral (BT) and cognitive-behavioral (CBT) perspectives, a similar process is called *experiential avoidance*, although in the BT and CBT perspectives less emphasis is placed on the unconsciously motivated aspects of avoiding and instead placed on the more conscious ones. In contemporary BT and CBT, rather than referring to these processes as *unconscious* when motivation is outside of one's awareness, they are instead seen as part of an implicit mental processing system. Historically, from a CBT perspective, implicit or unconscious processes have been much less emphasized than in PDT approaches. In BT, mentalistic references and explanations are avoided.

At the time the treatment began, there were no treatments with empirical evidence that had been designed or tested for those with HPD (which is still true currently). In the absence of any specific empirical literature to guide treatment choice, the author chose to employ an expressive/insight-oriented approach for a number of reasons. First, there is a long, rich clinical history and abundance of writing about using expressive/insight-oriented approaches with regard to treating HPD that the author could use to guide his work. Second, because HPD is a personality disorder, it seemed reasonable to the author to proceed with a treatment that had empirical evidence for treating a near-neighbor disorder such as BPD. Both are cluster B, axis II disorders (emotional and dramatic disorders), and the two disorders are often comorbid and share a number of conceptual similarities. For example, both disorders are characterized by shifting emotional experiences and difficulties

Thus, the author decided to work using a modified TFP approach. TFP is an expressive approach with empirical support for the treatment of BPD. The basic premise in this approach, as applicable to this case, is to focus on helping patients develop more differentiated and integrated representations of themselves and others, with the idea that doing so allows for a deeper understanding of oneself and others, better emotion regulation, and a better capacity to work toward goals. This stance was somewhat different from the approach Ms. Porter's previous therapist used. The previous psychotherapist employed what could be called a supportive psychotherapy frame. There are generally two types of supportive psychotherapies: those that are associated with psychodynamic psychotherapy and those that are not explicitly psychodynamic and are more generally supportive. These approaches often, but not always, derive from humanistic/person-centered approaches. All supportive approaches are similar in that they tend to focus on providing direct support to the patient through the provision of psychoeducation, helping or assisting with logistical concerns (e.g., helping the patient sign up for a needed service) as well as providing validation, reassurance, and even direct advice. There is an emphasis on building a collaborative relationship, positive alliance, and for the therapist to model healthy and normative behaviors and ways of thinking for the patient. From a psychodynamic supportive psychotherapies stance, these techniques are thought to help patients strengthen their adaptive defenses and rely less on maladaptive ones. In a supportive therapy, the therapist might regularly advise the patient to do certain things and warn him or her about doing other things. Although a more exploratory, less supportive approach would contain many of the aspects of a supportive therapy, such as emphasis on developing a collaborative relationship and the provision of a normative model, supportive treatment, with its emphasis on developing a positive alliance, can foster idealization, which is seen as a distortion rather than a realistic way of perceiving the self and others. Additionally, in contrast to expressive/insight-oriented psychotherapies that focus on exploration, supportive psychotherapies emphasize reflective listening and/or reflection of feeling, paraphrasing what the patient says and providing instrumental support (e.g., helping patients sign up for activities they are interested in).

The transition from a supportive psychotherapy to an expressive one with Ms. Porter was not easy. The psychotherapy with Ms. Porter got off to a difficult beginning. At the onset, she was feeling very distressed and overwhelmed by her situation. In the initial sessions, she presented as pressured, easily irritated, and frenetic. She began each session with a barrage of demands for advice that were peppered with frequent appeals for reassurance that everything would work out. She wanted immediate relief that psychotherapy often cannot provide. This was frustrating to her and increased her distress. Of course, it was impossible to provide given her current life situation, which, like her, the therapist was unable to magically fix for her. Reassurance was also difficult to provide in the first few sessions because the outcome could not be guaranteed. Thus, any reassurance would not be authentic and would probably not feel reassuring given that she might doubt the therapist's promise.

This stance of providing advice and reassurance in supportive therapy can feel very gratifying to the patient, and while there is no prohibition about gratifying the patient, sometimes that is not best. However, in expressive/insight-oriented treatments such as TFP, the goal is to take a nonjudgmental stance, one that allows exploration of all sides of the patient's experience, even those aspects that are difficult for him or her to tolerate. In this way, the therapist is modeling tolerance, acceptance, and the value of exploring the contents of one's mind. The supportive frame was also more consistent with the kind of treatment the patient desired, which also contributed to a rough beginning.

In therapy, Ms. Porter wanted more from the therapist and very early in the treatment showed both high levels of dependency and irritation at the therapist's stance. She had difficulty reflecting on her own internal experiences and looked to the therapist for feedback and reassurance. She wanted specific advice about which apartment lease to sign and whether or not she should hire a babysitter or put her children in day care. With regard to her bids for direct advice, the author explained to the patient that rather than giving her advice in which he would tell her what to do, he would work with her to help her clarify how best she wanted to handle her problems. This stance was also unsatisfying to her and seemed to increase her distress. She wanted answers and to be told what to do. The therapist stated, "I usually won't give you advice but instead will try to help you clarify and find out for yourself how you would like to handle your problems. I will help you clarify ambiguities, ambivalences, and weigh consequences of available choices. We may explore motivations that get in the way of achieving life goals. I may give direct advice if I see you getting into some kind of trouble. In those cases, I may warn you about it or even strongly suggest a particular course of action. Regardless, the final decision as to what to do will have to be made by you (even if it is to follow my advice)." The patient was frustrated with such explanations. Not so atypically, the patient also had many personal questions for the therapist. Of course, therapists should always answer questions about training and credentials, as patients have a right to such information. However, therapists can differ in terms of their comfort with disclosing personal information as a function of therapeutic orientation, treatment approach, or personal differences in comfort. My approach is typically to be willing to share personal information but wanting to discuss and understand the patient's rationale or concerns that prompt the question. I find that most of the time, exploration of motivations usually suffices. Ms. Porter wanted to know if I was married (I was) and if I had children (I did not at the time). Rather than immediately answer her, I told her that "I would be happy to share that information with you, but before doing so, I was wondering what your thoughts are about why this information may be of interest to you?" It turned out it was useful to have explored her concerns. She shared with me her fantasy that I was married to a waif of a woman who did not work outside the home, that we lived in an expensive suburb of New York in a big house, and that my stay-at-home waif of a wife spent her day taking care of the house and chauffeuring my children from one lesson to another, such as tennis and horseback riding. Her fantasy was quite a contrast from her life. I had an attractive partner; she was divorced. My spouse was helpful in taking care of the children; hers was not. Instead, she struggled as a single mother to care for her children in the context of a difficult coparenting situation. I had a luxurious living situation—a big house in a ritzy suburb; she lived in a small apartment in a crowded lower-middle-class area. She imagined the therapist to have a very different life than was the case. In actuality, the therapist's life was very different than she imagined. I too lived in a small apartment and not in a ritzy suburb. My wife and I were trying to have children but did not have any at the time.

I had an impulse to tell her that we were more alike than she imagined. But rather than disabusing her of her fantasy, we explored it. I wondered with her about consequences of her belief, that it sounded like she imagined my life to be so different than hers that I wondered if she might believe that I could not understand her situation or know how to help her. It made her mad to think that I had such an easy life, that I was wealthy and had assistance from a collaborative and engaged partner. She would yell at me. Further, I shared with her that maybe she felt my lack of understanding was so profound that I might judge her or be critical of her for the situation she was in. This was an important moment because she was able to share her concern that I was critical of her and disapproving of her for the choices and decisions she made. As the therapy proceeded, we explored her sense of my critical attitude, and over time she came to understand that it was not me who was critical of her but she herself who was critical of her. This was an important insight that allowed her to become more sympathetic toward herself and to externalize blame on others less.

There are a number of aspects to working in a TFP approach; one important aspect is the setting of the therapeutic frame. Setting the frame of the therapy includes a discussion and agreement about the structure of the treatment. This includes starting times, ending times, frequency of sessions, how to handle communication outside of session, how to handle vacations, schedule changes and missed appointments, fees, adjunctive treatments and contacts with other providers, contacts with other stakeholders (e.g., significant others, parents), and most important, the patient's and the therapist's respective responsibilities in session and to the treatment, as well as the therapist's explicit sharing of his or her understanding of the patient's difficulties in order to develop shared goals. And finally, the therapist provides the rationale for the treatment approach.

It is important to be explicit about the treatment frame and its components. Often, therapists, particularly with seasoned patients, neglect this step. Therapists assume that patients understand the "frame" of therapy; however, it is especially important with personality disordered patients to be explicit about the frame, problems, and goals of treatment as well as how the therapist will work with the patient. Therapies can differ, and patients' expectations can vary. Setting the frame also allows for the explorations of deviations from the frame. Without setting the frame, it is difficult to know if such deviations are meaningful or simply a result of lack of clarity.

Ms. Porter was very agreeable to the frame presented by the therapist. The therapist experienced her agreement as a combination of acquiescence and expedience. The patient's dependency contributed to part of the acquiescence and her high level of distress to her expedience. The therapist's attempts to address these concerns were met by reassurances to the contrary from the patient. The therapist felt the patient was quick to dismiss the concerns, but to push it further would risk alienating the patient. Despite the patient's reassurance about her acceptance of the treatment frame, very soon after the start of the treatment there were a number of tests to the frame. Some sessions, the patient showed up early and seemed put out when the therapist made her wait until the scheduled time. Other sessions, she showed up late and asked if we could meet into the next hour. There was an occasional missed session. She complained about needing more time and asked if we could schedule double sessions, on nice days she wanted to meet outside, and another time she suggested that we meet at a coffee shop. The therapist's attempts to maintain the agreed-upon frame were met with an attitude of condescension. She told me that I was too conventional, that her last therapist would meet outside on nice days and give her more time when she showed up late. I reminded her that we discussed starting and ending times, and that she agreed to this frame. She made light of her agreement and claimed that when she agreed she didn't realize what I was proposing. She just assumed that if she were early we could start early, and if she were late we could run over. Even when she didn't arrive late, she sometimes asked for more time. Her cavalier attitude about our agreement reminded me of the same attitude she complained about in her ex-husband with regard to picking up and dropping off the children. Although I felt it was too early in the treatment to share my thoughts about how she was acting in a way similar to the way she criticized in her husband, I was able to note her belief that I was being too rigid. More tests came. One night, it began to rain during session. When the session ended, she left. A few minutes later, she knocked on my office door. She asked if I could walk her to her car with my umbrella. Then in later sessions, she begged and pleaded with me to become her "coach." Her fantasy involved me coming to her home and work and helping her organize herself with respect to daily activities of life and work. She would become angry at me for not agreeing to become her coach. As this was going on, she inadvertently revealed that she was in other treatments. She was attending a lay group and meeting with a spiritual healer who used crystals to help her be more balanced, and she was getting benzodiazepines for anxiety from multiple physicians. These events were important to the treatment. The patient and I worked to understand how her behavior provided insights into what she was feeling, and these insights could be used by her to communicate her needs more clearly. I noted that on the one hand, she was being quite clear with me. Ms. Porter wanted more of me. She was consistently asking for more time with me. She wanted double sessions; she wanted me to be present at her home and work. She also wanted our relationship to be more casual and less formal. We could meet for coffee, enjoy the nice weather together, and be flexible about when we met. Given this desire and her feeling that my maintenance of the treatment frame was arbitrary and unnecessary rather than an effort to best help her, she felt rebuffed by me. I noted that if this was how she was feeling, then we could understand her seeking out other help through groups, healers, and psychotropic medication providers as a complex solution to her problems that at one level served many aims. She was distressed and needed more help, and these treatments offered her that. Engaging in these other treatments allowed her to minimize her need for me and may have been an attempt to maintain certain aspects of the frame herself (although clearly violating others). But I also hypothesized to her that her treatment infidelity was also a signal to me that she was unhappy with what I was providing and how I was doing so. I was reminded, although in a very different context, that this dynamic was similar to the ones she often experienced with romantic partners—wanting more from them, feeling overly dependent on them, seeking out others to supplement or provide for unsatisfied needs, and as a way to express anger and displeasure to others.

There were a number of nodal points in the treatment. One had to do with the occurrence of the 9/11 terrorist attacks that occurred during the course of the treatment. Of course, in the wake of the attacks, it was a stressful and frightening time. Most people in the NYC area were in a heightened state of vigilance and anxiety. However, it is safe to say that Ms. Porter's experience was much more intense. Following the attacks, she came into the next appointment highly dysregulated, frantic, pressured, and in a panic. She became furious with me for her perception that I was not sufficiently upset by the events that occurred and screamed at me, "How can you just sit there with all this going on?" This event allowed us to explicitly discuss what I perceived as a general issue but in the context of the current events, namely how out of control she felt and her desire to evoke the same kind of desperate, agitated, and hysterical state in others as a way of gaining distance from those feelings, as a sign that others understand and agree with her sense of a situation, and as a sign that others are mobilized to help her. And conversely, that anything short of sharing in such mental states was a critical rejection of her and a sign that others do not care.

The next nodal point in the treatment occurred as the patient began to improve. As she became more integrated and less defensive, she began to have more access to her internal world. She was less angry with others, less irritable and erratic in her behavior. She showed much better behavioral control and experienced a series of successes at work. Family life was becoming more enjoyable and she was less easily provoked by her ex-husband or others. While this change led to more consistent functioning and better tolerance of affects, particularly negative ones, it also left her capable of deeper feelings, which in turn left her with feelings that were new and could be uncomfortable at times. Additionally, as she progressed in the treatment, Ms. Porter began to become more depressed. As she became more integrated and aware, she began to realize that much of her grievances were unfounded and much of her suffering was a result of choices she made. This progression is not uncommon in therapy for those with personality disorders. With increased integration and coherence of mind, there is a movement from externalizing intolerable mental states into a more realistic, accurate, accessible, and reflective mode that allows for guilt, regret, and seeing oneself and others realistically but also with negative aspects. She began to blame herself for her problems.

As the treatment progressed, the depression began to resolve and the patient began to stabilize and function better. She made important changes in her life. Most notably, she was able to obtain a job more consistent with her education and she had sustained success at her job. She also became more emotionally engaged with her children and satisfied with providing care. Her relationship improved with her family and her ex-husband. She was more accepting and tolerant of their foibles. One area that she continued to struggle with concerned romantic relationships. She continued to find herself unsatisfied with her perceived options. She was more tolerant of physical imperfections in the men that she was dating, but she was still having a hard time maintaining a relationship. However, by the time treatment ended, she also was able to have a long-term relationship with a man her age, one with imperfections but to whom she was attracted both physically and emotionally. By all reports, he appeared to be a healthy person and a good prospect.

At the end of the treatment, the patient shared with the therapist her appreciation. She felt he had been very committed to the treatment, especially in the beginning when her commitment was tenuous. She shared that she always felt the therapist cared about her and wanted the best for her but that his ability to remain calm when she was upset in the end was most helpful. She acknowledged that this capacity in the therapist annoyed her at first and even made her mad, but in the end it helped her to believe that one could maintain calm and reflective thought through intense emotions. In retrospect, she recognized that a part of her was envious of the therapist's calm. However, as time progressed she became better able to appreciate the therapist's capacity to think clearly when she was upset and "all over the place." She was now able to recognize her own ability to think clearly in the kind of moments when she used to become disorganized and frenetic.

Outcome and Prognosis

The conclusion of the therapy coincided with the author finishing his postdoctoral training and the patient beginning a stable relationship with a man her age and tolerating his physical imperfections (as well as her own). As indicated earlier, the patient tended to be much less frenetic and instead became calmer. She was more tolerant of ambiguity with family members, her work, and life in general. Rather than becoming panicked in those moments and disorganized, she was able to continue to work toward understanding and clarity, and not behave in ways that contributed to the chaos only to create a vicious cycle. She was also more accepting of her own flaws, and her relationship improved with her family, her ex-husband, children, and coworkers.

During the therapy, she began working in a position that was more consistent with her intelligence and capacities, which as a result compensated her better, which not only reduced her financial stress and worrying but allowed her to do more of the things she wanted to do. The patient kept in periodic contact with the author over the next 15 years. In the first 5 years since the treatments ended, Ms. Porter continued to thrive in her job and was steadily promoted. She enjoyed her success and found her work both intellectually stimulating and rewarding. However, despite her sustained work success and satisfaction with her work, Ms. Porter continued to have the desire to work as a psychotherapist. This desire was a result, in part, from her capacity to aspire toward interests that were once defensively subverted as a young woman due to self-doubt but no longer defended and now available to her, and stoked by an appreciation of the opportunities afforded her through psychotherapy. She wanted to provide for others in a manner that she had been provided. Because she had an MSW degree, while continuing her administrative work and parenting, she began obtaining the supervised experience conducting psychotherapy that would allow her to become a licensed social worker and able to practice independently. After a few years of such experience, Ms. Porter was able to start her own private practice and is currently a licensed MSW-level social worker conducting psychotherapy.

Discussion Questions

1. Provide two to three reasons why bipolar disorder was initially considered as a diagnosis but then later was ruled out.

2. Describe the ways in which Ms. Porter's work patterns changed from the time she started psychotherapy until the years after her treatment ended. What other patterns in Ms. Porter's life changed during therapy?

3. Explain the pros and cons of using transference-based psychotherapy.

Anorexia Nervosa

Presenting Problem and Client Description

Dana was a single, Caucasian, heterosexual woman in her mid-30s who worked as an attorney at a medium-sized law firm. A petite individual, standing no taller than 5 feet, she showed up to her first appointment wearing a dark pantsuit that was at least two sizes too big and appeared tired and haggard with dark circles under her eyes. Dana's most conspicuous physical feature was her extremely deep tan, which likely contributed to her looking nearly a decade older than her stated age.

At her first psychotherapy appointment, she explained that she was seeking a new provider because her current psychologist, with whom she had worked for several years, had recently moved several hundred miles away to live closer to family. She explained, "I think I'm doomed to need therapy for the rest of my life because I always seem to revert back to my 'old ways' unless I feel like there is someone looking over my shoulder to keep me accountable." When I asked if she could say more about her 'old ways,' she replied, "Let's just say that having an eating disorder has made me do some pretty stupid things in the past, and I really don't want to go back to that ever again because, honestly, I'm not sure I'd survive another round." Thus, even from the first minutes of our very first meeting, Dana seemed to broadcast her fear that she could never hope to be emotionally healthy and well, regardless of how hard she worked at it.

Dana acknowledged that she was indeed a "hopeless workaholic," routinely remaining at her office until 10 p.m., long after her colleagues departed. She said that she didn't find practicing law particularly satisfying; nonetheless, Dana exuded uncharacteristic confidence in her belief that she was a very good divorce attorney who was well-respected by her colleagues. She said, "Now and then, one of my clients ask me if I'm divorced too, probably noticing that I don't wear a wedding band. And sometimes, sadly, I lie and say 'yes.' Isn't that pathetic!? You know you're unlucky in love when it feels better to lie about being divorced than admit I've never been married."

When asked about her current health status and eating behavior, Dana volunteered that she had been able to maintain what she considered a "good weight" by her standards, managing to keep it between 85 and 95 pounds for most of the past 10 years. She indicated that she achieved this by eating three highly regimented meals every day. The meals varied very little day to day, typically consisting of oatmeal, Greek yogurt, and coffee for breakfast, a deli meat sandwich for lunch, and some form of lean protein alongside vegetables every night for dinner. She said that she rarely strayed from this menu because it allowed her to avoid measuring her food, a behavior that created a lot of stress for her in the past. Dana denied ever engaging in any purging behavior, but she admitted that she continued to keep a running count of every single calorie she consumed. "It's just an automatic habit that I can't seem to shake," she lamented. Dana also reported drinking varying amounts of alcohol (anywhere between two to six drinks) several days per week. She said she always drank by herself at home after work in order to help her "unwind." After some exploring, she also admitted that she used alcohol to help her manage feelings of anxiety and depression that mostly stem from loneliness.

In terms of family history, Dana's parents divorced when she was 7. Dana described her father as a "hopelessly depressed alcoholic" who committed suicide when she was 11 years old. She said that she only saw her father a few times per year, mostly birthdays and holidays, yet she still felt a strong emotional connection to him and was deeply affected by his death. Dana described her mother as very aloof, perfectionistic, hypercritical, and emotionally dismissive. She said, "My mother always treated me like I was an accessory from her closet that she would wear because it always garnered compliments from others but all the while not really caring for it herself. . . . Let's just say we really never had a close emotional connection." For example, after Dana was seriously injured in a major car accident (discussed later in the chapter), her mother didn't show up at the hospital for more than 2 days and never offered an excuse or explanation for the delay.

Dana reported that her mother's family was wealthy, so after the divorce there was no real economic stress. Yet soon afterward, her mother chose to remarry a wealthy man who didn't have much interest in children. Thus, 9-year-old Dana and her 7-year-old sister were sent away to live and study at a boarding school that was more than a 3-hour drive away from home. It was there that Dana first took up gymnastics, and because she showed great promise as a gymnast, she transferred to a full-time gymnastics academy at 11, where all athletes were group-tutored at the gym instead of attending traditional schools.

Upon asking Dana to describe any other aspects of her early years that she felt affected her development, she shared that she had been a nationally ranked gymnast between the ages of 12 and 17, and it was, in part, a powerful desire to increase her competitive edge by keeping her weight down that spurred the early development of her eating disorder. She indicated that in addition to the physical and emotional pressures she imposed on herself, she had also felt pressured by her coaches to limit her food consumption in spite of maintaining an exhausting training schedule where she practiced gymnastics and related skills 8 hours a day, 6 days a week. Dana shared that she began counting calories when she was 12 years old, often restricting her daily limit to 800 calories—not nearly enough to support her demanding gymnastics training sessions.

Diagnosis and Case Formulation

Dana was first diagnosed with anorexia nervosa at age 17. She reported that she had been receiving treatment for it "on and off" ever since, including three inpatient hospitalizations. All of these hospitalizations were due to her weight becoming dangerously low and restricting calories to such an extreme degree that she was at risk of seriously damaging her heart and liver. Dana's first hospitalization was at age 17, and the other two hospitalizations occurred when she was in her mid-20s. Those hospitalizations occurred shortly after she broke up with her "boyfriend," whom she had been dating from ages 14 to 24. All three hospitalizations took place at a specialized eating disorder center where treatment included closely supervised weight-gain therapy achieved through eating staff-monitored meals and liquid protein supplements several times per day.

Dana described strongly resisting the treatment during her first two hospitalizations, denying that she was severely underweight and nutritionally compromised. She said that she was terrified of regaining weight, fearing that if she ate "normal" amounts of food she risked becoming obese and losing the love of her parents and boyfriend. During the few months before her third hospitalization, however, Dana learned that two of the friends she had met during her earlier inpatient treatments had fatally succumbed to anorexia nervosa. Dana indicated that this was a turning point for her, making a decision that she did not want to die.

Thus, she approached her last hospitalization quite differently. Rather than viewing treatment as an antagonistic battle between her and the therapeutic staff trying to help make healthy choices that would correspond with healthy weight gain (like she had in her previous hospitalizations), she viewed the staff more realistically, understanding their motives were genuinely benevolent rather than callous or malicious. Looking back at those years, Dana also appreciated that if she continued to follow the path of her deceased friends, she was very likely to die too, and ultimately decided that she did not want to share their fate.

During that third hospitalization, Dana also finally disclosed to her psychotherapist and her parents that her so-called "boyfriend," to whom she referred when she reached college but never allowed anyone to meet, was actually her married gymnastics coach. He was in his early 30s when he first began coaching Dana, and what was an emotionally exploitive relationship from the beginning became a sexual relationship when she turned 16. She successfully hid their relationship by spending time together under the guise of extra evening/weekend practice sessions. Throughout his relationship with her, he made promises that he would divorce his wife and marry her after Dana graduated from college. However, when Dana completed college, he broke up with her rather than marrying her. Her progress with the eating disorder crumbled at this point. Her weight plummeted from 105 pounds to 78 pounds, and she was involuntarily hospitalized twice, both times needing to be force-fed through a central intravenous line in her neck that delivered nutrients directly to her body. Fortunately, after revealing the huge secret about her coach, Dana's eating behavior slowly but steadily began to improve. And while Dana's body mass index remained low, she recovered her ability to eat nutritious foods with far less struggle.

Lastly, Dana also tanned far too much over the past 20 years, which contributed to her looking like she was in her mid-40s rather than her 30s. She admitted that she was "addicted to tanning" because she almost always felt cold, and laying in sunshine and tanning beds helped to warm her up. Dana also indicated the belief that most people assume individuals with tans are healthier than those without tans, and thought this was a way of "camouflaging" her eating disorder. Dana had already had a skin cancer removed the previous year and was told that she would almost certainly develop more cancers if she kept it up. Thus, it seemed clear that her tanning "addiction" was another risky behavior that should be addressed by the psychotherapy.

Course of Treatment

During the first month and a half or more of therapy, Dana and I focused on history taking and understanding what factors may have interfered with her achieving more progress during previous treatments. Specifically, Dana felt that even though her eating behavior no longer jeopardized her health or her life on a regular basis, she conceded feeling a protracted sense of sadness and dissatisfaction with her life. We agreed early on that her eating behavior had been an attempt to assert a sense of control in response to a range of feelings that felt both unacceptable and unmanageable, including sadness, anxiety, and anger (sometimes rage) toward herself and others. Previous therapies had more strictly focused on her day-to-day eating behavior, as well as her distorted body image. And she had greatly benefited from this work, recovering enough to stay out of the hospital as well as successfully attend law school.

Nonetheless, Dana's powerful desire and need to continue psychotherapy with a new psychologist was rooted in her ongoing struggles with dysphoria, poor self-image, and her fear that she was unlovable. And while a part of her was motivated and eager to tackle these concerns in a more direct manner than she had in previous therapies, another part of her was very scared that approaching these issues could result in her eating disorder resurfacing in a dangerous manner. We knew we both had to be alert to the possibility that Dana was at risk of "controlling" her eating and her weight in lieu of her experiencing her emotions that felt beyond her control. But we both agreed that this treatment would aim to acknowledge and credit her ability to support her physical health by maintaining a reasonable weight by relying on a treatment framework that would help prevent her eating behaviors from getting away from her in a dangerous fashion, as they had in the past.

Accordingly, the treatment included three protective components that she agreed to adhere to that are outlined here:

1. Dana's health and safety were the first priority—there couldn't be any treatment if she was too ill and weak to participate constructively. Thus, she agreed to have regular check-ins with a health care professional who would monitor her blood pressure, weight, and overall health. The treatment plan Dana agreed to specified that as long as her weight was above 90 pounds, she did not have to implement any nutritional interventions. However, if her weight slipped below 90, she agreed to consume nutritional supplements with the goal of getting her weight to 90-plus pounds. Finally, if her weight fell to 82 pounds, we would temporarily suspend the outpatient psychotherapy so she could attend an eating disorder partial hospital program and allow her weight/health to restabilize. This happened once for 2 months during a rough patch, but for most of the treatment her weight hovered a little higher than 90 pounds.

2. Relatedly, Dana and I agreed that we would not allow the therapy to become a battleground where we would engage in conflicts over her weight. All physical health issues would be "outsourced" to the same health care professional monitoring her health status. We agreed that we would both abide by the health care provider's assessment concerning whether Dana was adequately maintaining her health, and Dana would follow the provider's recommendations in order to protect the psychotherapy. This arrangement prevented me from becoming the "bad guy" if and when Dana's health vacillated.

3. She had to come to therapy; treatment avoidance had been a major issue in her previous therapies, so we had to create a contract that she simply had to come. This included that she would be charged for a full session of therapy if she did not show up without notifying me a day or more ahead of time.

During the treatment itself, Dana came to realize that the fear of weighing too much masqueraded a deeper fear that she was incapable of being loved, both by others and herself. Part of this realization came from a better understanding that the impact of her father's death and mother's distance impacted not only her childhood but also the assumptions that she brought to relationships in the present. She observed a historical pattern in herself whereby she tended to be attracted to people who were not available—such as due to already being married, as in the case of her coach and a more recent boyfriend. She likewise tended to be attracted to people who were not emotionally available, noting that she befriended both men and women who did not put as much time, energy, and/or money into the relationships as she did.

This dynamic often resulted in Dana developing resentments in her friendships that accumulated over time, eventually ending in their demise. Thus, much of the therapy looked at her cognitive distortions related to issues that made her feel unworthy of being loved and cared for by others. The therapy also helped her examine her motivations on a few more occasions when she repeated the pattern of putting disproportionate resources into new friendships she tried to develop.

The therapy helped her understand that her attempt to "buy friends" was both unnecessary and ultimately unsuccessful and damaging.

Another major facet of therapy involved exploring and understanding her extreme sensitivity to being rejected by others. This dynamic entered the therapy relationship on a few occasions when Dana accused me of rejecting and abandoning her by threatening to interrupt treatment when her weight began to drift lower. I responded by reminding her that the criterion was in place to protect the treatment. That is, she couldn't effectively participate in psychologically based treatment when she was physically starving herself. I also suggested that the opposite might be true—that she was essentially rejecting the treatment, rejecting my efforts to help her by controlling me by forcing me to prioritize her physical health over addressing her emotional health. In essence, dropping weight was akin to coercing me to do that, and that would be a threat to the treatment. During the therapy, I often needed to say something along the lines of, "So I think we need to get back to the emotional issues that you are expressing through punishing yourself by resisting nutrition." This theme came up a number of times in therapy. It was important to realize that part of her wanted to get better while another part was ambivalent about getting better. Getting better would allow her to do more of the things she wanted to do, but it would also require taking emotional risks that felt extremely threatening.

We had previously agreed that the eating behavior was a symptom of her bigger, very emotionally painful difficulties. Consistent with that premise, it became clear that the phases of therapy where she struggled more to maintain her weight coincided with times that she was holding back on some information. For example, some 10 months into therapy, she reported she was having an affair with someone at work who was married. Since both Dana and the person she was having the affair agreed it was just for fun (so she said), she lied by omission, insisting that she didn't think it was worth talking about in therapy. This was an opportunity to discuss how Dana would imagine the reaction of the therapist. She thought that the therapist would see her as bad and immoral for "luring a man away from his wife." She also feared I would be critical in a manner that echoed both her mother's and coach's chronic criticisms. Fortunately, instead it presented an opportunity relatively early on in the psychotherapy to dispel these fears and use it as a springboard to examine the complicated and unhealthy dynamics Dana brought to relationships. It also offered an opportunity to observe her strong tendency to misattribute her feelings to others. In fact, she said to the therapist that she could not tell me things because she believed I would reject her.

On the few occasions when her weight began to drop, she would accuse me of trying to control her and reject her with the requirement that she maintain a minimum weight.

An important part of therapy was to talk about what she wanted. One of the things she wanted was a stable, loving relationship. We discussed why she was drawn to people who were unavailable. We also discussed ways she interacted that were off-putting to others and made it difficult for her to cultivate close friendships that she wanted. Part of this was a discussion of the function of her workaholic lifestyle. Clearly, this was a way to fill her time and served as an ineffective proxy for feeling valued by her colleagues owing to the impressive income and positive reputation her work brought to her law firm. Her long work hours also tended to prevent her from having time to cultivate relationships that could feel threatening.

As we continued the ongoing process of examining her relationship dynamics in the therapy, a chance occurrence happened approximately 2 years into the work. An acquaintance through her job owned a dog that gave birth to puppies, and Dana impulsively adopted one of them. Quite unlike nearly all the human beings in her life, Dana was able to assume her dog was not excessively critical of her, and she rather quickly came to realize that he loved her. Dog ownership also opened up a new world of social opportunities; Dana met other dog owners equally smitten with their pets while attending puppy training classes. Her very cute pup also inspired positive interactions with other dog owners she encountered when she took her dog for daily walks. In a way that was rather unexpected, Dana's beloved pup provided a huge boon to the therapy by serving as a template for what an emotionally healthy relationship could look like. Previously in our work, Dana struggled to understand the concepts of genuine emotional and relational reciprocity; however, upon developing a very positive emotional relationship with her dog, this concept became much more tangible and accessible to her. Her sense of commitment and obligation to her dog also spurred Dana to take better care of her health, because she felt that jeopardizing her health was newly akin to putting his well-being at risk as well.

Outcome and Prognosis

The psychotherapy ended suddenly in response to Dana's deciding to relocate to a different community. At some point during her treatment, Dana had recognized that there was a certain irony in how she had been putting a tremendous amount of personal resources into understanding and enriching her interpersonal relationships, while during the same time in her work as a divorce attorney, she spent countless hours helping people dissolve their marriages. Accordingly, when a job opportunity "fell in [her] lap," one that she felt confident would be well within her skill set and provide much more satisfaction, she took it. The job was a 3-hour drive away, so our psychotherapy work could not continue. Per her request, I readily found her a new psychotherapist in her new community and have since learned that Dana continued to do well.

Discussion Questions

1. Dana attributed her desire to be a competitive gymnast when she was a preteen to the beginning of her eating disorder. During treatment with the psychotherapist, it became apparent that other issues contributed to her ongoing struggles with anorexia. What are at least three of these issues?

2. Dana's psychotherapist laid out a specific framework for Dana's ongoing therapy. What are examples from the case study of the ways in which the criteria for treatment proved useful?

3. Describe the pattern of Dana's relationships—both with friends and with her romantic interests. How did these patterns contribute to her ongoing battle with anorexia?

Bulimia Nervosa

Presenting Problem and Client Description

Sabrina left a message on my office voice mail around 10 o'clock the previous evening saying she was given my name from one of her former professors, whom she had stayed in touch with for several years since graduating. She said she was "sad, depressed, and feeling really bad about herself . . . and hoping that talking to someone could help." The tone in her message was tentative, nervous, and timid, so much so that when I called her back and answered the phone in a very cheerful, bubbly voice, I feared I had dialed the wrong number. But I hadn't; it was indeed Sabrina, and I made a mental note concerning the disparity between her voice message and how she sounded when we first spoke directly. She made it clear in our first conversation that although she worked long hours in the real estate business, she would readily make whatever changes in her schedule that might be necessary in order to meet as soon as possible. Thus, we arranged to meet the following week.

Sabrina was a petite 28-year-old Latina with long black hair. She greeted me with a big smile and automatically reached out her hand to offer a strong, confident handshake. She asked me how I was doing. I responded with a smile, gestured to a couple of chairs, and invited her to sit down. Without additional prompting, Sabrina launched into her story, explaining how until recently, she had lived in a city a few hours away, but she moved "back home" a few months ago and was seeking psychotherapy because some aspects of the adjustment had been "challenging." She offered that she had graduated from the local university as a communications major and had recently successfully taken and passed her real estate broker's test. She was the youngest of three children. Her father passed away 3 years ago, leaving her mother to operate the family real estate business on her own. Her oldest sibling, a brother, was a physical therapist who lived with his wife and family 30 minutes outside Chicago. She described her sister, who lived in Seattle and was finishing her last year of training to be an anesthesiologist, as her "best friend," and engaged to a man whom Sabrina regarded as "the perfect guy." "Sometimes I worry that I will never find someone who is as compatible with me as they are together," she sighed forlornly.

Sabrina continued on by describing how her previous jobs, first as an executive administrative assistant in a marketing firm and then as a paralegal for a law firm, had been insufficiently rewarding, both personally and financially. So earlier in the year, responding to the strong urgings of her mother and extended family, she moved out of her Pittsburgh apartment to return to the same suburb where she had grown up in order to join her mother's real estate business. Sabrina said, "It's both my mother's and my dream for me to learn the ins and outs of the real estate business, so over the next several years I can gradually take over." She explained how following years of mentorship, the family agreed that Sabrina's mother would then begin a well-earned retirement, allowing her mom to shift time and energy to hobbies and grandchildren. Currently, Sabrina was living with her mother, sleeping in her childhood bedroom, to save enough money to buy her own home. She said that she typically worked long hours, 10 to 12, both selling real estate and marketing/promoting the family business, but she offered assurances that she would still be able to attend regular psychotherapy appointments without difficulty.

Toward the second half of the appointment, in spite of having shared a fair amount of information, it seemed notable that apart from having made a major change in her life that seemed implicitly stressful, it still was not precisely clear what problem(s) had prompted Sabrina to seek psychological help. So I asked her, "Beyond what you've already shared, are there any other concerns that bring you to psychotherapy?" Sabrina responded that she was sad about her father's death, yet further discussion revealed that while she had grieved his loss, most of her concerns about this centered on her mother being "all alone now." Upon querying her again about any additional concerns that might bring her to psychotherapy, this time she said, "That's what's so strange because I really don't know. I actually don't see my problems as being any worse than anyone else's—in fact, I would say I have a better life than a lot of people I know. I have a new job that should give me a great future; and I have a supportive family who loves me to death—seriously, sometimes I think they might even love me too much! So I really, truly don't know what my problem is." At that point, she sat back in her chair in a manner that seemed like a curious mix of self-disgust and exasperation, the latter perhaps a response to my repeated probes. I said, "In the voice mail message you left me, you had called very late in the evening, and I noticed your voice seemed quite sad and tentative—very different from the way you have presented yourself so far today. Do you think you could help me understand that better—the difference between what you were doing then compared to now?"

With that statement, Sabrina began to weep silently, self-consciously turning her face away as if trying to avoid my gaze. After a minute or two, she apologetically collected herself and admitted that there was still a key piece of information that she had not yet shared due to feeling ashamed and embarrassed. Looking down, shedding intermittent tears and trying to minimize eye contact, Sabrina proceeded to share how she had developed problems with bulimia "on and off" during high school and college. However, she had successfully stopped bingeing and purging "for the most part" since age 22—that is, until fairly recently.

Back when she was in high school and college, Sabrina said she had not sought any kind of help because she did not view it as "a major problem." Rather, she interpreted her eating behavior as a way of managing stress, because the bingeing/purging became much more frequent during times of high tension in her life, such as before and during final exams, major events (e.g., family weddings, job interviews, etc.), and sometimes after arguments with friends or family members. When the stress subsided, she said that daily bingeing and purging decreased to weekly or even monthly occurrences. Sabrina reported that the bingeing and purging behavior had been "minimal" since graduating from college; however, it resurfaced as an undeniable problem over the past year or so.

She said that she had hoped "the total lack of privacy" she experienced while living with her mother would put a wrench in her bingeing/purging rituals and thus "force [her] to be good." But she tearfully admitted that the opposite had been true. She said that during the past 3 months, she had resumed a pattern whereby she consumed very large amounts of food, sometimes as much as 8,000 calories eaten over 1 to 2 hours, followed by 2-plus hours of purging. When asked about the long duration of her purging episodes, she said that she believed she purged 80% of what she could during the first 20 minutes of vomiting. However, having gained more than 10 pounds over the past few months, she felt an urgent need to "get rid of as much food as possible," even when the prolonged purging sessions left her feeling physically weak and exhausted.

Because it was difficult to binge in her mother's home for fear of being discovered, Sabrina concealed her bulimia by lying to her mother, telling her that she was going out to meet friends after work. Upon leaving work, she launched into the following routine: first, she would go to a grocery store, where she purchased a large tub of presliced watermelon, a loaf of bread, and a large container of hot soup. Next, she went to two or three different fast-food restaurants with drive-through lanes and purchased "combo meals" at each one, and then finally she drove to one of the neighborhood playgrounds, where she parked her car and began eating. By this time it would be close to dusk, the playground would be quiet, allowing her to secretively eat all of the food she had just assembled while listening, and often crying, to favorite songs on her car radio. After consuming all the food, Sabrina purged as much as she could in the playground's public restroom. Then Sabrina returned home, told her mother that she was utterly exhausted (which was wholly true), and retreated to her room until she went to sleep. According to Sabrina, she engaged in this routine three to four evenings per week.

While the dysfunctional eating behavior itself caused her a great deal of distress, she tearfully acknowledged her eating was also having a significantly negative impact on her relationships owing to the shame and guilt associated with hiding it from family and friends. Since returning to her hometown, she avoided reconnecting with old friends, declining invitations that would have typically involved going out to bars or restaurants. During the daytime hours and the evenings she did not binge and purge, she typically restricted her eating altogether in what had become an unsuccessful attempt to avoid gaining weight. Worse, from her perspective, on the few occasions she had accepted friends' invitations, she self-consciously overate in their presence (though to a lesser degree than she did when alone), then felt compelled to cut the evening short so she could privately purge. Sabrina had a sense that she was sabotaging her social life, which also contributed to feeling sad, lonely, and isolated.

During the evaluation phase of her psychotherapy, which took place over the first three appointments, Sabrina tentatively acknowledged a vague sense that there might be a connection between her eating disorder and the fact that she had been largely unsuccessful in her pursuit of a long-term romantic relationship. So far, the sum total of Sabrina's romantic experience was limited to three relatively short relationships with men, none of them lasting longer than 6 months. She indicated that in each relationship, she had been the one who initiated breaking up. She made sense of the pattern by explaining that she always seemed to attract men who were "too needy," and repeatedly found herself in positions where they were asking her to make "too many sacrifices." The sacrifices included the boyfriends' wanting to spend time alone with her rather than always going out with their larger group of friends, as well as "buying me gifts and things way too early—like they were already assuming we were going to end up together for the long term." When asked about her sexual history, she reported that she had chosen to be sexually active with each of her boyfriends, volunteering that she "liked sex a lot and there are definitely no problems there." At the same time, I observed how both times I introduced the topic of romantic relationships in her early appointments, Sabrina seemed to want to flee from it much more quickly than the many other topics we discussed. This seemed noteworthy, suggesting that she was more uncomfortable in this area of her life than she was prepared to address or deal with at that time.

Diagnosis and Case Formulation

When Sabrina sought treatment, she initially complained about feeling depressed, presenting vague symptoms of sadness and low self-esteem as her primary difficulty. Feeling intensely self-conscious and ashamed of her bingeing and purging behavior, she withheld this vital piece of information initially. It is not particularly unusual for people seeking help to omit or even deny certain issues or key details for fear of feeling overwhelmed or concern that the psychotherapist will judge them or find fault in a manner similar to how the suffering individuals often judge or fault themselves. A skilled and sensitive psychotherapist needs to strike a balance between being patient and providing clients with adequate time to feel comfortable enough to share their full stories while simultaneously maintaining a discerning ear and asking more questions when information doesn't add up to make a cohesive whole. Moreover, well-trained psychotherapists avoid making off-hand comments or observations that could seriously hamper a person making painful, sensitive disclosures. For example, if Sabrina had initially shared bingeing but denied purging when asked, it might have made it much more difficult for her to admit to the purging behavior if the psychotherapist had said, "Well at least that's great that you don't purge."

Although she reported feeling quite depressed at times, Sabrina's symptoms did not meet enough criteria to be diagnosed with major depressive disorder (MDD). She described her mood as "mostly okay" during the day, her mood usually only becoming anxious and depressed after she had resolved that she was not going to binge and purge on a given day and then failing to keep that promise to herself. In addition, her complaints of poor concentration and difficulty focusing, which can be symptoms of MDD, were consistently connected to her preoccupations with bingeing—that is, whether or not she would binge that evening and what foods she would or would not eat. However, there was no question about whether or not she met enough clinical criteria to be diagnosed with bulimia nervosa. She suffered from recurrent episodes of bingeing that occurred at least once per week, which were consistently accompanied by one or more inappropriate compensatory behaviors in an effort to "undo" the effects of purging. In Sabrina's case, she was bingeing much more frequently than once a week, and as is very commonly the case, self-induced vomiting was her compensatory behavior. Additional examples of compensatory behaviors include excessive exercise, misusing laxatives, as well as periods of fasting between bingeing episodes. Lastly, Sabrina's self-evaluation of her weight and body shape was distorted and disproportionately influenced her self-image and self-esteem.

Course of Treatment

From the beginning, it was clear that in spite of the long-term nature of her difficulties, Sabrina brought many strong personal assets to psychotherapy. She was a highly intelligent woman with a substantial capacity for hard work, both made apparent by the quick success she enjoyed during her first year working for her mother's real estate business. She was highly articulate, very personable, and had a broad array of social skills at her disposal, all of which served her quite well in a variety of social and business contexts. Accordingly, she appeared to approach her treatment with the same vigor and dedication that she used to approach other challenges. She invariably arrived on time for her weekly psychotherapy appointments, and she was consistently poised to share a large quantity of information concerning the happenings of the past week. In addition, in spite of some initial trepidation, Sabrina also agreed to meet with a local health care provider who specialized in working with individuals with eating disorders. Together, they collaborated to help Sabrina avoid some of the potentially serious health consequences of frequent and prolonged purging, such as monitoring her for signs of gastrointestinal complications, dehydration, and electrolyte imbalances that would increase her risk of cardiac arrhythmia—a sometimes lethal complication of eating disorders.

At the same time, another part of Sabrina seemed to battle against acknowledging certain aspects of her life in spite of strong evidence supporting their existence and problematic nature. For example, early on she needed help recognizing that while she came to sessions very energized to share stories about her week, her narratives tended to be so packed with small details that they risked distracting us from the central problems that brought her to psychotherapy in first place. After a while, Sabrina was able to see for herself how she tended to overwhelm the therapy with details in order to use up all the oxygen in the room, metaphorically speaking, and thereby smother the feelings she was trying to avoid.

Psychotherapy also revealed, rather swiftly, that while she projected a sense of confidence and swagger to the world, she tended to use it to camouflage deeply felt insecurities, as well as to shield herself from a wide range of emotions that she would rather disavow. Accordingly, during the couple months of psychotherapy, Sabrina and I spent a good deal of time exploring, recognizing, and reconciling these kinds of dynamics. We discussed a growing hypothesis that her bulimia was a symptom of her general distress rather than its cause. That is, it was not a simple matter of addressing the bingeing and self-induced vomiting and stopping them. Instead, we came to view these as maladaptive attempts to cope with and distance herself from very distressing feelings. The therapy proceeded in line with the proposition that identifying and addressing sources underlying Sabrina's distress, some of which were outside her awareness, would reduce her preoccupations and impulses connected with eating and help her cope with them much more effectively and adaptively than bingeing and purging ever could.

As such, we began spending less time scrutinizing and monitoring the day-to-day fluctuations of her eating. Instead, we worked from the assumption that Sabrina's eating behaviors stemmed from painful issues connected to her relationships with herself and others—the problem areas of her life that seemed to contain the roots of her distress. During this process, the following themes became apparent:

- Sabrina was very proud and protective of her mother and their relationship. When asked whether she might have felt some family pressure to join and ultimately take over her mother's business some years from now, she had a strong reaction, defending them saying, "My happiness is my mother's biggest concern . . . and nobody in my family would ever force me to do something that I didn't want to do!" Thus, at the start of psychotherapy, she insisted that she had zero ambivalence about this decision to move back home. But gradually she was able to acknowledge that she indeed felt pressure from her mother and siblings, although still confident it would not have changed her decision.

- While Sabrina understood her bingeing and purging as her way of dealing with stress, she tended to frame her "stress" in very general terms, such as working long hours and having very high expectations of herself. She seemed less aware of the possibility that her emotional distress and eating behavior were related to complicated feelings she had vis-à-vis her relationships with herself and others.

- In the early phase of treatment, Sabrina was aware of feeling ashamed and disgusted by her bulimic symptoms. However, she seemed less aware of its short-term "rewards," such as the positive lift she felt as she imagined the food that she would consume later in the day. The planning caused her to feel anxious but also excited. To a greater degree, she was able to acknowledge that the time she spent fantasizing about food helped distract her from some of her distress, albeit the bingeing/purging episodes themselves were also obvious sources of distress. This understanding underscored the importance of finding healthier ways of managing her distress, such as investing energy into her friendships rather than withdrawing from them.

- Sabrina struggled with feeling "like a fraud." She described how every day she was putting a significant amount of effort into "looking like I have my life all together," but inside she said she feels she was "totally falling apart," and the disparity contributed to her socially isolating herself from friends, coworkers, and family members. Therapy aimed at helping her reconcile this disparity by presenting a more realistic view of herself and appreciating the degree to which she had been projecting her negative feelings about herself onto others.

- Together, we observed how Sabrina consistently steered away from discussing her father and her father's death. Thus, we developed the hypothesis that their relationship and her feelings about his passing might be more complicated than she had realized prior to starting psychotherapy. She also discovered that her fear of loss was one of the reasons she had been avoiding romantic relationships during the past few years.

Thus, the early part of therapy was helping Sabrina discern the ways in which bingeing and purging was a maladaptive attempt to manage and regulate her emotions—feelings and emotions that felt unacceptable to her, including how she did not feel confident in her self-identity—which contributed to her feeling highly anxious, sometimes panicky, about taking over her mother's business. The thought that her mother would entrust the business to her helped her feel uncharacteristically close and connected with her mother. And because it turned out that Sabrina mostly liked the work itself, her leadership role in the business helped her solidify her sense of identity and improved her self-esteem. However, even several months into the treatment, she was still terribly scared that she would let her mother and the entire family down if she weren't successful. Thus, this was a central theme of the therapy that needed revisiting again and again over the 2 years of treatment.

In addition, therapy revealed how her bingeing not only provided temporary distraction and relief from feelings that she did not want to acknowledge, but the purging also provided a temporary sense of control when her life felt mostly out of control. Even deeper beneath the bulimic behavior were deeply conflicting feelings: both a hope and a deep fear that her bulimia would render her too disabled to take over her mother's business—in a sense, she would be off the hook due to an illness that "is out of my control." Interestingly, this dynamic came to light nearly a year into therapy when Sabrina had made so much progress that her bingeing and purging behavior had all but disappeared.

One day, she arrived for her appointment an uncharacteristic 20 minutes late, fell into her chair, and immediately began crying a puddle of tears. Between sobs, she shared that a policeman had stopped her for speeding on her way to today's appointment. She went on to explain that this was her third speeding ticket within a 12-month period, and the officer told her that in addition to a ticket she would be receiving a summons to appear before a judge who would decide whether Sabrina's driver's license should be suspended.

Sabrina was angry with herself and incredulous, struggling to understand her reckless behavior given that she had not been cited for a single driving infraction before this year. After some exploration, Sabrina came to understand that her irresponsible driving served to express feelings similar to ones that had been served by her bulimia. Because her livelihood in the real estate business largely depended on being able to drive herself and prospective homebuyers around town, losing her license would be a surefire way of putting herself in jeopardy with her mother and her job. This realization allowed Sabrina to put a cap on this behavior rather quickly, and fortunately, other than paying a fine, neither she nor others suffered any further consequences.

In addition to focusing on relationships with family and work, therapy eventually addressed Sabrina's challenges valuing and sustaining intimate relationships. On one hand, previously she had blamed her unsuccessful relationship history on her bulimia and associated insecurities about her physical appearance. On the other hand, therapy showed that Sabrina tended to choose men whom she came to describe as "shallow" and "emotionally unavailable." We discovered that she seemed to be drawn to men who at least appeared to have limited interest in developing close emotional connections because she too was afraid of emotional closeness. A close examination of her relationship anxieties and the reasons behind them (e.g., fears of not being "good enough," fears of being abandoned) helped Sabrina become less defensive and less dismissing of the men who crossed her path. Moreover, as she developed a better articulated sense of her own values, she was more successful in discerning the degree to which men she met did or did not share them.

Outcome and Prognosis

Sabrina attended weekly psychotherapy sessions for a little more than 2 years. Her bulimia nervosa symptoms improved in stages: After about 3 months, the frequency and duration of her binge/purge episodes decreased by 50%, and by the time she reached the 1-year mark, she binged and purged relatively rarely—less than once every few months. But although her bulimia symptoms had remitted, we both recognized that many of the dynamics contributing to the bulimic behaviors still needed attention, so the psychotherapy continued many months beyond when her eating disorder symptoms disappeared.

By the time she completed her treatment with me, Sabrina had achieved a much more stable and positive sense of her identity. She no longer tightly tied her value as a person to her physical appearance, recognizing that others were not judging her in the harsh manner she had judged herself. And she also newly appreciated the degree to which her other personal assets (e.g., high intelligence, capacity for perseverance, compassion for others, etc.) were much more important values to her and the people who loved her. This revelation, in turn, improved the quality of her relationships. Sabrina was less fearful of the idea of people wanting to be emotionally close her, and she resumed dating men toward the end of the psychotherapy.

Consistent with her plan, Sabrina gradually mastered all the skills needed to run the family real estate business, and she began to reap both the professional and financial rewards of her hard work. In my last direct contact with Sabrina, she shared that she had met and married a man whom she met while vacationing with her sister and brother-in-law. She also shared that she was 6-months pregnant with a baby girl and was both thrilled and relieved that her life seemed to be unfolding much better than she had once believed it would at the time we began working together. She said that she specifically wanted to let me know that her bulimia symptoms had not resurfaced during her pregnancy—an old fear of hers that had caused her to cast doubt on whether she would even try to become pregnant someday. Sabrina admitted that now and then, always during times of high stress, the impulse to binge crosses her mind. But she indicated that when this happens, she is able to regroup and refocus herself by drawing on the insight and knowledge she gained during her psychotherapy treatment.

Discussion Questions

1. During her initial appointment with the psychotherapist, Sabrina revealed a lot about the challenges of her recent move and her new job. However, about halfway through the appointment, her therapist was still unsure why Sabrina was there. What made the therapist believe there was more going on than Sabrina initially revealed? What techniques did the therapist use to help Sabrina discuss more about her concerns?

2. Explain why Sabrina was not diagnosed with depression even though she talked about feeling depressed and ashamed?

3. Why does the therapist choose to spend little time monitoring Sabrina's eating behaviors? What, then, does the therapist focus on during the early phase of Sabrina's therapy?

12

Borderline Personality Disorder

Presenting Problem and Client Description

Rasha was a 23-year-old single woman of Arab descent born in Syria, where she lived until age 11 when she moved with her mother and siblings to join her father in France. At the time she presented for treatment, Rasha was a full-time undergraduate at a local college majoring in finance and working part-time nights as an exotic dancer. Of Muslim descent, Rasha, from a religious family, was nonpracticing. She lived with a female roommate. Rasha presented to the clinic complaining of "personal problems" and concerns regarding her "career orientation." Rasha explained that for approximately 2 months, she had been experiencing problems with her "emotions," characterized by feelings of intense anger, irritability, and sadness with bouts of frequent crying that left her feeling "drained" and "not normal." Although Rasha did not directly connect the events at the time, she reported that the emergence of these feelings coincided with the beginning of her first romantic relationship with a man 10 years her senior who she met at the strip club. Prior to this boyfriend, Rasha reported having had approximately 20 sexual relationships, all "one night stands." Although clearly intensified in recent months, it became apparent during the intake that Rasha had difficulties regulating her emotions for many years.

Rasha also expressed concerns and misgivings about working as an exotic dancer. Of note, Rasha reported that she was sexually abused by her father between ages 12½ and 14, abuse that included intercourse. As a result of this experience, Rasha was removed from the household and placed in foster care. Rasha indicated some vague awareness that exotic dancing may not be in her best interest given the incest experience with her father. However, she stated that exotic dancing had considerable financial rewards that made it difficult for her to leave the job. At that time, there was little recognition that her initial attraction to exotic dancing and her difficulty extricating herself from it might also have had a psychological component.

In terms of mental status, Rasha presented as a tall, thin, attractive, casually-dressed woman whose manner and dress were consistent with her chronological age. In general, Rasha was pleasant and cooperative, yet at times she had an irritable edge. She had an above-average vocabulary, and she spoke in a fluent manner with a normal volume, rate, and rhythm. Her judgment appeared good. Rasha arrived on time for our meetings, appropriately dressed in jeans, sneakers, loose-fitting clothes, and a winter jacket. She wore glasses and had a serious demeanor. Her work as an exotic dancer seemed in stark contrast to Rasha's studious and almost nerdish appearance. She looked very much like a typical college student and projected a serious and purposeful attitude. Although her posture was closed and she wore her jacket for our entire first interview, she was cooperative, very open, and detailed in providing information. She was clearly very intelligent, but despite her collaborative stance, she did not appear particularly reflective or insightful.

At times, Rasha appeared appropriately troubled by the intensity of her feelings and the apparent randomness at which they occurred. Her irritation with others and crying spells occurred during class with fellow students and her professors, at work with bosses and coworkers, with her roommates, and with her boyfriend. Because these feelings occurred during so many different times and places, Rasha described not being able to understand the source of these feelings, which served to heighten her sense of feeling out of control, which was also extremely distressing to her. However, at other times, Rasha seemed cavalier, unconcerned, and sometimes even righteous or indignant about her feelings toward others. In addition to her problems with emotions, crying spells, and recent relationship problems, Rasha acknowledged a multi-year history of bingeing and purging, promiscuity without romance, and occasionally experiencing transient passive suicidal ideation during which times she thought it might be better not to exist; she denied homicidal ideation. However, in subsequent sessions, Rasha described a long-standing history of self-mutilation and suicidality and described having homicidal feelings toward her father, periodically dreaming of killing him, and at least one incident where she behaved homicidally toward her father by trying to run him off the road.

Rasha's boyfriend, whom she regarded as her first serious romantic relationship, was 10 years her senior. She had met him through her work as an exotic dancer; he was a customer at her place of employment, and the relationship was not developing as Rasha had hoped it would. Interestingly, she described having sex with him on their first date so that he would lose interest in her and leave her alone. However, Rasha went on to describe becoming obsessed with him, frequently calling him, badgering him when she did see him, and becoming very angry and tearful when she felt ignored by him. It appeared to the therapist from her description of the relationship that Rasha's "boyfriend" actually had very little interest in her beyond their initial night together and was actively avoiding her. Consistent with this idea, very soon after, they permanently broke up.

Rasha had one previous psychotherapy. The treatment occurred while in foster care between ages 14 and 18 and consisted of weekly sessions with a male therapist. She denied remembering the specifics of the therapy. She reported the therapy primarily focused on day-to-day concerns and did not spend significant time discussing the incestuous experience with her father.

Rasha was the oldest of nine children (six girls and three boys), born into a practicing Muslim family, living in what she described as an oppressive environment. She grew up very poor, in a socioeconomically depressed area of Syria, and when she was still an infant, her father immigrated to France in order to find gainful employment. Her father worked intermittently in factories and relied on public assistance, some portion of which he sent to Rasha's mother to support the family. Although Rasha didn't have much contact with her father during the next several years, seeing him rarely, she reported that her father's absence wasn't particularly distressing to her because many of her friends' fathers were also working abroad at the time, and the arrangement seemed "pretty normal." During his prolonged absence from the family, she described what sounded like a rather idealized, romanticized notion of her father. By her report, he was a greatly longed for, yet absent, figure who occasionally mailed her small presents and wrote her affectionate letters.

Rasha was raised by her mother and her maternal grandmother. She reported never having felt close with her mother and seemed to view her as uninteresting, weak, yet highly controlling. This experience and view of her mother made it difficult for Rasha to identify with her mother, and instead she described being competitive and antagonistic toward her mother. In contrast, Rasha expressed very warm feelings for her grandmother and frequently sought out her grandmother for attention and comfort. According to Rasha, her grandmother was the only person who consistently held a job and worked extremely hard for the family, qualities for which Rasha had tremendous respect and highly identified with. For nearly all of Rasha's life, her family, including her adult brothers, relied on public assistance to supplement her father's employment, a circumstance that she spoke very derogating of.

Rasha's life underwent a dramatic change when she turned 11. That year Rasha, her mother, and her younger siblings moved to France to join her father. Although Rasha was initially thrilled about the family reunion, her joy was short lived; within 18 months of the move, her father began coming to her bedroom at night, sexually abusing her in a manner that included intercourse.

After a little more than a year, Rasha revealed the abuse to her mother, who responded with disbelief and anger toward Rasha for saying such a thing. Additionally, Rasha's mother refused to take any measures to protect her, often leaving her home alone with her father. Feeling increasingly desperate, several months later, Rasha decided to share the same information with her favorite brother, the second-oldest child in the family, who likewise did not believe her and refused to help. A short time later, Rasha reported encountering a television program that portrayed the story of a young girl who was being sexually abused by her father and who reported the abuse to school authorities and received help. The very next day, Rasha packed her bags and brought them to school with the conscious intention of running away from home at the end of the day. At school, however, not surprisingly, one of her teachers inquired about the reason for her luggage, and Rasha told her about the ongoing abuse.

At that point, she was promptly removed from the home and placed in the French version of foster care (which sounded more like an orphanage). Rasha's father was arrested and jailed for a few months while awaiting trial, but during this time and for the next several years, Rasha's mother and siblings were angry with her for what they perceived as the trouble she caused for the family. Rasha's father was eventually acquitted, as it had essentially been her word against the family's (Rasha's mother and brothers all testified on behalf of the father). After the acquittal, Rasha reported that her mother acted as if all was better and expected Rasha would return home. Rasha's mother didn't understand why she refused to leave foster care and return home.

Rasha spent the rest of her childhood in French foster care. After aging out of the system at 18, Rasha found living in France in close proximity to her family to be difficult. After a couple of years working odd jobs, she decided to search for a better future for herself and made arrangements to take a position in the United States as an au pair. Rasha worked this job for a year, during which time she described spending much of her time going out at night, feeling put out and underappreciated by the family she worked for, and disconnected from the children she cared for. Rasha left her position as an au pair impulsively and moved in with an acquaintance. She stayed with this friend for 6 weeks until he gave her an ultimatum to leave. She then spent the next few weeks couch jumping from one acquaintance to another. She also was looking for a job, as she was unemployed. One day when walking down a street, she inquired about a job as a cocktail waitress in an exotic dance club and was offered a job as a dancer. By the time Rasha presented for psychotherapy, she had been working as an exotic dancer for more than a year.

Diagnosis and Case Formulation

At the time Rasha was evaluated, the *Diagnostic and Statistical Manual of Mental Disorders* (4th ed.; *DSM-4*; American Psychiatric Association [APA], 1994) was in use. Based on the assessment carried out over three sessions, Rasha was given the following diagnoses:

AXIS I: Posttraumatic Stress Disorder

Dysthymia

R/O Eating Disorder NOS

AXIS II: Borderline Personality Disorder (Principal)

AXIS III: None

AXIS IV: Moderate   —stress related to romantic relationship (acute)

—aftereffects of childhood sexual abuse by father (chronic)

AXIS V: Current GAF: 60

Highest past year: 70

Given Rasha's sexual abuse trauma history, one obvious consideration was post-traumatic stress disorder (PTSD). In order to meet criteria for PTSD in *DSM-4*, an individual has to meet six criteria (labeled A though F) that include (A) the experience of a defined stressor, (B) intrusive recollections or reexperiencing of the trauma, (C) avoidance/numbing of situations that are similar or remind one of the trauma, (D) hyperarousal in situations that are similar or remind one of the trauma, (E) the experience of these symptoms for a duration of more than 1 month, and (F) functional significance. Each of the six criteria have a number of subcriteria. Overall, there are 21 criteria. With regard to criterion A, the stressor criterion, the person has to have been exposed to a traumatic event in which he or she experienced, witnessed, or had been confronted with an event or events that involved actual or threatened death or serious injury, or a threat to the physical integrity of oneself or others, and the person's response had to involve intense fear, helplessness, or horror (the *Diagnostic and Statistical Manual of Mental Disorders* [5th ed.; *DSM-5;* APA, 2013] has removed this last requirement because it did not improve diagnostic accuracy). Rasha's sexual abuse experience and her response clearly meet criterion A, even under the *DSM-4* definition. With regard to Criterion B, Rasha displayed the requisite evidence of intrusive recollections/reexperiencing of the trauma required on this criterion. She described occasionally experiencing intrusive and distressing recollections of the sexual abuse, and although rare, occasionally she had dreams of the sexual abuse, which were also quite distressing to her. With regard to Criterion C, a person needs to meet three of the seven designated criteria. These criteria include (1) efforts to avoid thoughts, feelings, or conversations associated with the trauma; (2) efforts to avoid activities, places, or people that arouse recollections of the trauma; (3) inability to recall an important aspect of the trauma; (4) markedly diminished interest or participation in significant activities; (5) feeling of detachment or estrangement from others; (6) restricted range of affect (e.g., unable to have loving feelings); and (7) sense of a foreshortened future (e.g., does not expect to have a career, marriage, children, or a normal life span). Although Rasha often put herself in situations that were sexual, at other times she also acted as if the traumatic event was recurring, and at times she showed intense distress in sexual situations. Rasha's work as an exotic dancer could be seen as approaching rather than avoidance of stimuli associated with trauma; however, she did describe (1) feeling numb during sex and sometimes a combination of feeling numb and dissociated while dancing naked for men; (2) at other times, efforts to avoid thoughts, feelings, and conversation associated with the trauma; and (3) efforts to avoid places (her home) and people (her father, other family members) that led her to think about the experience.

A bit more ambiguous were the arousal criteria for Criterion D. For criterion D, two of five criteria indicating persistent symptoms of increased arousal must be met. These symptoms include (1) difficulty falling or staying asleep, (2) irritability or outbursts of anger, (3) difficulty concentrating, (4) hypervigilance, and (5) exaggerated startle response. Rasha did not describe a consistent period of difficulty falling or staying asleep, concentrating, or exaggerated startle response. However, she did meet criteria for hypervigilance and for irritability or outbursts of anger. Rasha described chronic irritability and frequent outbursts of anger; however, as will be discussed later, these symptoms seemed better conceptualizing as related to borderline personality disorder. Thus, this criterion was made tentatively. Nonetheless, all the symptoms, A through D, had persisted for many years and caused her clinically significant distress, and caused impairment, albeit she was still functioning relatively well. All things considered, Rasha was deemed to have met criteria for PTSD.

Another consideration given Rasha's complaints would be a depressive disorder. Rasha had described intense moments of sadness and bouts of crying that left her feeling drained. She also described more than occasional passive suicidal ideation and instances of self-injury. She also described periods of loss of appetite, but upon further inquiry, this symptom seemed related to a possible eating disorder. Upon detailed evaluation, it was determined that Rasha's depression was not consistent with that of a current major depressive episode; however, the pattern was consistent with that of what at the time in the *DSM-4* was called dysthymia, now called persistent depressive disorder in *DSM-5*. Although initially raised in the context of assessing neurovegetative signs in depression, the patient described an off-and-on pattern of bingeing and purging that required further assessment. It was clear that she did not meet criteria for anorexia nervosa, as she was not refusing to maintain her body weight nor did her body weight drop to 85% of expected weight. Additionally, she had some weight concerns, she did not have an intense fear of gaining weight, and she recognized that she was on the thin side within normal limits and wanted to maintain a healthy weight and appearance. Given her description of bingeing and purging, bulimia nervosa was considered; however, upon further evaluation, it was determined that she did not meet criteria for that diagnosis. Although she reported occasionally engaging in binge and purge behaviors for a period longer than the requisite 3 months, these behaviors did not occur on average twice a week and, importantly, her self-evaluation and resulting bingeing and purging were not influenced by her body shape and weight. Although she did not meet criteria for anorexia nervosa or bulimia nervosa proper, given her presentation she did meet criteria for eating disorder not otherwise specified (EDNOS). One can meet criteria for EDNOS when all of the criteria for bulimia nervosa are met except that the binge eating and inappropriate compensatory mechanisms occur at a frequency of less than twice a week or for a duration of less than 3 months, although what is not specified in the concept of EDNOS is how to account for her self-evaluation and bingeing and purging that occurred outside of the influence of body shape and weight. For this reason, EDNOS was noted as provisional.

Although the PTSD, dysthymia, and eating disordered behaviors were seen as clinically significant and important to address, Rasha's principal diagnosis was borderline personality disorder (BPD). Rasha's core complaints, as well as many of the symptoms of her other diagnoses, can be seen as a function of BPD. BPD includes nine criteria, of which an individual needs to meet at least five. BPD is characterized by a pervasive pattern of instability of interpersonal relationships, self-image and affects, and marked impulsivity beginning by early adulthood and present in a variety of contexts as indicated by five (or more) of the following: (1) frantic efforts to avoid real or imagined abandonment; (2) a pattern of unstable and intense interpersonal relationships characterized by alternating between extremes of idealization and devaluation; (3) identity disturbance: markedly and persistent unstable self-image or sense of self; (4) impulsivity in at least two areas that are potentially self-damaging (e.g., spending, sex, substance abuse, reckless driving, binge eating); (5) recurrent suicidal behavior, gestures or threats, or self-mutilating behavior; (6) affective instability due to a marked reactivity of mood (e.g., intense episodic dysphoria, irritability, or anxiety usually lasting a few hours and only rarely more than a few days); (7) chronic feelings of emptiness; (8) inappropriate, intense anger or difficulty controlling anger (e.g., frequent displays of temper, constant anger, recurrent physical fights); and (9) transient, stress-related paranoia or severe dissociative symptoms. Rasha described behaviors consistent with all nine criteria, although to varying degrees of severity.

For instance, she described frequently feeling abandoned by others, particularly this new boyfriend but also with friends and family. With her current boyfriend, she engaged in stalking-like behaviors and threatened suicide as a way to stave off his abandonment. She described a pattern of vacillating between idealizing and derogating others. This occurred with boyfriends, coworkers, peers, and professors. Although Rasha described a stable career goal in helping neglected children, she displayed other indicators of identity disturbance including having changed her major often, being unsure of what she believed in, having changed friends and types of friends frequently, and she did not behave in a way consistent with her stated beliefs, values, and goals. Although Rasha initially indicated that her problems with emotions had begun 2 months earlier, she presented with a long history of affective lability, and it was clear that these problems with emotions began many years earlier. Additionally, she frequently felt empty, and angry outbursts were common for her. Finally, as mentioned, she described dissociative experiences during sex. Rasha had indicated that she had a number of short-term, often one-night sexual experiences. During these encounters, Rasha described feeling numb, dissociated. She did not enjoy sex, was rarely desirous of sex, only engaging in it because she felt obligated.

Course of Treatment

The treatment began with my providing Rasha with feedback about my understanding of her difficulties so that we could develop a shared understanding and agreement on her problems and goals. Having such an understanding then leads into a discussion of how the therapy is designed to address the identified problems. In essence, what are the tasks of therapy to address the goals of therapy, the goals deriving from understanding the difficulties or problems that the patient is experiencing? This approach is very inconsistent with the ideas articulated by Bordin (1979) regarding the development of a working alliance between the therapist and patient.

When the therapist explains to the patient his or her understanding of their difficulties, including the diagnosis, it is important to do so in a way that resonates with the patient's phenomenological experience. I didn't want to simply tell Rasha she had borderline personality disorder, but I wanted to share with her at a phenomenological level what I understood from her and then try to provide a coherent conceptual understanding of how the various difficulties she shared fit together into a diagnostic picture. Doing so with BPD is especially important because there is often stigma associated with the disorder. Therefore, some patients respond negatively to the diagnosis. Many therapist are fearful of sharing personality disorder diagnoses, particularly BPD, with patients because they are afraid that the patient may respond negatively. While it is true that some patients do, I find that many patients are relieved that you have an understanding of their difficulties and may be able to help them. Many patients with BPD have spent years receiving treatments for the incorrect disorder and have thus suffered essentially untreated.

Rasha was very receptive to my conceptualization of her difficulties and the recommendations I made for how the treatment would proceed. However, even when the patient is in agreement with the therapist, often there can be ambivalence or even slight resistance to the therapist's proposed understanding and suggested approach. The ambivalence or disagreement about the conceptualization and/or approach is common and not necessarily a problem, but it needs to be addressed and resolved collaboratively. Collaboratively does not mean that the therapist either abdicates his or her professionally derived judgment or acquiesces to the patient's preferences, nor should the therapist simply impose his or her perspective on the patient. Sometimes, patients agree with the therapist's conceptualities and recommendations out of their own acquiescence. I was vigilant for indicators that Rasha was simply agreeing with me, particularly because she did not feel empowered to share her concerns with me. However, it was my estimation that what I had shared with Rasha resonated with her and that she was hopeful that my suggestions would be fruitful. The therapy I suggested to Rasha was transference-focused psychotherapy (TFP). At the time I was treating Rasha, TFP was one of two specialized and specific manualized treatments for BPD, the other being dialectical behavior therapy (DBT). Shortly after the treatment ended, another treatment, mentalization-based therapy (MBT), was developed, tested, and published. Today, there are a number of empirically tested and supported primary psychotherapies such as TFP, DBT, MBT, and schema-focused psychotherapy (SFP), among others. There are also a number of adjunctive group treatments and a generalist approach called good psychiatric management (GPM). Today, TFP, DBT, MBT, SFP, and GPM are considered the Big Five. A number of recent meta-analyses have found no differences between the treatments in terms of effects, no differences between those treatments classified as cognitive-behaviorally derived (e.g., DBT, SFP) and those that are classified as psychodynamically derived (e.g., TFP, MBT), or between DBT and other treatments.

With a shared understanding of her difficulties and the approach to be taken in therapy, we explicitly discussed each of our roles and responsibilities in the therapy. This included the logistics of the therapy—when appointments begin and end, how to handle lateness, absences, and the need to reschedule, as well as vacations and other events that might arise in the therapy. This part of the treatment is called the *frame setting,* and it is important for setting the foundation for any psychotherapy, but especially therapies with BPD patients (and/or therapy-naive patients) where subtlety and nuance should be made explicit.

Another aspect of the psychotherapy is the therapist's attitude or stance toward the patient. Here, there are two aspects that are important. TFP is delivered from a stance called technical neutrality. Kernberg (1976) coined the term *technical neutrality* to differentiate it from the psychoanalytic concept of neutrality. The psychoanalytic concept of neutrality derived from Freud's (1912/1958) statement that the therapist "should be opaque to his patients and, like a mirror, should show them nothing but what is shown to him." Freud was advising therapists to strive to remain as anonymous as possible to the patient, to be as much of a blank slate as possible, upon which the patient could project his or her unconscious fantasies, conflicts, and desire. Thus, Freud was suggesting that the therapist should try to avoid contaminating the patient's expression by injecting or imposing aspects of him or herself or his or her expectations on the patient. This was done to preserve that integrity of the transference and to ensure that the therapy was about the patient and not the therapist. The adoption of this approach, particularly in the United States, often led therapists to say very little and present as or be perceived as bland, cold, or indifferent. Documents suggest that Freud did not use the term this way, nor did he behave that way. For instance, accounts suggest that Freud was quite chatty in his own consulting room. In response to the detached version of neutrality, Kernberg (1976) suggested the term technical neutrality in order to distinguish between a "lack of spontaneity and natural warmth" and an "authentic concern for the patients [. . .] that protects their autonomy, independence and capacity to accomplish their work on their own" (p. 821). In Kernberg's conception, technical neutrality occurs within a background and attitude of warm concern and is about the therapist remaining equidistant from all sides of the patient's conflicts or "inner struggles." Thus, technical neutrality is not about being a blank slate, quiet, or passive; the therapist can be warm and active as long as he or she is not siding with a particular side of the patient's ambivalence or conflict. What Kernberg and others are suggesting is the adoption of a nonjudgmental stance toward the patient. A patient's wishes, desires, and inhibitions are complicated and fluid, as are his or her identifications and de-identifications with those associated with these struggles. Over the years, I have moved away from referring to this stance as neutrality or technical neutrality and instead call it *taking a nonjudgmental stance*. But taking a nonjudgmental stance can be complicated, particularly when working with a patient like Rasha, who has been severely sexually abused. Working with people who have been traumatized, particularly those who have been physically and/or sexually abused or where there is extreme malevolence, can evoke strong feelings in therapists who work with them. These feelings, called *countertransference*, can be quite powerful and push the therapist to want to act in ways that may not be best for the therapy. Typically, these feelings include empathy, sympathy, and concern. Therapists can also respond with feelings of sadness, hopelessness, and anger. Either way, the therapist may behave or act in a manner that runs counter to a nonjudgmental stance and interfere with the patient's expressing complicated feelings. In Rasha's case, I felt sympathetic toward this young woman who was striving for a better life in the face of what happened to her. I was not only saddened but was also outraged by what had happened to her and how her family responded. However, it is important for the therapist to metabolize these feelings so that they do not leak into treatment and potentially impose one's own needs onto the patient. When Rasha was angry at her father or mother, I often also filled with angry feelings and wanted to join her in condemning her parents. However difficult, it is important to maintain one's nonjudgmental stance in these situations too. A few examples illustrate why. Prior to treating Rasha, I had been involved in the inpatient treatment of a young woman who was hospitalized following a suicide attempt. Like Rasha, the patient was very compelling. The inpatient staff quickly liked her and sympathized with her. This connection deepened after it was found out that she was suicidal because she was sexually abused by her older brother. Staff were outraged at the brother and would sympathize with the patient, during which various staff members' anger toward the brother was often very palpable and obvious to the patient. The night before a family session in which the patient was going to confront her parents and brother about what had transpired, the patient made a serious suicide attempt and almost died. She had to be hospitalized in a medical unit, and some of the psychiatric staff went to visit her. Staff were concerned that maybe they pushed the patient too hard or fast to confront the parents. However, staff were shocked when the patient admitted the real reason she tried to kill herself. The patient shared that just as the older brother had sexually abused her, she had sexually abused a younger brother. What the staff did not realize is that every time they attacked the older brother, they were attacking the patient because she too had engaged in similar behavior. This is a very concrete example of a patient's untoward behavior, but identifications and de-identifications can be very subtle and not always well understood. For instance, another patient I treated described tremendous guilt about how she enjoyed her grandfather's attention and tenderness that would occur just prior to his fondling her. She was very confused and troubled by these feelings. Part of her enjoyed being singled out as special, and another part felt sickened by his behavior. She felt as if she was to blame for his behaviors, and she felt like an accomplice. I have found that other sexually abused individuals describe similar experiences in noting any tender or special feelings they had toward abusers or if there had been any sexual responsiveness in response to the perpetrator's abuse. By taking a nonjudgmental stance, the patient can bring up these complex and confusing feelings for discussion and resolution. With Rasha, I quickly discovered that I could not side with her against her father. She did not like when I shared in her anger toward her parents, particularly her father. She seemed to find it intrusive and overwhelming. I needed to give her space to experience it on her own terms from a nonjudgmental position that allowed her to move seamlessly back and forth between anger and forgiveness. She had missed and idealized her father prior to the abuse. She was eager to see him when she moved to France. She looked forward to having his presence and guidance. She did not know that he would betray her, and it left her with complicated feelings toward him to be worked out. Similarly, she was furious with her mother for not protecting her, but she also wanted to have a relationship with her.

Early on in session, Rasha was very compliant with the frame. She never missed a session and was always on time. She began sessions as we agreed by talking about her main concerns; she openly discussed her feelings of dysphoria and anger, her relationship difficulties, and her conflict about working as an exotic dancer. Her affect in session typically vacillated between feeling dysphoric, agitated, and crying, or energized, indignant, and angry at others. Despite the intensity of these feelings, she was dutiful in her schoolwork. In these early sessions, her distress was palpable and almost pleading with me to help her feel better. She complained about peers in her classes and coworkers at the dance club. She had a lot of conflict with others and was frequently agitated with others, looking down at others with disdain or crying about interactions with others. The early content mostly focused on her concerns about a boyfriend she had just begun a relationship with who was very much unavailable to her and her conflictual relationship with her mother.

During the early part of her therapy, it became quite apparent that one of the primary ways Rasha regulated her affect, especially her rage, was through geographical movement. Rasha would come to therapy and report how she was going to solve whatever problem that was most distressing to her at the time by switching classes and professors, leaving one strip club to dance at another, switching apartments and/ or roommates, changing friends, and so on. And she did change clubs she worked at when conflict arose, and she frequently moved from one apartment to another when she was no longer getting along with roommates. Rasha described how she had felt forced to make this recent succession of changes due to repeatedly encountering interpersonal conflicts with managers, fellow dancers, customers at the clubs where she worked, roommates, and essentially all of the people who populated her daily life. And of course, Rasha had successfully used this technique to help regulate her feelings vis-à-vis her family when she moved out of her house and into foster care and then again when she moved from France to the United States.

Despite all these changes, Rasha never discussed with me wanting to change therapists. At least not directly. There were a number of times early in the therapy when Rasha would contemplate moving to another city, where things would be better. I viewed Rasha's desire to move cities as a threat to the continuity of the treatment, which given her difficulties I saw as vital, which I had conveyed to her when we set the treatment frame. I also thought that bringing up her desire to move to another city might be a safe and covert way to express dissatisfaction with me as the therapist and the therapy in general. After all, although she was more stable and had a supportive outlet to vent, it was easy to imagine from her perspective that she was not much better, as she was still frequently distressed. I tried connecting these ideas for her, but she rejected them. From the beginning of the therapy, she had tended to idealize me or at least steered clear of criticizing me. I felt she was protecting me from her wrath because she was dependent on me as a benign person in her life. She didn't dare risk the sanctuary our meetings provided. Any gentle suggestions that she had concerns about therapy were met with strong denials. I was reluctant to push this idea too hard out of respect for Rasha's needs and decided to approach the problem indirectly.

Relatedly, one of the greatest challenges during this period of the treatment was to help Rasha recognize the source of her tremendous rage as being located inside her, rather than being an inevitable response to what she perceived as being a collection of uniformly corrupt, callous, and morally despicable people in her environment.

This was achieved, in part, by my gradually helping her see that despite all changes involving places and people, the concerns and feelings she brought to therapy largely remained the same. Gently, I shared with her the idea that no matter where she moved to or who she was involved with, these concerns were located in her, and we had to tease out how best to understand and resolve them. I said to her, "No matter where you run to, you take your conflict with your mother and your father with you. You can't simply outrun it; we have to work to understand it and resolve it, so that you can truly be free of it. When you can disentangle what is a current upset from what is past upset, then you will be free and have more relief." I wanted to be careful how I delivered this intervention because I didn't want it to seem as if I were blaming her for the feelings she experienced. Instead, I wanted the intervention to validate the struggle she was experiencing. She calmed down and became reflective. She responded by indicating that aspects of this intervention resonated with her, particularly the futility of trying to outrun her concerns. She too had awareness about this.

Also, in great contrast to Rasha's mother, who was unable and/or unwilling to listen to, never mind respond to, her distress, Rasha began to trust my ability to tolerate her feelings. Rasha's trust was building slowly as she became upset in session and I was able to sit with her, help her calm through gentle reflection, and she learned to better tolerate her upset. I remember one time toward the end of one particular session that one could describe as affectively stormy, to say the least. Rasha noticed that she was feeling a new, uncharacteristic sense of "lightness" and relief, when she suddenly remarked, "My God, you *really can* take anything that I throw at you, can't you!"

For understandable reasons, she was genuinely surprised that I could listen to her and respond empathetically to her tirades without recoiling and/or rejecting her in the manner that she had previously been accustomed to. But through having this experience with me time after time, Rasha grew to realize that her feelings were not as dangerous or damaging as she feared—to me or to her. Rather than continuing to come to therapy and using it as an opportunity to vent about a long list of angry rants in response to day-to-day events, she increasingly was able to tie her in-the-moment feelings and ways of relating to people in the context of long-standing ways of viewing herself and others, and patterns of reactions. She came to understand her emotions not as earthshattering disruptions but as subtle and sometimes not-so-subtle indicators to attend to her experience in the moment. Anger toward a friend was now a signal to bring up her concerns with her friend so that they could be discussed rather than an indicator that the friendship should be ended.

Another aspect of Rasha's treatment involved her long-standing tendency to binge and purge. I struggled with how best to address her bingeing and purging—that is, how much emphasis to put on it in the context of her other problems. The amount of bingeing and purging she engaged in varied quite a bit, with long periods of time without any and other times where it was much more problematic. At the beginning of treatment, Rasha experienced her bingeing and purging behavior as occurring in a random way that was totally disconnected to anything going on in her life. Typically, she would report that she had been going about her usual routine when she began feeling "bad" (early on in therapy she often described her feelings in terms that were very broad and undifferentiated), and in response to feeling bad, she binged on a huge quantity of food. Bingeing only made her feel better for a short period of time and sometimes made her feel worse, a problem she would then solve by forcing herself to vomit. While she reported that this binge/purge pattern provided her with some relief, she also recognized that this "dysfunctional" behavior was bad for her physically, and it was also in conflict with her desire to perceive herself as a person who could control and handle things, as she often experienced this behavior as out of her control. I understood her bingeing and purging, in part, as another attempt to regulate her affect and feel in control. As we explored the precipitants and dynamics of her bingeing and purging cycles more thoroughly, it became apparent that what preceded bingeing were feelings of being depressed, empty, and longing for intimacy and a caring other, particularly her mother. Sometimes, still unsatisfied, she would call her mother. She described that most times her mother said something to disappoint her or upset her, which led to Rasha ending the conversation abruptly and then feeling the need to purge. It was as if she binged to emotionally fill herself up, and then once filled, she felt imposed upon or intruded by the feeling. At the beginning of treatment, it was difficult for Rasha to acknowledge that she longed for her mother to soothe and comfort her during times that she was feeling lonely and distressed. At first she would deflect, if not outright reject, attempts to discuss her longings, but as treatment progressed, she began to recognize that part of her was indeed interested in some connection with her family, including her mother.

In Rasha's case, her bingeing served as an intrapsychic proxy for her intense wishes to be nurtured and protected, especially by her mother, longings that were almost uniformly unfulfilled and disappointed. Rasha responded to the intense disappointment by rejecting the maternal introject through vomiting. In this fashion, Rasha symbolized the conflicts over feeling punishing and being punished, being the rejecter and being rejected.

As the psychotherapy continued, toward the end of the first year of treatment, another dominant pattern emerged concerning her eating disordered behavior. Ten months or so into the psychotherapy, after nearly a month-long interruption in the treatment during August, Rasha reported after a 2-month remission in symptoms she had resumed purging on a weekly basis during a vacation. Upon further exploration, it became apparent that each occasion of bingeing and purging occurred within a day of the appointment times during which we would have normally met. I pointed this out in a matter-of-fact way and invited her to reflect on that with me. She acted annoyed with me and said that the association was merely coincidental. I acknowledged that it was possible that her bingeing and purging resurfaced coincidently to our break in the treatment but also suggested that it might be worth considering other hypotheses too. Sensing that it would be too difficult for her to acknowledge her dependency on the treatment and me, I began by exploring the surface meaning of the behavior and slowly brought up possible underlying motivations.

She observed that after purging she felt relieved, her mood lightened, and she felt that she could temporarily ignore the emotions left in her, yet it troubled her because she also sensed that this relief was a false emotion. She was also able to talk more directly about how she used bingeing and purging to control her feelings. It seemed that her ability to take what she wanted and to expel something uncomfortable made life sufficiently tolerable so that she didn't feel she was risking too much by coming to me for psychotherapy. In this discussion, she acknowledged being angry with me for not being available during the vacation. She further acknowledged that when she was bingeing, she felt defiant and that the defiance was directed at me. She indicated that she felt like she had no control over the vacation and that her bingeing was a way of taking that control back from me. She believed (correctly) that I would not have wanted her to binge, so she defiantly did so knowing that I could not stop her. She was in control of her behavior, even if the behavior was about being out of control. And there was nothing I could do. However, she then shared what she thought was a strange feeling. She said at some point she felt both controlled by me, as if I were forcing her to act this way, and she felt distant from me, as if her behavior would push me away. She became fearful that I would end the treatment because she binged, and in what she described as a panic, she began to purge, with the hope of undoing what she had done and repairing our relationship. We began to examine this dynamic, not just in relation to me, which was useful because it was in the here-and-now of the consultation room, but also as it related to her functioning in general—how, for her, absence felt like rejection, rejection out of her control, and bingeing was a way of being in control and out of control at the same time. It transformed out-of-control feelings into feelings in control. It allowed her to feel powerful when feeling weak, to feel indignant and independent toward those she felt dependent on. But there were a number of costs and edged a slippery slope. As we discussed these dynamics and Rasha was better able to articulate, tolerate, and accept her feelings, her bingeing and purging began to decrease and eventually ceased.

The bingeing and purging appeared to transform into a healthier behavior with a similar dynamic. Normally very punctual, Rasha began a pattern of being 5 to 10 minutes late to sessions. On those days that did she arrive on time, she would announce to me that she was on time in a manner in which she seemed to be asserting control. It was kind of like she was saying, "I'm on time because I unilaterally made the decision to be on time," as opposed to being the time that I designated as the time we meet. Over the course of 2 or 3 months, we discussed the possibility that Rasha was using being late as a way of managing her feelings of dependence and control. As our discussions continued, Rasha continued to increase and deepen her capacity to discuss difficult dynamics. Lateness gave way to timeliness. She began talking about our relationship in a realistic manner and was able to both bring up things about me or the way I worked that she did not like as well as express gratitude toward me.

These changes coincided with changes in her capacity to relate with others outside of therapy. It was around this time that Rasha met a man through a friend she worked with. She became interested in this man, and within a few weeks they began dating. The man seemed genuinely interested in her, not merely as a sexual being. They did activities together, went out with friends, and she met his parents. He was bothered by, but tolerant of, her job as an exotic dancer. She described wanting to be sexually intimate with him in a desirous and reciprocal way that was uncharacteristic of past sexual relationships, although she still had a lot of concerns about her responsiveness and performance, and worried about both his enjoyment and judgment of her. She sometimes became very jealous of his friendship with both men and women and sometimes became quite suspicious of his intentions, wondering if he was using her for sex. But the relationship struck me as the most involved and intimate relationship in which I knew her to be involved. It was not without its problems, but because of their mutual and authentic interest in one another, differences and fights were able to be resolved in relatively reasonable ways. Her fights with him were no longer characterized by angry outbursts, throwing objects, bingeing and purging, and threats of suicide and self-injury. Instead, she cried and pouted but also expressed herself. As a result, issues were resolved and the relationship continued and deepened. She was developing friendships through his friends. Rasha's boyfriend's family was important to him, and Rasha began attending family events. At first, she was competitive and jealous of his family members, particularly his sisters and mother. But these women also embraced her, and she began to realize their motivations were not competitive with her but genuine, despite any faults they may have had.

As she developed a more integrated sense of herself and others in her life, leading to better control over her emotional experience and the capacity to progress in her studies, and a deepening in her relationship with her boyfriend, she became more future oriented and began to envision a satisfying life. She began an internship related to her interests and became less interested in the strip club lifestyle. We began discussing her pursuit of nonclub employment, and her success on her internship contributed to her capacity to pursue such opportunities.

Outcome and Prognosis

Rasha made excellent progress during the course of the treatment. Concretely, she was able to complete her degree in a timely manner and with solid grades. She was now involved in a relationship with a man who was interested in a committed and emotionally intimate relationship with her, and most important, despite the financial benefits, she stopped working as an exotic dancer, taking a much lower-paying entry-level internship position related to her career goals. Rasha was not completely happy in her relationship with her boyfriend, but she was much happier than in the past, and importantly, she was now able to talk directly with him about her concerns. Her contact with her family was less tense and characterized by greater levels of resolve on her part. She was able to become closer to her siblings, viewed her family less negatively and more realistically, and thus was more sympathetic to their struggles. After the therapy ended, Rasha periodically contacted me by letters to the clinic. Although I was no longer working at that clinic, the letters were forwarded to me. Early letters expressed gratitude and made reference to her continued relationship with the boyfriend, as well as educational and work achievements. After a few years of these periodic letters, Rasha began contacting me directly by e-mail. These e-mails were every 2 or 3 years at first, the last e-mail being about 8 years ago. Over time, Rasha described work success, then attending a graduate program at a prestigious university program, and later letting me know she graduated and obtained a very high-level and high-paying position that interested her. She told me she had not experienced any subsequent suicidality, had only rare bouts of self-doubt and depression, which were short-lived, and no angry outbursts. Additionally, she shared with me a very insightful thought that has impacted both my clinical and research work. She told me that when she first entered treatment, she fantasized about being someone else, someone with a different life, someone whose father had not sexually abused her and someone whose parents had supported her. Someone whose boyfriend loved her for who she was, and someone who had not been an exotic dancer. Over time, she experienced herself differently. It was subtle at first but very noticeable as treatment went on. As this change occurred, she felt better about herself despite her imperfections, she felt better about her boyfriend despite the things about him that bothered her, and she felt better about her mother despite her limitations and betrayal. She could not forgive her father nor did she want to be in a relationship, but psychologically she was disentangled from him. She did not think of him often, she could better tolerate her mother and siblings mentioning him, and the abuse and homicidal dreams stopped. And then she shared a thought that was so profound. She wrote: "I cannot change what happened to me, but I was able to change how I think about it." She went on to explain that it was not to say that she developed a Pollyannaish view of what happened, but that she developed a more contextualized one that allows her to appreciate herself and others more fully and realistically. And then she ended by thanking me for tolerating her when she could not do so, for aspiring for her when she could not, and for helping her come to a new view of herself—"it made all the difference." I have not heard from her since, but I am confident that she is now capable of having the kind of life she aspires toward. Tolstoy said one can live magnificently if one knows how to love and work. My hope and belief is that Rasha is living magnificently now.

Discussion Questions

1. Even though Rasha's principal diagnosis was BPD, she had other clinically significant behaviors. Explain why the psychotherapist focused on the BPD in Rasha's treatment. In doing so, be sure to provide examples of Rasha's behaviors that were not considered clinically significant.

2. Summarize technical neutrality in psychotherapy, and explain how it was used during Rasha's treatment.

3. Describe the ways in which Rasha's complicated relationship with her mother and father played a role in her problematic behaviors. How did the way in which Rasha's therapist interacted with Rasha become part of her treatment?

References

American Psychiatric Association. (1994). *Diagnostic and statistical manual of mental disorders* (4th ed.). Washington, DC: Author.

American Psychiatric Association. (2013). *Diagnostic and statistical manual of mental disorders* (5th ed.). Washington, DC: Author.

Bordin, E. (1979). The generalizability of the psychoanalytic concept of the working alliance. *Psychotherapy Theory, Research, and Practice, 16,* 252–260.

Freud, S. (1958). Recommendations for physicians on the psycho-analytic method of treatment. In J. Strachey (Ed. & Trans.), *The standard edition of the complete psychological works of Sigmund Freud* (Vol. 12, pp. 109–120). London: Hogarth Press. (Original work published 1912)

Kernberg, O. F. (1976). Technical considerations in the treatment of borderline personality organization. *Journal of the American Psychoanalytic Association, 24,* 795–829.

13

Antisocial Personality Disorder With Comorbid Narcissistic and Borderline Personality Disorder

Presenting Problem and Client Description

Bill was an attractive and affable 30-year-old white heterosexual man who was referred to me by a colleague who had seen him briefly following his release from prison. Bill had spent 2 years in prison following his arrest and conviction for identity fraud. He had stolen the identity of an ex-girlfriend who had a gender-ambiguous name. Armed with her Social Security number and previous addresses, he applied for and received credit cards in her name. He controlled his spending on those cards while they were dating, but once they broke up, he began spending heavily on them, including on an expensive vacation to Hawaii. By his report, he was arrested in the airport upon his return from Hawaii. In total, he had spent over $50,000 with these fraudulent cards in less than 1 year. This was not Bill's first time using other people's credit cards, and he was sentenced to 2½ to 5 years in a state penitentiary. Previously, just after his father's death and before his will went to probate, he used his father's credit cards, running up $50,000 in debt. The purchases were discovered by a sibling. At that time, Bill claimed to have engaged in this spending as part of a manic phase of bipolar disorder. His attitude was very dismissive toward his siblings, who were irate. He could not understand why they were so upset. He argued that he was sick, didn't know what he was doing, and couldn't be held responsible. Moreover, Bill didn't think it involved them—they were just being controlling and greedy. And he further justified using his father's credit cards because he believed his father would have wanted him to do so for having taken care of him prior to his death. This pattern of excuses and rationalization is common in those with antisocial personality disorder (ASPD). Those with ASPD often use a logic referred to as "kettle logic," which is a rhetorical device wherein one uses multiple contradictory arguments to defend a point, or in the case of those with ASPD, to externalize blame. The logic of the kettle story told by Freud in the analysis of Irma's dream in *The Interpretation of Dreams* goes like this: A man rebuked by his neighbor after returning a borrowed kettle with a crack in it replies first that he had returned the kettle intact; second, that it was damaged when he borrowed it; and third, he never borrowed it in the first place. Bill's siblings were upset because paying back the credit card companies would need to come out of the father's estate and thus, in large part, from the siblings' share of their inheritance. Additionally, his siblings contended Bill had not taken care of their father and, in fact, had been less involved than they were. Bill had also used his father's credit cards years earlier when in college to pay for phone sex, running up a bill of a few thousand dollars. When these charges to the credit card came to light, Bill reported he was suicidal and was hospitalized. In the hospital, he claimed to have multiple personality disorder, that he did not recall the phone calls and it must have been one of his other personalities.

While in prison for his most recent incident, he was able to convince the prison authorities that he suffered from bipolar disorder and was accorded various special considerations, such as being housed in a psychiatric unit within the prison. With the support of prison staff, he was able to successfully petition for early release due to his mental illness. Upon his parole from prison, his parole officer suggested that he be in treatment because of his bipolar disorder. Bill resisted and stalled until the parole officer became insistent and made it a requirement. At that point, he began treatment, court mandated, with my colleague. However, he did not attend regularly, frequently missing sessions. My colleague, growing frustrated by what he perceived as the patient's lack of true interest in therapy, asked that I assess him to determine his motivation and capacity for treatment and for the possibility of my picking him up as a transfer.

I agreed, and it was in this context that I met with Bill. Bill arrived for our meetings on time, dressed casually but appropriately. He was polite and appeared forthcoming in conversation. He looked to be at ease, but he was also gamely haughty. As he answered my questions, he seemed engaged and cooperative; however, he acted very familiar with me, as if we were colleagues, and as we continued, I increasingly realized that despite the tenor of our interactions and his apparent cooperation, I often was not getting the information I was interested in obtaining. I had to frequently clarify his comments and seek additional information, which seemed to make him feel uncomfortable.

Between sessions, I discovered that Bill had been in treatment at our clinic when he was a young child. I was surprised by this because I had asked him about his previous treatment history, including as a child, and he had failed to mention this particular treatment. In fact, he denied having any psychological problems until his early 20s when he had his "first manic episode" that resulted in using his then-alive father's credit cards for phone sex. When I asked him about what I had found out and why he had not mention this, he responded in a very cavalier manner and tried to brush it off. As I persisted, rather than get frustrated or upset with me, he tried to charm and flatter me with the idea that he hadn't shared it because he knew I was so competent that I would find out anyway. As he described his situation, the narratives were tinged with the idea that it was he who was a victim rather than others.

Bill grew up in a middle-class family; his mother was a registered nurse and his father an insurance executive. He described being close to his mother, although it did not sound like a very emotionally close relationship. He indicated that his father was a good but distant man. He neglected to mention to me that his father had been arrested, charged, and convicted of embezzlement from the company he worked for and served many years in prison himself, which left the family with financial strain and humiliated in his community. Bill described knowing that he was charming from an early age and realizing that he had the ability to use his charm to manipulate others. Although he shared with me that he knew it was wrong to manipulate others and he would never do such a thing, he nonetheless went on to describe manipulating others. He also described tricking friends and other children, lying to others including adults, often to get out of trouble but sometimes for no reason other than to see what he could get away with. He described stealing from friends and neighbors, and as he got older, he described coercing both male and female peers into having sex. In all these instances, he was indifferent to indignant to other people's concerns.

Without much awareness, he described experiences that seem common among those who develop ASPD. For instance, although he described his mother as a very meek woman, he also described a number of instances where she seemed to take pleasure in his aggressiveness and bad behavior toward others. He described her affect as bright, alive, and reinforcing when he cut in front of other kids or took advantage of others, or even hit another child. This meek woman also used to stand up to the principals of his schools when Bill found himself in trouble for bad behavior. Bill shared that his mother supported him unconditionally and described situations in which he articulated that he was the victim of others. In addition to her enjoyment of his aggression toward others, which may contribute to what is called *ego-syntonic aggression* in those with ASPD, Bill described numerous instances of noncontingent aggression. With regard to his mother, in a rare moment of derogation toward her, he described an instance where his mother became angry with him and hit him when he was a young child. He was walking with his mother and a sibling when Bill decided to kick his brother in the back of the leg, causing his brother's leg to buckle. His mother, seeing this, grabbed Bill by the arm, lifting him off the ground, and smacked him hard a number of times while angrily repeating the phrase through clenched teeth "You don't hit others, don't hit others." Bill referred to his mother as a hypocrite for the apparent contradiction between her hitting him and her admonishments to do otherwise. Bill also described how his father would get upset with him, not for the things he did wrong but because his bad behavior had an impact on the father. Bill described that he knew being bad or aggressive was okay as long as his father or mother were not negatively affected by it. Experiences like these contribute to a lack of contingency between aggressive behavior and consequences as well as an attitude that others are corrupt and only care about their own self-interests.

Early on during my interview with Bill, he told me he had graduated from a prestigious university with honors. He described his course work and his experiences on campus in detail. After completing his degree, he indicated that he started and ran a number of successful businesses, which he described losing as a result of being the victim of unscrupulous partners, manic episodes, and most recently from having to go to prison. He told me he would be a millionaire by now if not for his unfortunate arrest, completely ignoring the fact that his prison sentence was due to his own dishonesty. As the interview proceeded, I had a sense that he was not being truthful with me. Most of what he was telling me was believable with a few exceptions (e.g., the way he described his arrest in the airport seemed embellished), although he was clearly grandiose about his ability and prospects. At one point, he was telling me about a new business he wanted to start but that he couldn't get a business loan because of bias against him due to his prison record. My clinical intuition doubted what he was telling me, but because I had no tangible reason to doubt him, I did not want to simply accuse him of fabricating so I listened carefully like a detective lying in wait listening for inconsistencies. He also assured me that he would soon be a millionaire and began telling me that he developed a detailed business plan that he was going to take to another bank. He mentioned that he even had a name for the business, at which point I quickly pounced, asking him the name of the business. By this point, I felt confident that he did not have this business plan or a name and that this would be exposed for us to discuss. However, without any latency, Bill proclaimed "Pure Imagination" was the name of the business. I had to chuckle to myself. I doubted the veracity of what he was telling me but was impressed with his quickness and thought the business name might be a good metaphor for the material he was providing to me during the interview. As Bill continued, I was reminded of the movie *The Usual Suspects*, and I began to feel like Chazz Palminteri's character Special Agent Dave Kujan sitting across from Kevin Spacey's Roger "Verbal" Kint. At this point, I felt Bill was just making things up, but I couldn't tell for sure. This is another aspect of working with those with ASPD, which is that you begin to feel unsure of what information is real and what information is made up. This experience is often referred to as *gaslighting* in the popular media in reference to the 1944 movie *Gaslight* staring Charles Boyer and Ingrid Bergman, which is based on Patrick Hamilton's 1938 play *Gas Light*. In the movie, Charles Boyer plays Bergman's husband and manipulates events in order to make Bergman's character doubt her sense of reality. This is done in order to distract her from his criminal activities. Because it can be difficult to detect a lie, it is important in general, but particularly when there is any hint of ASPD, for the evaluating clinician to check with informants and collateral data.

Therefore, before I completed the interviews, I sat down with my colleague to discuss my impressions and to check details. I also spoke with Bill's mother, his parole officer, and requested hospital and prison records. In speaking with my colleague, he looked puzzled. It was not my diagnostic impression that was bewildering, but many of the details I shared with him were inconsistent with the details that Bill shared with him. For instance, according to my colleague, Bill had not graduated from a prestigious university with a business degree but had an associate's degree from a local community college. While I had doubted some of what Bill was telling me, that was a detail I found believable. He was clearly very bright, articulate, and knowledgeable. He used phrasing that struck me as consistent with someone who attended an elite university. Later, in consultation with the person prescribing Bill's psychotropic medication, my colleague and I discovered that all treaters had different versions of various "facts." Because I had obtained signed authorization to speak with Bill's mother and parole officer, I was able to obtain important informant information that helped to clarify the extent of Bill's lying.

With all the information in hand, I met with Bill once again. During this session, I shared my initial impressions as well as the feedback I received from the various collateral informants. I pointed out that it was difficult to understand his providing me with such misleading information because he had to know that I would speak with his current treaters at the very least, and that he had provided me with consent to speak with his mother and parole officer. At first, he tried to convince me that other people misunderstood or that I misunderstood, or that he never said what I thought he did, or that he meant something different. He would try to convince me that what he said to either me or another was really the same if you narrowed or expanded the meaning or scope of what he said. Once again, it felt like the logic of the kettle.

In addition to not being truthful, there were a number of instances where it was clear that his social empathy was impaired. For instance, he often saw himself as the victim of those he was victimizing. One such example that illustrates the level of impairment in his social empathy came to light after therapy had begun. Bill developed a long-standing scheme for saving money on rent, of which he was quite proud and which he had pulled off many times periodically, beginning during his college days. He would find a group of people through advertisements who were seeking a roommate, typically a group of people who knew each other, had a precipitous vacancy, and needed a sublessor quickly. He would use his pleasant and affable manner to charm and put them at ease. Because he was very likeable, he was quickly chosen by those looking for a new housemate. As customary, he would pay his first month's rent and any required fees and deposit when signing the lease but then would fail to pay subsequent months' rent. He would stall for months with excuses and promises. Eventually, the roommates would petition the courts for eviction, and he would leave just before the sheriff would be called to remove his belongings. In this way, he would have a place to live for 6, 7, or more months but only pay 1, 2, or 3 months of rent at most. Not only was he unconcerned with the problems he caused for others, he thought this was a very clever idea and also often felt indignant and justified in his mistreatment of them because of perceived grievances, such as they were overcharging him or that his roommates were nags for insisting that he pay his rent. Sometimes, he even described feeling the victim of these roommates, which was the case with his most recent targets. One session, he came in very upset and angry. He thought he had found a new set of roommates on the heels of being evicted from his current apartment, but at the last minute, the prospective roommates backed out of the offer. Apparently, one of the women, for some unexplained reason, became nervous and developed cold feet. She was able to convince the others to go with a different sublessor. This created a problem for Bill, who needed to vacate his current apartment before the sheriff arrived. He was furious at this woman and her roommates, and was very angry in session, cursing and threatening them and calling them all sorts of names. He then became angry at me because he perceived that I was not on his side about his plight. I acknowledged that I could "see how upset and angry he was about the situation" but gently shared with him that "it was difficult to empathize with his anger given that these women just dodged a bullet in that his intention was to rip them off." Bill was surprised by my comment but also reacted well to it. He shared with me that often others, including previous therapists, either did not know how to respond to him in these kinds of situations or that they would empathize with his distress. In describing his previous therapists' reactions, he appeared filled with disdain for them as he questioned what kind of therapist would support someone ripping off others, suggesting that either the therapists were weak, stupid, or corrupt themselves. Bill raised an important issue in the treatment of those with ASPD, namely the importance of not siding with or colluding with the patient's antisocial behavior. Although such an admonishment would seem obvious, those with ASPD can be very adept at creating situations where therapists collude with them, often unintentionally and even without awareness. On more than one occasion, while treating ASPD patients like Bill, patients have shared with me details of crimes or planned crimes in which failing to confront the patient through silence or even exploration can be interpreted as collusion. In that moment with Bill, I was keenly aware that even listening quietly could be perceived as tacit acceptance of his behavior or as fear of confronting him. If I was to empathize with his anger, I would show myself to be without an ethical backbone, which might be seen as dangerous to him or confirm for him that either I was naïve and foolish or corrupt too. As we continued to talk about his intentions, he laughed and seemed to take pleasure in the idea that I might be too smart to fall for his attempts to corrupt me.

He also told me about affairs he had with women who he perceived as vile: a high school teacher, a mental health worker at the psychiatric facility he was hospitalized in as a college student, and also an English professor (who turned out to be a graduate teaching assistant). In each case, he spoke of them with a mixture of disdain and glee. In an angry and insulting manner, he talked about how easy each of them were to seduce and how easily corruptible they were because of their own base desires. Although he spoke with delight and pride about his prowess, he also reviled how the high school teacher took advantage of a minor, how the mental health worker broke a professional boundary, and how the graduate teaching assistant was married and thus an adulterer (not recognizing that he too was an adulterer).

Throughout the interview, he spoke with little empathy for others and little remorse for any of his wrongdoings, but he was very sensitive to even very small slights. He told me how he would go to bars and flirt with heavy women or those he perceived as less attractive. How he would sit at the bar and the women would buy him drinks, and then at the end of the night he would excuse himself to go to the bathroom but instead leave with a woman he perceived as more attractive. He laughed as he told me this and with derision indicated that the women back at the bar deserved what they got because they were trying to get him drunk and seduce him. In addition, his descriptions of others, including his mother, father, siblings, girlfriends, and friends, were impoverished. At one point, I was asking him to describe a woman he indicated was his best friend. The response was vague and lacking. I asked him if he thought he described her in a way that I could get a sense of what made her unique. He responded as if he recognized he had not and tried again. The subsequent description was just as lacking.

Diagnosis and Case Formulation

Based on all the information I had about Bill, it was clear that he met full criteria for ASPD. In the *Diagnostic and Statistical Manual of Mental Disorders* (5th ed.; *DSM-5;* American Psychiatric Association [APA], 2013), as in *DSM-4* (APA, 1994), there are four requirements:

1. A pervasive pattern of disregard for the violation of the rights of others occurring since age 15, as indicated by three or more of the following: having hurt, mistreated, or stolen from another, for which there are seven criteria.

   a. Failure to conform to social norms with respect to lawful behavior as indicated by repeatedly performing acts that are grounds for arrest;

   b. Deceitfulness, as indicated by repeated lying, use of aliases, or conning others for personal profit or pleasure;

   c. Impulsivity or failure to plan ahead;

   d. Irritability and aggressiveness, as ideated by repeated physical fights or assaults;

   e. Reckless disregard for safety of self or others;

   f. Consistent irresponsibility, as indicated by repeated failure to sustain consistent work behavior or honor financial obligations; and

   g. Lack of remorse, as indicated by being indifferent to or rationalizing.

2. The second requirement is that the individual be at least 18 years old.

3. The third requirement is evidence of conduct disorder with onset before age 15 years.

4. The last is that the occurrence of antisocial behavior is not exclusively during the course of schizophrenia or a manic episode.

From the various sources of information, including Bill, there was a clear pattern of disregard and violation of the rights of others, including having hurt, mistreated, and stolen from others. These behaviors, as reported by his mother and as contained in clinic records, began before age 18.

Bill also met criteria for narcissistic and borderline personality disorder (NPD and BPD). With regard to NPD, Bill reported or displayed all nine of the criteria, including: (1) a grandiose sense of self-importance (e.g., exaggerates achievements, talents, expects to be recognized as superior without commensurate achievements); (2) described being preoccupied with fantasies of unlimited success, power, beauty, and ideal love; this criteria showed in his claim that he would have been a millionaire had others not sabotaged him and that he will be a millionaire soon; (3) described that he is "special" and unique and can only be understood by, or should associate with, other special or high-status people (or institutions); this criterion showed in his lying about attending an Ivy League university; (4) described a clear need for excessive admiration; (5) displayed a sense of entitlement (i.e., unreasonable expectations of especially favorable treatment or automatic compliance with his expectations), which showed in his expecting special treatment in jobs and then feeling indignant when fired; (6) periodically was interpersonally exploitive, taking advantage of others to achieve his own ends; (7) lacked empathy, was unwilling to recognize or identify with the feelings and needs of others; (8) was often envious of others and believed that others were envious of him; and (9) at times behaved or displayed an arrogant, haughty behavior and attitude.

Not unexpectedly, Bill also met criteria for BPD. Bill described a pattern of unstable and intense interpersonal relationships characterized by alternating between extremes of idealization and devaluation. He would see women who he felt were perfect and pursue them. Once in a relationship with them, he would alternate between idealizing and derogating them; eventually, he would break up with them because he devalued them. Bill also described a somewhat unstable sense of self characteristic of identity disturbance, although his identity disturbance was more in line with what you see in narcissistic and antisocial individuals. That is, it was more stable than what is typically seen in BPD but still inaccurate, characterized by what Kernberg (1974) called *pathological grandiosity*. Still, Bill had a difficult time with consistency of his desires and investments that suggested identity disturbance. He also had a difficult time maintaining a consistent moral code. The identity disturbance could also be seen in his flipping from one idea to another without apparent awareness or with denial when confronted. Bill endorsed impulsivity with regard to spending, sex, and substance use, although this criterion is isomorphic with the impulsivity seen in ASPD and probably should not be double counted. Although not particularly frequent, Bill also met criteria for recurrent suicidal behavior, gestures, or threats, and self-mutilating behaviors. These threats or actions tended to occur during major crises such as when he had been caught stealing or arrested, and often appeared insincere and overtly manipulative but other times seemed to occur in the context of feeling hopeless, demoralized, and overwhelmed. Bill clearly showed affective instability and marked mood reactivity, although the typical oscillations involved moving between normal mood and irritability and anger. Still, at other times he was aware of feeling empty. Clearly, Bill had inappropriate, intense anger or difficulty controlling anger, although again, this criterion was isomorphic with criterion d of 1 for ASPD and should not necessarily be double counted. Although Bill did not fully meet criteria for transient stress-related paranoid ideation or severe dissociative symptoms, as his paranoid ideation was not so transient or stress-related and his dissociative symptoms were not severe, he did on occasion report transient dissociative and psychotic symptoms from time to time. For instance, one session he arrived in a panic clasping his ear and thinking he had a brain tumor. He complained of a bump behind his ear that was large and could only be a brain tumor. I had never seen him in such a panic. He would not settle and wanted me to see the tumor, which was placed in such a way he could not see it but only feel it. When I looked behind his ear, I saw the bump. But rather than a large protrusion suggestive of something to be concerned about, it was a little pimple. As soon as I told him that, he was able to feel the bump and perceive it as a pimple and calm down, but he was unable to do so on his own, which struck me as a transient psychotic-like mentation.

Course of Treatment

At the time the assessment was arranged, it was explained to Bill that I was someone with expertise in the kind of issue he was grappling with and that I would be assessing him in order to make recommendations about how best to proceed, including the possibility of transferring his case to me or another therapist. After the assessment, I provided feedback to Bill and his therapist in a joint meeting. During that meeting, I did not mince words, and I was both very direct and used clear examples to explain to Bill my understanding of his difficulties. With antisocial patients, it is important to be explicit, clear, and thorough, and to not shy away from difficult issues and harsh realities. I typically end my assessments with asking if there are any other issues that I had not asked about that are pertinent to the patient's situation—anything I should have asked but didn't, anything the patient should tell me but that did not come up, anything at all that the patient might seek treatment for or another person might believe he or she should share in order for me to have all the information to be most helpful. With Bill, I further elaborated, asking if there were any lies, inconsistencies, or omissions that I was not aware of as yet.

He began the treatment pleasant and obsequious with me. He would compliment me, flatter me, and sometimes even fawn over me. I perceived this as disingenuous and as an attempt to keep the tenor of our relationship not just pleasant but the treatment as neutered. My sense was that therapy was something he thought he had to do to make his parole officer happy and that I was another person to get over on. His transference toward me was typical of those with antisocial personality and narcissistic personality disorders. As the therapy continued, he would frequently rail on about grievances and injustices—his bosses were unreasonable at best and frequently aggressive and corrupt, using their power to toy with him. He would get fired from one job after another for showing up late, not showing up, failing to follow direction, breaking rules, and being provocative with bosses, coworkers, and even customers. He had very little insight about how his behavior might impact others or that the very things he accused others of doing, he himself was doing. He saw others as provincial and prudish when they balked at his sexist comments or complained about his watching and showing others pornography at work. He saw them as hypocritical and that he was the truly honest person because he said and did what everyone wanted to say and do. This view of himself as honest was in direct contrast to his dishonesty, deceptiveness, and manipulation of others.

When I would confront him about his actions, he would respond by suggesting that I was naïve. With certainty, he would tell me that my naïveté was understandable because I had an easy life and my parents were rich and spoiled me. Therefore, I had no idea what the real world was like. He would regale me with clichés such as "it's dog eat dog," "either you're a predator or you're prey," and "a good defense was a good offense." He would tell me that it is good I didn't grow up on the "mean streets" like he did because I would have been taken advantage of with my trusting attitude. All this despite my diplomas on my wall that indicated I went to state and city universities rather than elite private schools. Other times, rather than naïve and foolish, I was dishonest and corrupt, especially when I would confront him with a detail that might interfere with his naïve and foolish representation of me. For instance, one time when I again suggested to him that it might be easier for him to think of me as naïve and foolish, and himself as cunning and savvy, than to think maybe I had a point and he was thinking about thing in ways that unnecessarily pitted him against others, he quickly flipped and began accusing me of being the deceptive and exploitive one. He shared that the only difference between me and him is that I had this good gig (being a psychotherapist) and that I was just going through the motions, taking the state's money to see him. Thus, we were no different, we were both wasting time and fooling the state. He continued that he understood what I was doing after all, and shared he would do the same if he were in my position. I shared with him that he either saw me as naïve and in need of his protection or corrupt and not trustworthy. I reminded him that I didn't just stumble into this gig, that I make thoughtful choices that require discipline and commitment, and many years of hard work and evaluations, including many proposal and defense meetings along the way. But I followed this with the idea that maybe that does not matter because it is not that I am corrupt in his mind because I am a complete fraud who fell into a good gig, but maybe in his mind it is worse than that. Despite my apparent capacity for discipline and commitment, he still thought I was being duplicitous with him. He leaned in, enthralled by what I was saying. I went on. I hypothesized that maybe he thought my duplicity was in treating him when there was no hope he could change for the better. He readily agreed. What I said obviously resonated with him as he sat across from me looking smug and righteous. I told him that I thought there was someone in the room who thought he couldn't change and get better, but it wasn't me. And that part of him that doubts if he can change interferes with the treatment. It keeps him from engaging and honestly sharing with me and committing to the process, and it turns this process into a sham. I shared with him what I told him when we began treatment, that I did not know if he could get better but that it was possible, and I was committing to trying and helping him. But if there was to be any chance, he needed to be committed and honest, and that would be difficult, trying, and even painful at times. For the first time in the treatment, he seemed authentic and looked anxious about a psychological issue. This interaction became a turning point, and I was more hopeful than ever. However, within weeks, he reported to me that he had something to tell me but that I could not tell anyone. He wanted me to promise, but I told him I could not do so, not knowing what it was that he might tell me. He soothed himself by telling me that it did not involve suicide, murder, rape, abuse, or any impending crime and, therefore, I could not break his confidentiality. Nevertheless, I did not feel soothed. What he told me is that years earlier he had been arrested for robbery and that his plea deal required him to make restitution. However, the police only knew about a portion of the money, and he only returned that portion. It was not that much money, but he still had the unreturned part. I thought to myself, wow, what a complex event. I was unsure if having kept some of the money constituted a crime, and if so, was it a past crime or an ongoing, and therefore reportable, crime? I would need to consult with a lawyer. While I appreciated his honesty and thought it was important to the treatment, it also created a bind. I had asked him to trust me, but now I was faced with betraying that trust in needing to report him or at least encouraging him to report himself, which could result in his going back to prison. If I did not pursue acting honestly, then I was possibly breaking the law, and even if not, I would be acting as corrupt as he often thought I was. After speaking confidentially with an ethics adviser and lawyer, in session I brought up that I was glad he brought this to me. I imagined he recognized that this would be a difficult situation to deal with, but hiding it would interfere with the therapy and his recovery. At first, he seemed to take pleasure in my uneasiness. I continued with my belief that he needed to inform the authorities and return the money. He quickly protested, believing that he would go back to prison if he did. I asked if he had spoken to his lawyer about the situation. Bill laughed; now I was being naïve again. I told him that it was important to explore options before deciding what to do. He mocked me, calling me naïve and stupid if he thought he would turn the money over and risk prison. I corrected him and said I expected that he would explore options and talk to a lawyer. Again he scoffed, and with certainty he angrily told me he knows as much as any lawyer and he does not need to waste his money for advice he already knows. I told him I understood that he believed he already knew what a lawyer might say and that it would cost money to discuss this with a lawyer, but we did not know what a lawyer would say and that there may be ways of making restitution that would preclude prison. I also indicated that to not explore options would essentially destroy the treatment by turning it into a sham and forcing me to either be corrupt as an after-the-fact accessory to the crime or be his policeman. Angrily, he accused me of secretly loving the power I was wielding over him. I told him to the contrary, I found my position painful and uncomfortable despite having a clear sense of what I thought was the way forward. He said it was easy for me to see the way forward because it didn't affect me directly. I agreed.

Outcome and Prognosis

We continued to discuss this for the next couple of sessions when the issue became moot. Bill was drunk one night and coming out of a bar pummeled an innocent passerby. When the police came to break up the fight, he resisted and assaulted them. He was restrained, arrested, and considered in violation of his parole. Because he violated parole, Bill was not able to get bail. He sat in jail waiting to be tried and sent back to prison. Ironically, his lawyer was able to use the unreturned money to get a reduction on his sentence.

This case was not selected to illustrate a good outcome but instead to illustrate many of the behaviors and dynamics associated with ASPD. As such, the outcome is unclear. What can be seen in this case presentation is why treating those with ASPD is so difficult. It is difficult to engage in a process when you believe that not only is the process corrupt but so are the individuals involved.

Discussion Questions

1. What are at least three behavioral patterns or characteristics from Bill's life that are indicative of ASPD?

2. Discuss some of the difficulties raised by Bill's therapist in treating someone with ASPD.

3. Bill's therapist says Bill meets all nine criteria for narcissistic and borderline personality disorder. What are at least three examples from the description of Bill's life that stand out to you as indicative of this diagnosis?

4. What techniques does Bill's therapist use in conversations with Bill, which Bill's therapist says are important to use when working with people who have ASPD?

5. There is a point in Bill's treatment that his therapist calls a "turning point." Given what you know about what comes after this, do you agree with this assessment? Why or why not?

References

American Psychiatric Association. (1994). *Diagnostic and statistical manual of mental disorders* (4th ed.). Washington, DC: Author.

American Psychiatric Association. (2013). *Diagnostic and statistical manual of mental disorders* (5th ed.). Washington, DC: Author.

Kernberg, O. (1974). Further contributions to the treatment of narcissistic personalities. *International Journal of Psychoanalysis, 55,* 215–240.

14

Childhood Depression With Selective Mutism

Presenting Problem and Client Description

James Arlow presented as a serious and taciturn yet friendly 5-year-old boy of African American descent. James was rather short for his age and thinly built with short, tightly curled black hair, big brown eyes, and a long face. There was some almost undetectable indication of a lazy left eye and droopiness on the left side of the mouth suggesting that James may have had Bell's palsy. James's posture was good, he walked with an easy, fluid manner, and he appeared coordinated. James and his twin sister, Barbara, were referred to the clinic I was working at by a consulting psychologist at a therapeutic nursery that James and his sister attended after school. The consulting psychologist was concerned about James's level of depression. He described James as a well-groomed but reticent and somewhat languid little boy. The consulting psychologist also noted James was markedly cautious and emotionally constricted, particularly in novel situations, and only mildly less so in familiar surroundings, such as his classroom. In the classroom setting, James was at times willing to respond to people asking him direct questions; however, at other times he would not respond, and he rarely initiated conversation. Periodically, he would withdraw to an extent that he appeared indifferent to the interactions among others in his environment. The consulting psychologist was particularly concerned about his flat affect and limited behavioral expressiveness. James was able to participate in classroom activities and follow routines, but when not engaged in a specific activity, he was observed to have slow physical movements and to be very reluctant to initiate interactions with others.

Additionally, James's teachers described his behavior as growing increasingly "sulky" and "pouty," particularly in his interactions with adults. They also noted that James was overly sensitive. For example, he could not tolerate being corrected or making mistakes and often withdrew in response to such experiences. He was similarly sensitive to reprimands and redirection. Furthermore, after withdrawing, James was often unresponsive to adults' attempts to reengage him. Episodes such as these were increasing and at the time of the referral typically occurred 3 to 4 times per day. At times, his behavior reportedly appeared to be motivated by a desire for attention. The consulting psychologist believed that while James possessed a sound core of academic and intellectual skills, his depressive symptoms and associated impaired motivation limited his ability to interact with teachers, peers, and adults, and ultimately was hurting his school performance.

I was immediately struck by his unusually taciturn and sober manner. James was quite unlike most of the more effervescent 5-year-olds I had met prior to him. He was also not the typical referral at the clinic, who came in due to attentional or behavioral problems. By most outward appearances, things seemed to be going relatively well for James. At home, he appeared to have a positive relationship with a loving, devoted foster mother whom he had known and referred to as "Mommy" since birth. At school, he was not provocative, demanding, or antagonizing toward his teachers or fellow students. There were no reports of fights or violence, no verbal aggression—just a rather small-for-his-age, pleasant child. Nevertheless, James appeared depressed—his affect was flat, he was somber, quiet, and inhibited. It was as if he did not trust that the adults in his world would be able to help him feel better. His teachers reported he rarely spoke in class—that for all intent and purpose, in school he was selectively mute.

Diagnosis and Case Formulation

James was referred with the diagnoses of depression and selective mutism. However, although the *Diagnostic and Statistical Manual of Mental Disorders* (4th ed.; *DSM-4*; American Psychiatric Association [APA], 1994) allowed for the adult mood disorders criteria and diagnoses to be applied to children (with some slight modifications), the term *childhood depression* was not an official *DSM-4* diagnosis. Upon review, it was clear that James did not meet full *DSM-4* criteria for major depression. *DSM* classification relies upon a descriptive symptom-based approach. With regard to depression, *DSM4* distinguishes between major depression, dysthymia, and depressive disorder not otherwise specified. *DSM* criteria for major depression include:

For a two week period, and represents a change in functioning.

1. Depressed mood characterized by reports of feeling sad, low, blue, despondent, hopeless, or gloomy; or

2. Anhedonia, that is, the inability to experience pleasure; and

3. Significant weight loss or gain when not dieting;

4. Insomnia or hypersomnia nearly every day;

5. Psychomotor agitation or retardation nearly every day (observable by others);

6. Fatigue or loss of energy nearly every day;

7. Feelings of worthlessness or excessive or inappropriate guilt nearly every day (not just about being ill);

8. Diminished ability to think or concentrate, or indecisiveness, nearly every day (observed by others); or

9. Recurrent thoughts of death, suicidal ideation with or without a plan.

Furthermore, *DSM* rates the severity (mild, moderate, severe) and whether there are psychotic features, mood congruent or mood incongruent, and whether or not the depressive episode is in partial or full remission, and whether this is a chronic pattern. Lastly, *DSM* specifies whether the current episode is melancholic or not. Although the *DSM-4* does not contain an explicit category for childhood depression, it explicitly acknowledges the existence of childhood depression and permits clinicians to use the criteria for adult depression to diagnose depression in children and adolescents. James met the first criteria for sure, appeared to meet the second one, at least not when home, he possibly met criteria 7, and certainly met criteria 8 at times. This pattern would leave James at a subthreshold level for major depression or meeting criteria for depressive disorder not otherwise specified, which can be used when the patient is subthreshold on the number of symptoms or in cases where another clinician has provided a major depressive diagnosis but which cannot be fully confirmed.

Another consideration would be what was called dysthymia at the time, now referred to as persistent depressive disorder in the *DSM-5* (APA, 2013). Dysthymia occurs when depression is chronic rather than episodic. In adults, the chronicity lasts at least 2 years, but in children and adolescents the criterion is at least 1 year. The main diagnostic features of dysthymia are depressed mood for most of the day, for more days than not, as indicated by either subjective account or observation for 1 year in children. In children, the depressed mood can also be irritable. In addition, the child must exhibit two or more of the following: poor appetite or overeating, insomnia or hypersomnia, low energy or fatigue, low self-esteem, poor concentration or difficulty making decisions, or feelings of hopelessness. During the year period, the child cannot be without depressed mood/irritability or two of these six additional symptoms for more than 2 months. The child cannot have had a major depressive disorder in the first 2 years of the dysthymic disorder, cannot have ever had a manic episode, and the disorder does not occur during the context of a psychotic disorder or the effects of substances, and the disorder has to result in clinically significant distress, impairment in social, school, or other important areas of functioning. Although James met many of the criteria for dysthymic disorder, it was unclear if he met the full criteria set needed or for the full time period required. Nonetheless, James was experiencing significant depressed mood and affect that impacted his general happiness, his relatedness with others, and his school functioning, and thus a diagnosis of depressive disorder not otherwise specified seemed warranted.

James also met criteria for selective mutism as follows: (1) consistent failure to speak in specific social situations such as school despite speaking in other situations (such as home), (2) the disturbance interferes with education achievement or with social communication, (3) the disturbance lasts at least 1 month and not limited to the first month of school, (4) failure to speak is not due to lack of knowledge or comfort with the spoken language, and (5) the disturbance is not better accounted for by a communication disorder (e.g., stuttering).

Although only 5 years old, James had already had life tougher than most. His biological mother and father were heavy drug users who met and conceived him and his twin sister in a drug haze. They were never in an emotional relationship, and the pregnancy was unwanted for both of them. His biological mother continued to use drugs while she was pregnant, and he and his sister were both born testing positive for a range of illegal drugs. Because of that, the children were immediately removed from her care. James's father was also using drugs and unavailable to care for him and his sister. A relative was contacted and approached about serving as a foster parent to the two children. Ms. Arlow, in her mid-40s and the mother of grown children, agreed to become James's and his sister's foster kin mother. At the time, she was unmarried. Both James and his sister suffered a number of physical sequela to being born drug positive, including low birth weight, needing to be detoxified, and suspected neurological and possible learning issues. Now 5 years old, depressed, and selectively mute, James seemed at a critical nodal point in his development. His consulting psychologist, teachers, and school officials were concerned that James might be suffering from lingering learning problems. It was difficult to disentangle James's learning difficulties from his emotional ones.

According to James's foster mother, Ms. Arlow, James's behavior at home was much different than his behavior in public. In contrast to the quiet, inhibited child that the consulting psychologist described and that presented to the clinic, at home James was reportedly a verbal, active child who asked lots of questions and readily asserted his wants and needs. Other behaviors, however, seemed to be consistent at both home and school: James's foster mother reported that James often experienced feelings of impatience and frustration to which he was quick to respond by becoming pouty and sulky.

Since birth, James and his twin sister, Barbara, lived in foster care with a distant relative and that relative's two children, 19 and 17. The older foster sibling attended a local college but lived at home. The foster mother was the only adult participating in James's treatment and the sole source of historical information sans medical records, the consulting psychologist, and teachers. James was reportedly born 4 weeks prematurely weighing 4 pounds, 2 ounces. Significantly, his toxicology screen at birth was positive for cocaine, and he required treatment for congenital syphilis. After a 1-month hospitalization, James and Barbara were placed in kinship foster care with Ms. Arlow.

The foster mother was a well-dressed, early 40s African American woman of average height and medium build. James's foster mother worked full-time as a receptionist for a large company for many years. Despite full-time employment and being a single parent, James's foster mother was extremely responsive and available for James and Barbara's care. She presented as an intelligent, articulate, dutiful woman who was appropriately concerned and very maternally invested in the twins; however, at times she had difficulty seeing and acknowledging James's emotional struggles. She was very organized and took care of the children's instrumental needs with efficacy and care but was less available emotionally. While her affect was generally upbeat and positive, she could often be somewhat nervous and guarded when discussing the children, and at times she appeared to be somewhat on the controlling side.

At the time I began seeing James, his birth mother was in her 30s. James's foster mother reported that James's biological mother may have as many as eight children, ranging from as young as James and Barbara to "adult children." James's birth mother had reportedly been sober and drug-free for approximately 2 years and was employed, living alone in a one-bedroom apartment. These major gains notwithstanding, James's birth mother saw the twins only sporadically, approximately every 3 to 4 weeks for an hour or two. This has been a longstanding visiting pattern in spite of the fact that she has more frequent court-approved visits scheduled with the children. Additionally, James's birth mother was also permitted to have overnight weekend visits with the twins in her own apartment, an opportunity of which she had never taken advantage. James's foster mother indicated that she worried that the birth mother may seek full custody of the children one day, although she recognized that the visitation pattern would have suggested otherwise. Ms. Arlow did not directly share her concern with the twins; however, it was not entirely clear how much of her anxiety was transmitted to them indirectly.

At the time I began seeing James, his birth father had also been sober and drug-free for a number of years. However, he too showed little interest in gaining custody of the children. James and Barbara saw their father sporadically, mostly at family gatherings, but recently they have expressed confusion as to why "Mommy" (Ms. Arlow) and "Daddy" don't live together. Ms. Arlow often seems to have a rather idealizing, Pollyannaish attitude toward James's father, a relative of hers. For example, she describes Anthony as being a big-hearted, idealistic person who thoroughly loves the children, yet she has great difficulty reconciling these sentiments with the fact that he has made very little time and contact with the children even though he only lives a couple of blocks away. James had a strong longing for his father in particular. In a typical interaction during the therapy, James created some special artwork for his "Daddy" in eager anticipation of seeing him on Father's Day, but at the very last minute, Anthony canceled claiming he was ill.

Course of Treatment

James was seen as a child back in the mid-1990s for childhood depression and selective mutism. At the time, most children with James's presentation were treated in either a humanistic or dynamic form of play therapy. Both humanistic and psychodynamic play therapies tend to be characterized as nondirective play therapy as opposed to directive forms. Briefly, play therapy is based on the assumption that children can safely express and communicate conflicts and concerns through play and games. With guidance from a trained person, play can be used to express, work through, and resolve issues, and accept normative behaviors in themselves and others. The understanding of the importance of play as a natural, self-guided, and healing process has a long history dating back to Plato, who quipped that one can learn more about another from observing play than in conversation. Similarly, Rousseau stressed the importance of observing play for understanding children. In the case of Little Hans, Freud (1909) first stressed the importance of using the child's play to provide helpful insights into the child's concerns. It is through play that children master the situations that concern them. Children often play out conflicts in their play such as separation and reunions, discipline, and dealing with life's impositions. Other psychoanalysts such as Melanie Klein (1929, 1961) and Anna Freud (1946, 1965) began to elaborate theories of play therapy. Similarly, Carl Rogers (1942, 1951) and Virginia Axline (1947) began to explicate child play therapy from a humanistic/client psychotherapy perspective. In more recent years, a number of parent-child play therapies have been developed and have shown promising efficacy.

Behavior and cognitive behavioral treatments that were commonly used for externalizing disorders such as ADHD and behavioral problems were beginning to be formulated for internalizing disorders such as depressive and anxiety disorders, particularly cognitive-behavioral treatments. At the time, medications were rarely used to treat depression in children as young as James, although about that time, case reports, open label, and small-N randomized control trials were beginning to appear in the literature.

Nonetheless, because of the array of depressive symptoms expressed, a medication consult was discussed with James's foster mother. Ms. Arlow was very reluctant to proceed with a medication consult and even became teary during our discussion. She shared that the thought of this tiny boy on powerful adult medications scared her and made her feel sad. I reviewed with her my understanding of the literature, which was quite cautious. But I felt that given the circumstances of his birth and the neurological and physical symptoms James experienced, that it might make sense to have a medical work-up that addressed the question about the need for medications. I wanted to remain sensitive to her concerns but at the same time be thorough in approaching the treatment. I shared with her that I understood her concerns and even shared in them, which I pointed out was evident in my presentation of the literature at the time. She indicated that she recognized that and asked if I would be in attendance for the consult. I told her that I could be present. The physician I found for the consult was a well-respected child psychiatrist at a local medical school. After a lengthy evaluation that included meeting with the foster mother, me, and James in various combinations, the psychiatrist concurred with my recommendation to begin with a dynamic play therapy. Similar to my sentiment, she felt that the risks of medications far outweighed the potential benefits unless James continued to remain depressed or became worse after a viable time/dose of psychotherapy. This conclusion is consistent with the growing literature base that suggests although antidepressant medications can be helpful for young children, the empirical data from randomized control trials is equivocal, and a number of untoward side effects, including manic-like behaviors and suicidality, are frequently observed.

With medications off the table, I proceeded with a psychodynamic-informed non-directive form of play therapy under the supervision of an experienced psychodynamic play therapist and supervisor. This decision was standard practice at the time and justified by the existing empirical literature, which consisted mostly of some large uncontrolled studies. There were some small-sample randomized controlled trials (RCTs) of cognitive-behavioral therapy (CBT) for children with depression, but at the time, these studies suffered from a number of problems that limited the inferences that could be drawn from them. However, in the early 2000s, there were better-designed larger sample RCTs that began to suggest the value of a CBT approach. This occurred in the context of few RCTs of psychodynamic treatments (PDT). However, more recently, there have been a number of RCTs examining PDT, including comparisons with CBT that have found efficacy for psychodynamic treatments and equivalency with CBT treatments. Thus, a decision based on standard practice and a relatively impoverished data base now appears well justified.

During his first few months of twice-weekly psychotherapy, James was quite shy, well-behaved, and cooperative during sessions. He typically chose to play with puzzles, board games, and toys that required him to piece things together. He showed remarkable adroitness, concentration, and tenacity in completing puzzles and building things. Once in a while, James would indicate that he needed my assistance, but only in the mildest ways. Extremely intent on being a "good boy," James meticulously cleaned up one activity prior to beginning the next one without any prompting. Occasionally, James initiated spontaneous conversation; however, these were typically short two- or three-word sentences or questions. And although he would act as if he were about to continue speaking, he usually did not elaborate on these modest overtures. Throughout these early sessions, he was quiet, shy, hesitant, and appeared quite depressed.

As he began to feel more comfortable during sessions, he moved from playing with games and puzzles to more motoric activities such as shooting basketballs, throwing a football, tumbling on a gymnastic mat, and using action figures to act out fights. At this point, sessions with James were characterized by his showing off and trying to impress me. His motoric activity clearly seemed to be acting as a manic-like defense against profound feelings of sadness, smallness, and inferiority. He rarely engaged me in shooting baskets with him. There was never any ambiguity in the fact that he was the player and I was his audience. Even when we threw the football together, I was more his audience than a teammate. He continued to strive to impress me with his physical dexterity, quite fearful that I might not like him otherwise. James frequently wanted to make absolutely certain I saw his athletic exploits, frequently inquiring "did you see me do that?" or "see how I did that?" Sometimes, he would repeat his actions in slow motion complete with narration so that I could more fully appreciate the intricacies of his feats. I commented frequently on how important it was to him that I saw how good he was at doing things, comments to which he could only respond with a subdued facial expression and silence.

As his treatment progressed, James gradually became less concerned with impressing me. His play became somewhat less motoric and solitary, and became more symbolic and collaborative. In a game with action figures, James repeatedly played the role of Batman while the therapist was consistently instructed to play the role of Spiderman. Together, the two figures collaborated in fighting other assorted action figures that were designated as the "bad guys." A central theme included James's action figure needing to be rescued by the therapist's action figure, especially by catching the figure as he was falling. Alternately, James's action figure with swords in both hands would come to the rescue of the therapist's action figure. In this game, James was clearly working diligently to develop a representation of the therapist as a person who would protect him, keep him safe, and consistently be there during times of both potential and actual crisis.

During this phase of the treatment, James also repeatedly initiated playing hide-and-seek. In this game, he would hide under a gymnastics mattress and the therapist would search the room saying "Where's James? He was here a second ago." During the first few times playing this game, James could barely tolerate the therapist's searching for him, fearing he would not be "found." Instead, after only a few seconds of being searched for, James would energetically pop up from his obvious hiding place and shout "Here I am!" Next, it was James's turn to search for the therapist, and so the therapist would hide under the mattress and James would pretend to search for the therapist saying "Where's Ken? He was here a second ago." During this phase of treatment, James developed an increased sense of security that even if he remained "hidden," the therapist always found him.

One aspect of treatment related to this brand of play that has been continuously difficult for James has been not having a secure sense of when he was going to see his therapist again. Reassurances such as "I'll see you next Monday" have done little to soothe him, because with the exception of "I will see you tomorrow," most concepts of time cognitively eluded James. Compounding James's difficulties was the fact that there have been multiple occasions when Ms. Arlow has not brought him to his scheduled sessions, which at those times lent an increased sense of tenuousness and uncertainty to his treatment. In engaging in the game hide-and-seek, James seemed to be attempting to master issues of separation and object constancy. Not only was the act of being "found" tremendously satisfying, but also the therapist was providing James with a model of how to tolerate absence. Interestingly, during this phase of the treatment, James had little difficulty ending sessions and cleaning up.

Another game frequently initiated by James was a game he called "Space Jam" based on the cartoon movie of the same name starring Bugs Bunny and Michael Jordan. In this game, initially he would pretend to be either Michael Jordan or Bugs Bunny and the therapist was instructed to play the alien space monster (by making "monster" noises), but in a playful way. Another part of this game included James's taking a tremendously deep breath and "blowing" at the alien space monster so as to render him powerless. Later, James and the therapist would team up as Michael Jordan and Bugs Bunny to beat the alien space team in a crucial basketball game. Beating the alien monsters both alone and in tandem thrilled James and seemed to provide an outlet for some of his oedipal strivings. It was interesting to note that at this time, previous themes of attack and rescue, as well as falling and being caught, reentered the play, perhaps as a way for James to reassure himself that despite "defeating" his therapist, he remained protected and safe from harm.

Around the same time, James became increasingly interested in initiating physical contact with the therapist and would often hold my hand, hugging me at the beginning and end of sessions, and reach into my pockets feeling for my keys and touching my pocket that contained my wallet. During sessions, James would try to orchestrate the play so that he might touch me. He frequently requested the therapist to hold his hands so he could flip himself or have me bend over to pick up a ball, at which time he would take the opportunity to climb onto the therapist's back. One time, after having climbed onto the therapist's back, he asked to be carried over to the other side of the room piggyback style. He whispered "I got you now" in a soft voice as if he were talking to himself.

Approximately 5 months into the therapy, James had developed a strong connection to the therapist. However, it was at this time that sessions also became more difficult for him. He began to mildly protest the ending of sessions and often needed much cajoling. During these occasions, he would say goodbye to the room and the door of the room. James fantasized that his and Barbara's therapists lived in the therapy rooms at the Psychological Center, and he also made an oblique reference to the therapist having children, which James hoped would elicit this mysterious yet threatening information. Occasionally, James's protests were more severe and he would refuse to clean up. The therapist would acknowledge how difficult it was to end sessions and how equally difficult it was for the therapist to miss James between sessions (part of helping James tolerate negative feelings was modeling for him by the therapist's taking them on).

During a period where Ms. Arlow became more erratic in bringing the children to sessions, sometimes bringing them 20 minutes late or not bringing them at all, it became quite difficult for James to begin sessions. He would arrive to the clinic sleepy and crying, and needed much cajoling to begin his sessions. During this period, James would often spend up to 20 minutes crying with little response to the therapist's attempts to comfort him and engage him. When James pulled himself together, he would usually direct the therapist to draw him some picture on the blackboard. Directing and giving orders to the therapist was a way for James to assert control and comfort himself.

During this phase of treatment, James would sometimes pretend to fall to the floor, particularly after some basketball exploit such as beating the monster from "Space Jam." He would lie quietly, pretending to be seriously injured or dead. James would direct the therapist to coax and cajole him to come back to "life," and James would then come back to "life," usually for a short period and then repeat the play sequence. Through his "dying" and then requesting to be coaxed "back to life," James poignantly demonstrated his ongoing struggles with profound feelings of depression and his concomitant desire to reach out to an adult who might help him transcend them.

After a few productive meetings with the children's therapists, Ms. Arlow began to bring the children regularly and timely. As a result, James's relationship with the therapist became more secure, and James's expressions of emotion were less labile. James began to express much more interest in knowing the therapist's mind. Play centered on drawing collaboratively and more direct verbal exchanges between James and the therapist. For instance, James became very interested in knowing how the therapist knew certain things and conversely in asking the therapist to guess how James knew certain things. During this phase, he would also ask the therapist how he knew how to draw certain things, frequently asking me to draw things that he could not draw well, like hands. Eventually, my verbalizations such as "hands are hard to draw" and "it took me many years to learn to draw hands well" seemed to help him tolerate feelings of anxiety, allowing him to make statements such as, "I can't draw hands. Can you show me how?" James would often ask the therapist to draw a picture, and then he would turn it over and trace the outline of the drawing. Other times, he would use the therapist's drawing as a model for his drawing and would ask the therapist to draw certain aspects of the picture that he had difficulty with.

Finally, the break for summer vacation was extremely difficult for James and also very telling in terms of how he typically handles such difficulties. Whenever the therapist would approach the subject, James would respond angrily, "I know that!" He did not want to talk about it. Sometimes, he would loudly instruct the therapist "don't talk! . . . I said no talking!" in an effort to avoid the subject and its associated feelings. James had difficulty ending the sessions prior to summer break, often wanting to take toys from the room home with him. The therapeutic task was to respectfully accept his defenses and help him to tolerate his feelings.

At the end of their final sessions prior to the August break, James and Barbara returned to the waiting room, both very upset. Barbara immediately crawled into Ms. Arlow's arms where she molded to her Mommy's body, wept quietly, and appeared to find comfort. In great contrast, James dejectedly walked over to the window where he stared steadily out at the Manhattan skyline. When this therapist approached him and asked him what he was doing, James replied, "I'm looking at the Empire State Building." At first, the therapist thought James must be mistaken because the silhouette of the specified building seemed nowhere in sight. But then slowly, as the therapist followed the direction of James's gaze, he found himself vaguely able to distinguish the hazy outline of the Empire State Building from among the thousands of buildings in the distance.

This interaction seemed to be a sad yet appropriate metaphor for how James experiences his world. James is desperately yearning for something that remains tantalizingly visible, yet distant and painfully unattainable, namely a father; thus, it is not surprising that when he searches the distant horizon, his eyes settle on one of the biggest, grandest landmarks on the island. Instead, he is the "odd man out" in a household with his sister and foster mother, a woman who loves him but often could not emotionally reach him the same way Ms. Arlow can connect with Barbara. As the therapist prepared to leave the room, James said suddenly and forcefully, "I don't have training wheels on my bike anymore." With this statement, James seemed to be trying to achieve two things. It was almost as if he momentarily regressed and thought if he could impress with a great achievement, there was a chance his therapist might reconsider this upcoming month-long separation. Yet at the same time, James seemed to be conveying to the therapist, as well as trying to convince himself, that he was going to be okay without his therapist (i.e., his training wheels).

With regard to school, James's teachers reported that his skills are at grade level and he does extremely well on artwork. He follows direction well and is inquisitive. James's teacher reported that he has made good improvement in the social realm of school, and he is able to collaborate with his peers. Although James is still quiet, his teacher noted that he is well-liked, sought out by other children, and has made many friends. In contrast to his previous functioning, James now seemed to have more interpersonal confidence and enjoy interacting with peers. James had been promoted to the first grade.

Over the course of the treatment, there were a number of important nodal points that occurred with James's foster kin mother that were essential to treatment. Early on, the therapist, in collaboration with James's sister's therapist, supported Ms. Arlow in her desire for James and Barbara to attend the same school and helped facilitate this both with regard to the logistics of the school and vis-à-vis the therapeutic nursery's consulting psychologist, who recommended that James and Barbara attend different schools. The idea of transporting James and Barbara to and from different schools would be very time consuming and was overwhelming to Ms. Arlow. However, the consulting psychologist felt strongly, given James's reliance on Barbara as a mouthpiece, that it was in his best interest to be in a separate school from Barbara. This recommendation led to a rupture between Ms. Arlow and the consulting psychologist right as James and Barbara's treatments were beginning. For a number of reasons, the supervisor of the two therapists felt it was important to side with Ms. Arlow. First, logistically it would be difficult and understandably burdensome to transport two children, the same age with the same school start time, to different schools in different parts of a large city. Second, there was a solution to the consulting psychologist's concern that could be accomplished at one school: that is, ensure that James and Barbara were in separate classes. Third, Ms. Arlow needed to feel supported by James and Barbara's therapists, and to not do so on this issue might lead to a rupture that could doom the treatment. Having supported and facilitated Ms. Arlow's preferred solution, a bond was strengthened between the therapist and the family.

A second important event with James's foster kin mother was around sensitively presenting to her and tolerating her concerns and anxieties around the medication consult and the neuropsychological testing. Both needed to be done in order to figure out how best to proceed, but both consults carried large concerns for her. Rather than imposing the consults on her, I took the time to hear her concerns. I validated them without reinforcing any distortions and joined with her in the concerns she expressed, expressed openness about the results, and gently nudged her toward moving forward with them. My sense is that she perceived me as on her side and not simply another bureaucrat imposing their will on her.

The third event may have been the most important because it indicated a shift in Ms. Arlow's perspective. The therapist experienced Ms. Arlow as a very attentive and responsive parent, particularly concerning educational and instrumental needs, however, less so with regard to James's emotional needs. Some of this seemed to be rooted in stereotyped gender roles, seeing James as a "little man" who was tough and not in need of the same kind of emotional support as Ms. Arlow saw Barbara needing. Some of the lack of emotional attention appeared grounded in Ms. Arlow's own defensiveness and intolerance of James's emotional states and her failures. During one meeting, she told me that it is important to her to parent James and Barbara correctly and that she works hard to provide them with resources. She further elaborated that she could not tolerate the idea that she had somehow contributed to either of their problems. During our meetings, I worked gently with her to be better aware of James's internal work and mental and emotional states. Overall, I found it frustrating and slow going. There was a rigidity to her way of thinking that I reckoned served her well in raising children in a complex urban environment but with some cost to the capacity to reflect and process her and her children's internal world and concerns. A change was occurring, but it was not noticeable until one unfortunate event. One day, Ms. Arlow failed to bring the children for session. This was unusual, as lateness and missing of sessions had been resolved a while ago. After the session, I received a call from Ms. Arlow. She explained that they had been in a car accident on the way to therapy. The taxi they were riding in rear ended the car in front of them at a red light. It was a minor accident, but the driver of the other car was irate and reached into the taxi and pulled the taxi driver out of the car and proceeded to hit him. People intervened and the police arrived. Ms. Arlow was concerned that James might not mention the incident to me and wanted me to know so I could look for any signs that it was bothering him. She said he had been rather stoic about the event. She shared with me that it was very scary, that she was scared, and that she imagined if it was scary to her it must be even scarier to the children. Upon her sharing that, I experienced an epiphanic moment where I realized something had changed for her in terms of her capacity to reflect on James's mind. We discussed that event further in our meetings, and it became an intersubjective moment for us in recognizing her capacity to empathize and tolerate his emotional states.

James continued to improve and became better able to tolerate feelings of vulnerability, smallness, and weakness. He became less reticent and more motivated to communicate and verbalize his thoughts and feelings. It is as if he had more faith in the efficacy of verbal communication and for reaching out to others for comfort. James was beginning to allow himself to yearn for close attachment with caring others. James had been afraid of opening the floodgate of feelings associated with connectedness but now seemed more secure that such closeness was available to him and not dangerous. He was spontaneously speaking more, initiating interactions with peers in school, and doing well academically.

Throughout my work with James, and through the play and surrounding conversations, I wanted to gently and respectfully help him to become aware of his "in-the-moment" feelings and the ways in which he defends against allowing these feelings to emerge. As the treatment took hold in the play, we became partners for accessing and processing his impulses, fantasies, defenses, and pathological modes of relating. These conflicts and his ways of dealing with them could now be grappled with in a safe environment with a helpful other. By working with James's feelings in the "here and now," I have helped him to tolerate a fuller range of affective states, to bring fantasies associated with these states into the treatment, and to bring to bear more mature levels of organization to what were once unconscious and threatening thoughts and feelings. Increasingly, James could tolerate and integrate previously split-off, unacceptable aspects of himself that he had defended against and enacted through withdrawal and affective constriction. Additionally, James began performing better with regard to academic functioning and social relationships at school.

Outcome and Prognosis

James had been seen in twice-weekly individual play therapy for 2 years between ages 4½ and 6½ in order to treat his depression and selective mutism. In addition, treatment addressed improving his tolerance for frustration and making mistakes, as well as his tendency to sulk and withdraw when frustrated or not getting his way. Early on, treatment was geared toward providing James with positive regard, showing interest in his activities and concerns, and helping him express himself through play and conversation. As James began to feel understood, he was able to better modulate his feelings without acting on them through activity or denying them and withdrawing. In addition, James's foster kin mother, Ms. Arlow, was seen as needed conjunctive to James's and his sister Barbara's treatments in order to assist her in better understanding James's needs and become more constructively involved in helping James deal with his feelings, as well as continue to build a therapeutic alliance that will facilitate James's and his sister's treatments. During treatment, James became steadily more verbal and able to express his wants and needs more directly. This capacity in session translated to his home and school. Reports at school and home indicated that his capacity to express himself, engage with peers and adults, and function all improved. His expectations changed from a little boy who felt emotionally alone to a child who could take risks in expressing himself and reaching out to others. Strikingly, his academic functioning improved dramatically. James went from a child who was thought to be learning disabled and of only average ability to one who was recognized as very bright, capable, and advanced in his thinking and academic skill. He began to develop friendships and, according to his teacher, even began showing a sophisticated sense of humor for his age, recognizing context and irony. After treatment ended, Ms. Arlow kept in contact with the therapist through the clinic for a number of years. She reported that James was doing well in school and that he seemed happy. She indicated that she enjoyed him and felt more attuned to his needs separate from her own. Ms. Arlow reported that James was generally at expected educational levels and was even in advanced classes for some subject matters. Furthermore, she reported that teachers liked him and that he had many friends as he was a funny, generous, smart, and kind child.

Discussion Questions

1. Describe the factors in James's prenatal development and his family situation that likely played a role in his symptoms of depression.

2. Provide three or more examples of the ways in which James's therapist used play therapy to help him better express himself and resolve issues in his life.

3. On several occasions, Ms. Arlow was late in bringing James and his sister to therapy appointments or she didn't bring them to their appointments at all. Compare how James's behavior changed during the periods when he was late or missed appointments and the times when Ms. Arlow was more consistent about getting the kids to their appointments on time.

References

American Psychiatric Association. (1994). *Diagnostic and statistical manual of mental disorders* (4th ed.). Washington, DC: Author.

American Psychiatric Association. (2013). *Diagnostic and statistical manual of mental disorders* (5th ed.). Washington, DC: Author.

Axline, V. M. (1947). *Play therapy.* Boston, MA: Houghton Mifflin.

Freud, A. (1946). *The psychoanalytic treatment of children.* New York, NY: International Universities Press.

Freud, A. (1965). *Normality and pathology in childhood.* New York, NY: International Universities Press.

Freud, S. (1909). The origin and development of psychoanalysis. *American Journal of Psychology, XXI,* 181–218.

Klein, M. (1929). Personification in the play of children. *International Journal of Psychoanalysis, 10,* 193–204.

Klein, M. (1961). *Narrative of a child analysis.* London, England: Hogarth Press.

Rogers, C. R. (1942). *Counseling and psychotherapy.* Boston, MA: Houghton Mifflin.

Rogers, C. R. (1951). *Client-centered therapy.* Boston, MA: Houghton Mifflin.